# Seeking Gaddafi

# Seeking Gaddafi

Daniel Kawczynski

**dialogue**< >

First published in Great Britain in 2010 by
Dialogue, an imprint of
Biteback Publishing Ltd
Heal House
375 Kennington Lane
London
SE11 5QY

ISBN 978-1-906447-05-2

10 9 8 7 6 5 4 3 2 1

A CIP catalogue record for this book is available from the British Library.

Set in Bembo
Printed and bound in Great Britain by TJ International Ltd, Padstow, Cornwall

To my uncle Jurek Krysiak, who worked in Libya
for many years and inspired my interest in the country.
He died while I was writing this book.

# CONTENTS

# FOREWORD

Libya is the land, more than any, where the forces which have shaped the modern world collide.

An orphan child of Empire, shaped by the colonial legacy of Italian rule, a testbed for Marxist thought, a vanguard nation in the struggle against the West and a nursery for Islamic radicalism, it was a state sponsor of terror and a pariah power. But Libya is also an oil producer fuelling contemporary capitalism, a crossroads nation which champions both Arab and African interests, a society in which women play a much more prominent role than in other developing nations, and a pragmatic ally of the West in combating al-Qaeda.

And the complexities of Libya's position go further still. While it has abandoned its pursuit of weapons of mass destruction, it supports the genocidal regimes of Sudan and Zimbabwe; while it seeks to combat Islamist terrorism, its role in the Lockerbie bombing is a crime for which no proper reckoning has been made; and while it seeks to live with the realities of modern liberal economics, it also persists as a brutal tyranny which operates by the rules of clan loyalty rather than attempting to move towards anything resembling democracy.

The man at the heart of all these contradictions is Libya's enigmatic ruler – the great survivor of Arab nationalism, Muammar Gaddafi. Seeking the truth about Gaddafi is, like following tracks in the shifting sands of the Sahara, no easy task. But my colleague Daniel Kawczynski has brought his characteristic tenacity, passion and energy to the task. The result is a fascinating portrait of a land and its leader, with illuminating detail on every page and telling insights culled from Daniel's own work on international development and human rights.

Daniel's picture of Libya, for all that land's complexities and contradictions, does reinforce one overarching lesson. While Libya has been blessed with fabulous material and mineral wealth, the absence of democracy has held the country, its people and its neighbours back for decades now. Across the Arab world, millions live under tyrannies and autocracies, denied the opportunity to speak, think, work and love freely. Their talents are given no proper outlet, their voices are stifled, their futures blighted.

I know how passionately Daniel feels about the need to extend the hand of friendship to all those Arab peoples who have suffered so much under rulers indifferent to freedom and hostile to democracy in the last sixty years. And this book is testament to his love for Libya and its people, a land which has been blessed and cursed in equal measure over the last six decades but which has in Daniel a staunch and sincere friend.

*Michael Gove* MP
*January 2010*

INTRODUCTION

# SEEKING GADDAFI

April 1984 was an ugly month of violence in both Britain and Libya. In Tripoli, on the fifteenth, Libyan citizens watched in horror as that most barbaric of human ceremonies was enacted before them: a public hanging. The victims were two young undergraduates at Tripoli University. The reasons for their deaths were murky and poorly understood but certainly connected to the escalating paranoia of a leader determined to stamp out all opposition. It was neither the first nor the last state murder Gaddafi would present as a warning to his subjects, but its ramifications were to be profound.

Even in those pre-internet days, news of these students' deaths quickly reached Libyan expatriates all over the world. In London, members of a dissident group called the National Front for the Salvation of Libya decided to mount a public protest against the hangings outside Libya's embassy, which, in accordance with the dictates of revolutionary correctness, had recently been renamed the London people's bureau. Inside, the revolutionary zealots of highly uncertain diplomatic credentials who had seized control of the bureau earlier that year made their own plans for handling this unwelcome display of dissent.

On the morning of 17 April, the dissident demonstration went ahead in the normally staid and respectable surroundings of St James's Square. The protestors were angry but peaceful, chanting slogans and waving banners. This was to be no normal demonstration, however: at 10.20 a.m., participants and passers-by witnessed flames bursting from the first floor of the people's bureau, and heard the drumming of a ten-second volley of machine-gun fire. Eleven of the anti-Gaddafi protestors, the intended targets, were injured.

The only fatality was a young British woman. Twenty-five-year-old Constable Yvonne Fletcher had been deployed that day alongside her fiancé to police the protest, and tragically ended up an unintended victim of the cowardly Libyan agents, whose real intention had been to silence their unarmed, peacefully protesting compatriots. Fletcher's helmet, left behind as she was rushed off in an ambulance, rested on the pavement for days, a potent symbol of the atrocity that was flashed on news broadcasts around the world. I was only twelve years old when Fletcher died, but as for many British people, the sight of her helmet lying in the no-man's land between the police lines and the Libyan people's bureau was burnt in my memory. Even a small boy could recognise the potential for chaos and fear inherent in this bizarre murder of a serving police officer.

PC Fletcher's murder marked the beginning of a steep slide in British–Libyan relations: diplomatic representation was withdrawn on both sides; two years later Margaret Thatcher supported a belligerent President Reagan in his decision to bomb Tripoli; the IRA benefited more and more from Libyan money and Libyan explosives; and in 1988 Pan Am Flight 103 exploded over the skies of Lockerbie, perhaps the worst yet of the atrocities to be attributed to the Gaddafi regime.

Fast-forward to twenty years after the murder of PC Fletcher, and we see an entirely different scene. A characteristically dapper but increasingly frayed-at-the-edges Tony Blair is meeting a triumphant Colonel Gaddafi in his preferred theatre: a Bedouin tent set up in the Libyan desert. Relations with the Arab world in general are in tatters following an invasion of Iraq justified by a set of weapons of mass destruction (WMD) that are starting to seem a figment of the Western political imagination. Libya, at this point, has presented itself as a rare diplomatic victory for Blair. The two leaders shake hands as cameras flash, having discussed oil deals, the case of PC Fletcher, the atrocity over Lockerbie and WMD. The handshake marks what is seen by many as a triumph of courageous British diplomacy, the reintroduction of a cowed, co-operative Gaddafi into international politics. A dictator, presiding over an extensive and secret weapons programme, with allegedly high-quality intelligence on al-Qaeda, has been brought meekly into the fold, and British businesses stand to profit most handsomely. There are those crying foul, saying that the bloodstained Libyan record has been washed clean by rivers of oil. They take the desert handshake as further evidence of Blair's descent into ethical oblivion. But the fact remains that Gaddafi has reinvented himself yet again, and a new era in British–Libyan relations has commenced.

Ours is an age in which the West has dealt closely and sometimes violently with regimes it has understood only poorly. We do not grapple enough with what the Arab societies we engage with, in whatever way, are really like. I wanted to write this book to dig deep into the realities of Libya and of Colonel Gaddafi, and to present some of the really difficult dilemmas of our relationship with the Libyans. After all, buried in our relationship with Libya are most of the problems that the modern Foreign Office faces. While journalists so readily and so graphically talk of oil versus blood, they are less ready to confront the really unpleasant truth that we need to get oil from somewhere, and few of those marketing it are easy-going democracies. Business contracts are decried as a foul and lowly consideration to take into a meeting with a dictator, but if we decided that we were only going to do business with the democrats of the world, British profits would be dented rather dramatically. Isolating the dictators of the world is often counterproductive, and by exchanging ideas, technology, visits and cultural insights, an argument goes that we can help to encourage change for the better.

Yet the fate of the millions of people subject to the whims of dictatorial regimes cannot be forgotten, either. We have a responsibility as a free society to remember those clapped in jail or 'disappeared' for speaking out. Libya is a country where journalists vanish, political prisoners are secretly murdered and freedom of the press is vigorously restricted. By doing deals with dictators, we may be propping up regimes that should have been toppled ignominiously years ago. Gaddafi since readmittance to the West is immeasurably more solid and stable in his power at home, and we must face up to that.

As shown so graphically by the brief life of PC Fletcher, the brutality of foreign dictators tends to impinge on the lives of ordinary people in unexpected ways. The families of the British citizens who have been exposed to the evils of Gaddafi's policies over the decades – the Fletchers, the Lockerbie victims, IRA victims, murdered dissidents' families – rightly demand that their government stand up for them and seek justice actively. Individual tragedies resonate in the pages of our newspapers, and politicians are deservedly criticised when they callously set them aside. So the microcosm of the Britain–Libya relationship graphically illustrates the difficult tightrope walk faced by the Foreign Office and its ministers in many of its key relationships. What is clear, though, is that knowledge is everything. The Blair government and the Foreign Office screwed their courage to the sticking place in reopening the relationship with Libya, but they could not have done it without a set of diplomats who had an intimate, painstakingly acquired knowledge of the realities on the ground in Libya. Put simply, we have to know Gaddafi to deal with him well.

Knowing Gaddafi is no easy task. The stories are legion, and the personal vanity of the man seems to know no bounds. Few other world leaders have had a fashion spread in *Vanity Fair* depicting the unique extremes of their wardrobes. Articles on Gaddafi are almost obliged to begin with a carefully constructed description of the outfit chosen for a particular meeting. A blinding white suit covered by an Arab *bisht* for the 2009 G8 summit, an aviation-themed leather and fur ensemble for a visit to Versailles in 2007, a long shirt emblazoned with photographs of African heroes to see President Mubarak of Egypt in August 2005, flowing peach and purple silk robes to meet the Portuguese Prime Minister, Antonio Guterres, in April 2000: Gaddafi's outfits seem to be getting increasingly bizarre in the twilight years of his reign. Many have commented on the thick layers of make-up he wears, and also on the carefully judged height of his shoes. A Saudi businessman, discussing my book project, informed me soberly that I would never secure the interview I wanted with Gaddafi, because the Colonel would look ridiculous if he adjusted his boots to match me at 6 feet 8 inches, and so, my friend felt, we were unlikely to meet.

As a young, tanned, healthy army colonel, new to the air-conditioned corridors and plentiful lunches of power, Gaddafi could carry off these fashion excesses. Nowadays, they are more a visual embodiment of the air of corrupt grandiosity and self-promotion that surround his rule. Since Gaddafi's rehabilitation into international acceptability, Western politicians who shake his hand seem to have cultivated a certain expression. They just barely smile, they stand as far off as possible, and they look as though they feel slightly ill. Hopefully, they must think, this will satisfy Gaddafi while fending off tabloid attack at home. It is hard, though, in many of these photos, to judge whether the look of slight queasiness is down to the policies of Gaddafi's regime or to the glaring tastelessness of the outfit he has chosen that day.

Gaddafi visits are also characterised by excessive, inconvenient and belligerent displays of the Leader's fondness for luxury and his Bedouin character. His hosts scramble to find suitable locations to set up the obligatory tent for receiving dignitaries and, in some cases, to find fodder and shelter for the camels Gaddafi has in the past had flown in to accompany him. In 2007, the French found the Leader and his 400-strong entourage a spot to pitch his heated tent next door to the Elysée Palace, and *Paris Match* was invited to photograph the Colonel relaxing within its canvas walls. Later, pedestrian bridges over the Seine were closed to allow the Leader to take a cruise, accompanied by his famous all-women bodyguard, while disgruntled tourists were herded out of the Louvre to allow him to gaze on the *Venus de Milo* in solitude. The kitsch of a Gaddafi visit is always enthusiastically enjoyed by the local press, and it ensures that the Libyans' travels get extensive media coverage.

Should Gaddafi be visited at home in Libya, the visitor will without exception be held up in Tripoli, shuffled onto an unexpected and uncomfortable flight into the wilderness, and then, usually, driven out to meet the Leader in an authentic tent in an authentic slice of desert. In Gaddafi's mind, it seems that this emphasises both his rugged Bedouin nature and his ability, as supreme leader, to delay and inconvenience

Western luminaries as he wishes. It is a rather petty and bullying habit, particularly as the length of the delay and the extent of the inconvenience are dished out in direct proportion to the visitor's level of importance. It is also, probably, counterproductive. For most visitors, it does nothing but reinforce the unfortunate impression of Gaddafi as deeply weird and Libya as a humorously inefficient fiefdom.

Gaddafi is also compulsively disruptive and an incurable lover of chaos, and is thus an unpredictable presence at any international meeting. Seemingly, there is an internal struggle going on, in which he craves acceptance within international forums but also desires desperately to express his disdain for structures he sees as fatally tainted with neo-imperialism. In September 2009, given his first ever chance to address the United Nations, he spoke for an hour and forty minutes (having been given a fifteen-minute slot), tore up the UN Charter, speculated that swine flu was a biological weapon, and offered his thoughts on the assassination of President Kennedy.

There is, therefore, an awful lot of white noise surrounding Gaddafi. So extreme are his eccentricities, so bizarre his pronouncements, that the real nature of the man and of his ambitions gets buried. It is very difficult to know what kind of a man hides beneath the clothes, the tents, the female bodyguards and the directionless rantings. In the course of researching my book, I found that, to an extent, each of the people I talked to makes their own Gaddafi. For the diplomats, Gaddafi is a calculating, rational man who can be explained by reference to his ideological tract, *The Green Book*, and by his pursuit of Libyan national interests. For Libyan dissidents, Gaddafi is an evil genius, his ideology a sham, his purpose to hold onto power and to maintain a reign of fear over his citizens. For journalists, Gaddafi is a bumbling, farting, demonic madman, a fountain of idiotic eccentricities and a pleasurable embarrassment with which to beat their own political leaders.

Gaddafi himself revels in constructing different personas and rotating them. Coming to power at the age of just twenty-seven, and serving as Guide to the Revolution for forty years, he has fashioned successive roles for himself, inhabiting each with gusto. First there was the ardent Nasserist. Seizing the reins of power in 1969, he proclaimed himself merely the agent of Nasser's pan-Arab vision, and declared his aim to be the unification of Libya with Egypt. Closely associated with this was Gaddafi the anti-colonialist and the defender of freedom, under which guise he showed a remarkable inability to discriminate, dishing out funds to pretty much every movement or individual out there proposing liberation as their goal, from the IRA to Carlos the Jackal, Abu Nidal to the African National Congress.

Alongside there has always been Gaddafi the authentic, austere Bedouin, receiving guests in tents and promoting his need to disappear into the desert to meditate in mystical solitude. Gaddafi's roots are indeed authentically Bedouin and of the desert – he was born to the family of an impoverished, illiterate goatherd, and is not even sure of the year of his own birth – but it is very hard to know where the genuine desert mystic ends and the image-manufacturing PR man begins. Lately, we have also had Gaddafi the African King of Kings, revelling in his role as chairman of the African Union and seeking to guide Africa into a European Union-style framework, with the currency to be the 'afro' and the leader, presumably, Gaddafi.

Then there is the Colonel as political philosopher. Gaddafi heralded his *Green Book* as the ultimate achievement in the evolution of democracy and convened scholarly conferences, at which the universities of the world somewhat strangely managed to produce professors willing to write papers venerating Gaddafi the democrat. To this day, Gaddafi continues to claim that *al-Jamahiriyya al-'Arabiyya al-Libiyya al-Sha'abiyya al-Ishtirakiyya al-'Uzma* – the Great Socialist People's Libyan Arab *Jamahiriyya* – represents the pinnacle of democratic development. His concept of the *jamahiriyya*, the state governed through consultation and popular participation, has, in his view, superseded the tired and exploitative old path of representative democracy. Citizens forced to attend lengthy, tedious and ultimately unproductive committee meetings designed to endow dictatorship with a stamp of legitimacy might disagree.

How much, though, do all these carefully proclaimed ideological commitments and painstakingly constructed images really capture the man? It is my view that all that can really be pinned down about Gaddafi is that he is essentially power-seeking and deeply vain. His twin goals are to maintain his position in Libya and to be commemorated by the historians as a world thinker and a respected statesman of influence. Everything serves those two goals, the first of which is thus far a resounding success, the second rather less likely.

Gaddafi's vanity and lust for power hit the visitor to Libya directly in the face: the entire country is festooned with garish billboards venerating the great Leader. As with Nicolae Ceauşescu, the Colonel's image barely ages. He is shown young, wrinkle free, at the peak of his virility. His wise revolutionary words are emblazoned on walls and green arches: 'With him we live, without him we die', 'Falcon of Africa – Thinker and Leader', 'To you alone, O Leader, love and adoration', 'The Liberator – Dawn of Freedom'.

Of course, a ruler's motivations and character are less important than the way in which he proves himself able to serve his country. This is the part that often gets forgotten when it comes to Gaddafi – reams of newsprint are spent on Lockerbie, PC Fletcher, the IRA connection, his posturing in international forums, but relatively little on what it has been like to live as a citizen of Gaddafi's Libya. And in some ways, life is good. Compared to neighbouring states, health and education are vastly superior, pretty much universal, and free. Libya is a literate country where almost all citizens have a house and a car, and in which women are far less restricted than in most Arab states.

These days, Gaddafi's hand at the tiller is light. He has always claimed to play no official role in Libya's governance, a claim few have believed. It does seem, however, that through his four decades in power, he has learnt to leave the detail to his often highly capable ministers. He listens to those who serve under him, and they give him frank advice. All of this happens within limits, of course, and there are a number of unsayables – no-one discusses the succession, Gaddafi's own position or the role of Islam.

This ability to delegate reflects a key aspect of Gaddafi: his flexibility. Other dictators have erred by believing themselves infallible, but Gaddafi has proved uniquely able to learn from his mistakes and adapt to changing times. He can back away from his errors and do the necessary to correct them. Bringing Libya in from the cold after the tragedy of Lockerbie was a slow and painful process, but Gaddafi showed himself willing to take every single step, no matter how humiliating or unjust he perceived it, in order to restore Libya to the international stage. The unpalatable reality was that if he did not, Libya's crumbling economy threatened to bring him down along with it, and Gaddafi was able to act on this reality in a thoroughly decisive manner.

Gaddafi won himself a record in the early 1970s as a firebrand in the world of the international oil trade, galvanising OPEC into negotiating fairer prices for its members. Since then, however, he has largely ensured that the oil industry has been run smoothly and conservatively. Upsetting it would mean undermining the entire foundation of his rule – the construction of a rentier state channelling money to citizens as efficiently as possible to buy their compliance in his schemes for governance – and so the oil companies have been very carefully shielded from the crazy experiments enacted on the rest of Libya's economy. King Idris I, Gaddafi's predecessor, bequeathed him a prolific and well-governed oil industry, and Gaddafi has protected this precious legacy at all costs.

It must also be said that Gaddafi has ensured that this sparsely populated country, which today is home to just six million people, has punched well above its weight in international politics. Gaddafi has given Libya a remarkably high profile, and Libyan dissidents frequently bemoan the willingness of the Tony Blairs and Condoleezza Rices of this world to meet Gaddafi on his own terms. Of course, the other side of this coin is that Libya spent the 1980s being viewed as a far more lethal and capable enemy than it really was, culminating in the American decision to bomb Tripoli and Benghazi in 1986, an act of war many thought far in excess of the actual threat posed by the Libyans.

Despite all this, Gaddafi will not be remembered as a wise or a beneficent ruler. History has traditionally been something that happened to Libyans, who have been subjected to wave after wave of colonial intervention, culminating in the brutal, murderous rule of the Italians from 1911 until the Second World War. Gaddafi is, perhaps, yet another disastrous event to befall Libya, stifling the energies of its people still further and preventing its oil wealth from being used to create a dynamic, happy nation. Libya under Gaddafi has not been fashioned into a confident society. Political participation has been a carefully constructed façade, and the 1980s are particularly recognised as a decade of fear and deprivation. Small businesses were banned, savings accounts seized, critics of the regime murdered, and the result of it all was that much of Libya's educated, skilled middle class got up and left. Those who stayed behind lived under the constant surveillance of the sinister revolutionary committees and endured an atmosphere of complete repression, with no non-government media and a minimal civil society. For a long period, even sports teams were banned. Things might be better now, but few Libyans really trust the man who showed himself so willing to use his people as guinea pigs in a chaotic and random series of socio-political experiments.

The 1980s were also a decade of war, death and bloodshed, although this was perpetrated outside Libya's own borders. Gaddafi poured Libya's oil money into sponsoring conflicts around the world. Not only did he fund subversive groups in shameful attacks against civilians, he also mounted an incredibly expensive war against Libya's southern neighbour, Chad. The objectives of the war were complex and obscure, the main rational motive seeming to be possession of the Aouzou Strip, a remote and barren piece of land that was thought to contain valuable uranium reserves. Having purchased much of the world's most advanced military hardware, Libya was ultimately defeated in 1987 by its impoverished, internally riven Chadian foe. This was humiliating in the extreme and represented something of a nadir for Gaddafi. Along the way, thousands of soldiers lost their lives, including, it is thought, many Palestinians and itinerant labourers of various nationalities plucked at random off the streets of Libyan cities to serve in the war. This was an ugly, cruel and embarrassing episode for Libya: so much money lost, so much blood shed, all for nothing.

Gaddafi has not done well for Libya. He may not be the worst of the world's dictators, and other peoples of the world have suffered more than the Libyans over whom he has ruled. Leaders, however, must be judged on the materials with which they work. Gaddafi had immense oil wealth, from which it might have been expected that he would help his people to build a safe and profitable society. He has not done this. These days, outside the oil industry, the economy is stagnant and in desperate need of difficult reforms, which Gaddafi appears incapable of enacting. Libyans continue to live without meaningful political representation and without a free press. Whatever Western leaders priding themselves on their rehabilitation of Libya like to think, Gaddafi's chief motivation remains his paranoid fear of the emergence of any sort of opposition to his rule. There is no plan for the succession, and chaos looms when the Colonel passes.

By working with Gaddafi, by profiting from the financial opportunities available in Libya, by taking the valuable intelligence he has provided, has Britain extended his rule? Possibly. At the same time, I do not feel in any way that Tony Blair made the wrong decision by bringing Gaddafi in from the cold. What his successors have done, I feel less sure about. I am not convinced that Gordon Brown and David Miliband have been assertive enough in asking the Libyans to pursue PC Fletcher's killer, or in seeking justice for the victims of Libyan-sponsored IRA attacks. Broadly, though, Blair put us on the right path with Libya. Principled disengagement offers us very little. Principled engagement, in which we keep raising our concerns with the Libyans, and in which we allow the people of our two countries to join together to create profits and to share knowledge and expertise, offers us an awful lot, not least the chance to be there and to be listened to as Libya forges a new path in a post-Gaddafi era.

# THE MAKING OF GADDAFI

Who is Colonel Muammar Gaddafi? What made him the man he is today? Gaddafi has devoted so much of his forty-year period in power to creating a cult around his own personality that the truth of the man now seems lost in the choppy and uncertain waters of his own mythologies. We have Gaddafi the Bedouin, Gaddafi the acolyte of Nasser, Gaddafi the enemy of neo-colonialism, but we know little about the traumas, the mistakes, the small early successes, the family conversations that led to the formation of a man of such overweening ambition. Much can be learnt by going over the facts of his origins and by understanding the exciting historical and political climate of the time, but ultimately we are faced with the fact that the deep truth about the nature of the man, if any exists, is likely to be buried under the mountains of his own rhetoric. We are left with only one incontestable truth: the life of Gaddafi has been one devoted from the outset to getting and keeping power.

Certainly, a ruler like Gaddafi would not have been possible anywhere else in the world. He is a product of the Libya into which he was born – poor, bereft of educational infrastructure, deeply scarred by the traumas of colonisation, devoid of talented and skilled leaders; in fact, one of the poorest countries of the world. Yet at the same time, it was a nation poised on the edge of freedom, a nation that had clung on to some of its proud tribal, Bedouin heritage, a nation seized by the excitement of an Arab world that was reasserting its pride and influence.

Libya's fate has long been shaped by its privileged geo-physical circumstances. The discovery of oil was to be a spectacular manifestation of this, but long before that, its location at the top of Africa and only a few hours from Europe had shaped its fortunes and brought prosperity. For centuries, Libya was home to a string of vital trading posts, and over the millennia it saw a succession of invasions by powerful foreigners keen to benefit from its useful Mediterranean positioning. Foreign rulers, however, mainly perched on the lucrative and fertile coast, while the indigenous Berbers and later Bedouin Arabs lived relatively freely in the scrubby desert of the interior regions.

From 1551 until the Italians arrived in 1911, much of Libya was under the rule of the Ottoman Empire. As rulers, the Ottoman emperors' agents in Libya could be brutal at times, but their control was often patchy and tenuous, growing more so as the nineteenth century progressed and tensions within the declining imperial state loosened its hold on its colonial possessions. The Turks and the Tripolitanians developed an uneasy mutual accommodation, while other parts of modern-day Libya remained almost untouched by Ottoman edicts.

It is important to recognise the historically very divided nature of the three main regions of Libya – Cyrenaica in the east, Tripolitania in the north-west and Fezzan in the south-west. These three regions experienced waves of colonisation very differently. Coastal areas tended to co-operate with foreign rulers and to prosper from an often healthy trade between Europe and Africa, while resistance was often stronger out in the desert regions of Cyrenaica and Fezzan. The interior reaches of Fezzan were rarely completely conquered, and have been a constant source of tribal rebellion against the ruler of the day. These rebellions were often led by the Berbers, the indigenous people of north Africa. Cyrenaica, rather than Tripolitania, emerged as a centre of resistance to Italian colonisation.

From Ottoman Cyrenaica sprang Libya's only modern resistance movement. This was the Senussi, an Islamic religious faction that was later to furnish Libya with its first and only monarch. The Senussi movement emphasised strict adherence to the Koran and drew on Sufism, a mystical school of Islamic thought. It was the creation of a man called Sayyid

Mohammed bin Ali al-Senussi, known as the Grand Senussi. The Grand Senussi was an Algerian born at the end of the eighteenth century, who claimed descent from the Prophet Mohammed's daughter Fatima. After studying religion at Fez and Cairo, he moved to Mecca to establish his first *zawiyya*, or religious lodge. Within three generations, the influence of his movement had spread as far as India, Syria, Turkey, Sudan, Egypt and Arabia. The Senussi's stern, austere approach appealed strongly to the Bedouin in Cyrenaica, who similarly stressed simplicity and piety.

The Senussi came into their own as the leaders of resistance to the most brutal episode in Libya's history, colonisation by Italy. The Italians, keen to carve a niche for themselves in the European scramble to divide up Africa, had been putting out feelers in Libya from the late nineteenth century, establishing banks and commercial centres and promoting Italian culture. On 29 September 1911 the Italian Prime Minister, Giovanni Giolitti, declared war on Libya's Turkish colonisers and dispatched troops to the ports of Tripoli, Benghazi, Derna, Tobruk and al-Khums. After a brief period of combined resistance by the Turks and the Libyan tribes (who preferred their fellow Muslim nation as coloniser) the Turkish conceded a peace treaty. The Turks signed Libya over to the Italians in October 1912, without the involvement of any Libyans.

The Libyans, understandably resenting their exclusion from the negotiations and questioning the right of the Turks to sign them over in this fashion, resisted Italian rule vigorously over the next two decades. The human cost of this resistance was extreme. In an early act of violence, the Italian forces murdered 4,000 men, women and children over three days in October 1911, in retaliation for a defeat inflicted on Italian troops by a combined Turkish and Libyan force. An early researcher of colonial rule in Africa collated eyewitness accounts of this massacre, which recorded that 'Tripoli has been the scene of one of the reddest dramas in the history of wars', that there had been 'a veritable carnival of carnage' in which 'crazy soldiers armed with revolvers . . . were shooting every Arab man and woman they met', and that parties of Italian soldiers were 'shooting indiscriminately all whom they met without trial, without appeal'.[1] With brief interludes in which varying degrees of regional autonomy were experimented with, violence and oppression became par for the course over the 1920s and 1930s.

Some of the worst crimes of Italian colonisation were committed from the late 1920s, following the rise to power of the fascist dictator Benito Mussolini. Mussolini saw Libyan opposition as a threat to the assertion of a renewed Italian pride, and in 1930 dispatched his general Rodolfo Graziani to solve the ongoing problem of Senussi-led resistance. Graziani was to find a permanent place in the annals of Libyan history as the violent, cruel face of Italian colonisation. It is recorded that his forces bombed civilians, raped women, tortured prisoners and violated copies of the Koran. Under Graziani, around 12,000 Libyans were killed each year in what Libya expert Geoff Simons describes as 'an Italian campaign that had assumed a genocidal character'.[2] Desert nomads were herded into concentration camps, where many perished, or else they were subjected to poison gas, and it has been estimated that in total 750,000 Libyans were killed during the Italian conquest of Libya, a figure which, if accurate, would amount to nearly half the original population. These years of suffering had a personal impact on Gaddafi, as his grandfather died in the resistance and 300 members of his Qadhafiyya tribe fled in terror to Chad.

It was against the Italian colonisers that the Senussi movement had its finest moment in Libyan history, led by one of Gaddafi's great heroes, Omar Mukhtar. Mukhtar was a religious man, an expert on the Koran and a highly gifted military strategist. His rebel force of around 5,000 soldiers combated the might of the Italian army with astonishing success, particularly in the late 1920s and early 1930s. Mukhtar was regarded by Graziani as the 'origin of the malady' of Libyan resistance, and the focus of the Italian military was on capturing him. In 1931, the elderly Mukhtar was finally caught, gunned down from the air while riding across the desert with ten fellow soldiers, mounted on horses that were close to death from starvation.

Large-bellied Italian dignitaries in suits and uniforms posed for photographs in which they contrasted unpleasantly with the aged and exhausted prisoner, who was clad in voluminous traditional robes and manacled by heavy iron chains. The significance of Mukhtar as an opponent to the Italian regime was reflected both in this enthusiasm for souvenir photographs and in the triumphalist tone of his execution. After a cursory excuse for a trial, he was hanged in front of 20,000 Bedouin, who had been rounded up and forced to watch the demise of their leader. Libyan resistance was left in tatters following his death, destroyed by an extreme campaign of violence and unable to regroup without its charismatic leader. Without Mukhtar, the remainder of the 1930s saw little opposition to Italian policies. By the end of the decade, 110,000 Italians had emigrated to Libya and had ensconced themselves happily on farms and in pretty villas built just like those at home. In 1937, Mussolini rubbed salt into Libyan wounds by bestowing on himself the unlikely title of Protector of Islam. *1911—*

Mukhtar was to recur time and again as one of Gaddafi's favourite symbols, his defiance of colonialism presented as one of the Colonel's great inspirations. Visiting Italy in 2009, Gaddafi pinned a large photograph of Mukhtar to his lapel, an uncomfortable reference to the two nations' shared history, and a somewhat confusing gesture given that the Colonel then proceeded to accept a large aid and development package from Libya's old enemy, and to sign extensive agreements on economic co-operation. Mukhtar was the centrepiece of many of Gaddafi's speeches over the years, and the Hollywood film *Lion of the Desert*, starring Oliver Reed as Graziani and Anthony Quinn as Mukhtar, was shown nightly during the 1980s on Libyan television.

Of course, all of this ignores the fact that Gaddafi had deposed Idris I, grandson of the Grand Senussi and leader of the movement Mukhtar had given so much to promote, as well as the fact that Gaddafi has spent much of his reign in mortal dread of Senussi-led opposition, a paranoia which resulted in the prolific persecution of Mukhtar's Senussi successors. Gaddafi, however, has never been one to shy away from a contradiction.

The conduct of the Italians in Libya is vital to the story of Gaddafi. If Italy had been a different type of coloniser, it might have been that a figure like Gaddafi would never have emerged – an under-educated, undoubtedly naïve, blustering character without any experience as a leader. For Italian rule was characterised by cultural, intellectual and civic impoverishment. Libyans were given a reduced version of full citizenship, which provided no rights outside Libya and fewer than Italians received inside Libya. Libyans were not at any stage allowed to occupy a role where they might supervise Italian subordinates, and in 1949 there were only sixteen native university graduates in the entire country. The Senussi movement had been banned and tribal councils abolished. At the end of World War II, just 10 per cent of the population was literate and industry was virtually non-existent. Not only had the Italians done little to set up the institutions of a modern state or to train the Libyans in governing one, they had also destroyed most of the existing local political systems. The first US ambassador to Libya, Henry Serrano Villard, described the economy and reserve of political experience as 'subnormal'. In 1969, the year of Gaddafi's coup, the country was still recovering from these brutal years, struggling to build a modern politics for a people who had never experienced such a thing. There were still very few educated, capable leaders available for Libya – in such a vacuum of talent, education and experience, the powerful ambition of an army captain in his mid-twenties was enough to take him to the pinnacle of power.

★

One of my most enjoyable tasks as an MP has been working with a group of veterans in my constituency who fought with the Allied coalition of forces termed the Desert Rats. Famously, the Desert Rats held the port of Tobruk in eastern Libya over the course of a 240-day siege by the forces of the German general Erwin Rommel in 1941. I have learnt much from these men about the realities of fighting far from home and family in an inhospitable and deeply foreign environment, and I am always humbled by their unassuming courage and pragmatism. When in Tripoli, my interest in the Desert Rats and the military history of the region led me to visit the British war cemetery there. The cemetery was an oasis of order – the grass was a rich and healthy green, all was impeccably maintained, the gravestones dazzlingly white under the African sun. The contrast to the rest of Tripoli – where any attempts at lawn were sparse and burnt brown and the streets were cluttered with rubble and garbage – was deeply moving. It took several hours to walk all through the cemetery, a sad reflection of the immense loss of young lives. For the north African theatre of war was hard fought and hard won, and many thousands of British, Australian, New Zealand, Indian, Polish and Czech soldiers perished there.

Yet many accounts of the events at Tobruk and the other historic battles that took place in Libya during the 1940s refer to the location of the conflict merely as 'north Africa'. As is perhaps to be expected in the vast international drama that is world war, the unfortunate local inhabitants of the countries where that drama is played out are often seen as minor characters, to the extent that their countries may not even be named in accounts of the bloody battles fought there. Oral histories recorded by Allied soldiers will refer tangentially and briefly to 'bands of Senussi Arabs' that caused periodic problems for Allied troops fighting the Italians and the Germans. From the Libyan perspective, of course, they were not part of the backdrop of the conflict, but the victims of a massive and destructive visitation of the might of the industrialised world. The Libyans had a relatively small role in fighting the war, although the Senussi did form a Libyan Arab Force of five infantry battalions to support the British. They suffered a great deal, however, from its consequences. A large proportion of the country's infrastructure was completely wrecked. More than a thousand air raids hit Benghazi alone during the course of the conflict. Thousands of Italians fled, leaving agriculture and trade in disarray. By 1943, when the Axis forces had been comprehensively defeated in the region, Libya had been uncomfortably carved up between the French in Fezzan and the British in Cyrenaica and Tripolitania.

The Cyrenaican leader of the Senussi movement, Sayyid Idris al-Senussi, grandson of the Grand Senussi, had meanwhile manoeuvred himself into an excellent negotiating position. He had from the pre-war years argued in favour of dealing with the British, a loyalty that stood him in good stead. With some reluctance, the Tripolitanians eventually agreed to allow Idris to negotiate on their behalf, and some rather uncertain guarantees were extracted from the British in the 1940s that Libyan territories would not be allowed to return to the Italians. Crucially, Idris had emerged as a convincing and articulate Libyan leader, someone that the Allies could reasonably negotiate with in a region extremely short of capable leaders. Despite the nervousness of the Tripolitanians, fearful of handing their fate over to a leader of such pristine Cyrenaican heritage and loyalty, Idris would become the acceptable face of the new Libya that was to emerge from the ashes of a troubled history.

What to do about Libya was a headache for the post-war world. Italy was persuaded to give up its sovereignty in 1947, but that still left a country administered in part by the French, in part by the British, and with a range of stridently divided Libyan opinions to account for. The Cyrenaicans feared their fate under a unified state, as the Tripolitanians far outnumbered them, and many preferred an independent, Senussi-controlled Cyrenaica. The Tripolitanians, meanwhile, wanted a union, but were wary of being controlled by the Senussi and of the possibility that their own quite vibrant, metropolitan politics would be suppressed. In Fezzan, many wanted French administration to continue, seeing it as a way to ensure their economic survival in a region where many were desperately poor, while others were opponents of colonisation and supported a union. Meanwhile, the French were rather keen on remaining in Fezzan, the British were somewhat inclined to keep a function for themselves in Cyrenaica and many Italians in Tripolitania were determined to stay on and to retain a role for their country. Local opposition to the parcelling up of Libyan territories between Western powers, however, was fierce, and the proposal to share the country out in this way, devised by the British and Italian Foreign Ministers, Ernest Bevin and Carlo Sforza, proved a much-needed mutual focus of resentment which finally brought the Tripolitanians and Cyrenaicans together. The Bevin–Sforza plan was defeated in the UN after much Libyan lobbying. To celebrate, a street in Tripoli was named after the UN's delegate from Haiti, Emile Saint Lot, who cast the deciding vote against the plan.

Ultimately, the UN found in favour of sovereignty for an independent Libya. The Dutch UN commissioner, Dr Adrian Pelt, was given the job of leading Libyans to devise a constitution for this new state. His task was unenviable, as the Tripolitanians and Cyrenaicans battled for influence every step of the way, to the extent that it proved impossible even to decide on a single capital, and Benghazi and Tripoli became joint capitals. Libya finally achieved its independence in October 1951, a federal state with an income of £3 million per year, a meagre sum almost wholly derived from the rents on British and US military bases. In years to come, Gaddafi was to term this a false dawn for Libya, a fake independence delivered by ill-intentioned and self-interested Western midwives, who foisted on the region a Libya that would do as it was bid.

★

In the early 1940s, as the Allies battled the Axis forces to wrest control of Libyan territory, Muammar Gaddafi entered the world, born in a tent on the edge of the Sahara. His father, Mohammed Abdul Salam bin Hamed bin Mohammed (known as Abu Meniar), scratched out a living herding goats and camels, light years away from the elites of Libya's coastal towns and inland oases. He and his wife Aisha had four children, of whom Muammar was the only son. The family relationship seems to have been strong, as Gaddafi kept his parents close until they died (his father in 1985, at the age of ninety, and his mother in 1978). One's tribe is important in Libya, and Gaddafi was born into a small and relatively weak one, the Qadhafiyya (which translates literally as 'spitters of blood'). The Qadhafiyya had declined in power and influence over the centuries, being pushed gradually west, away from the fertile pastures of the Cyrenaican plateau into the arid deserts around the town of Sirte.

Relatively little seems to be known about the influence of his family on the adult Gaddafi. The clues that we get from Gaddafi himself relate mainly to the claimed formative influence of his exposure to austerity. Throughout his life, Gaddafi has presented his rough desert childhood as a touchstone of authenticity and a kind of moral compass-point. He puts his hatred of corrupt officialdom and his distrust of dependency on the state down to his fiercely independent and physically harsh youth among his Bedouin family and tribe. In later life, at times of trouble he was to say that he sought solace in the desert, apparently retreating to meditate and draw inspiration from the peace of its sands.

Gaddafi is a man of many contradictions, however, and this austere Bedouin persona was to be counterbalanced by the decadent showman. Agreeing with his claim of a spiritual connection to the Libyan desert

is difficult when he ruthlessly milks Bedouin culture for every drop of
political capital and ultimately turns it into a joke, posturing in foreign
capitals and causing incredible inconvenience with his entourage of tents
and camels. Moreover, he now boasts a large posse of frequently badly
behaved (and certainly extremely wealthy sons,) most of whom enjoy the
full range of Western luxuries, so his personal commitment to austerity has
begun to seem risible now, in the sunset years of his rule. Separating the
truth about the resonance of his desert origins from the bizarre political
fiction of the great Bedouin leader has now become impossible, probably
even for Gaddafi himself.

As foreign powers negotiated the future of Libya in the late 1940s, the
young Muammar Gaddafi entered primary school. According to Blundy
and Lycett's biography, he was the first member of his family to receive
an education, and was immediately a 'serious, taciturn, pious' student.[3] He
attended school in Sirte, a pretty coastal market town perched between the
sea and the stony expanses of the Sirte Desert. It would certainly have been
an enormous financial stretch for this rural family to send a son to school,
and Gaddafi was lucky compared to many other Libyans of the era, who
went without schooling. He slept during the week in the local mosque and
walked or hitched the 20 miles back to his rural home on the weekends.
As a Bedouin boy from the home of a goatherd, he was one of the poorest
pupils in the school, and likely learnt some powerful lessons about the
place of his family in Libyan society. It was a serious and responsible life,
one would think, for the average ten-year-old, and one wonders about
the experiences of loneliness and the steely determination that must have
characterised this childhood routine. The French writer Mirella Bianco,
who travelled to the Gaddafi family home in the early 1970s, found that
none of his sisters, parents and cousins expressed any surprise that their
relative had risen to such dizzying political heights: all seemed to feel that
he had always been a uniquely serious person, born to lead.[4]

At the age of fourteen, Gaddafi and his family moved to the town of
Sebha in Fezzan, where his father took a job as a caretaker to the local
tribal leader. The school in Sebha seems to have contributed much to the
formation of Gaddafi the ruler. A teacher quoted by Blundy and Lycett

described Gaddafi as 'gifted, conscientious and solitary, with a sobriety bordering on asceticism'.[5] This serious student, however, was also popular with the other boys. Gaddafi made important friends at this school, whom he would carry into his political life and rely upon heavily as trusted allies. Key among these was his best friend, Abdul Salam Jalloud, who was his most trusted advisor for many years.

At the Sebha school, Gaddafi the orator took shape. It is reported that his fellow students carried around a small stool for him, in case he should wish to step onto it and deliver an impromptu speech. Gaddafi and his friends demonstrated frequently and vigorously, over issues ranging from the Algerian revolution to the deposition and murder of Patrice Lumumba in the Congo. He was thrilled and inspired by the achievements of President Nasser of Egypt, and devoted hours to listening with his friends to Radio Cairo broadcasts and enthusiastically distributed forbidden political literature and little postcards of Nasser. In 1961, Gaddafi and these comrades joined together to mount a demonstration in support of Egypt, following Syria's breaking of an agreement of unity. The demonstration, which led to the arrest of twenty students, resulted in Gaddafi's expulsion from the school. Drawing on the influence of some powerful associates, he managed to get a place at another high school in the town of Masrata, east of Tripoli, where he completed his secondary education. At each of the schools the young Gaddafi attended, he analysed the strengths and weaknesses of those around him, and carefully gathered the allies he felt would be needed when he made his play for power.

Throughout Libya, the populace shared Gaddafi's feelings towards Nasser. Nasser, who led a military coup that deposed King Farouk I in 1952, was undoubtedly one of the twentieth century's most influential men. With his powerful oratory, his Arab nationalist politics and his espousal of the Non-Aligned Movement for the promotion of third world interests, he reinvigorated and renewed Arab self-esteem, and restored dignity and purpose to a people humiliated by centuries of imperialist rule. In resisting the British, French and Israeli attacks following his nationalisation of the Suez Canal in 1956, he became a hero to Arabs and anti-colonialists everywhere. His philosophy – culturally Islamic and Arab but emphasising the secular, focused on modernisation, flavoured with socialism, and anti-Western – inspired leaders across the region.

It is difficult to exaggerate how thoroughly the Libyan coup was fashioned on the revolution and the philosophy of Nasser. Gaddafi had spent hours of his ascetic childhood memorising the Egyptian president's speeches, and he adopted Nasser's actions as a virtual blueprint for the planning of his own uprising. The Libyan revolution borrowed its symbols from Nasser – the coup was led by army men calling themselves Free Officers, and, as the Egyptian revolutionaries had done, the leadership named itself the Revolutionary Command Council. It was not just a question of influence, however: Gaddafi actually planned, after taking power, to approach Nasser with a view to subsuming his country into Egypt, forging a partnership between small, oil-rich Libya and its large and politically influential neighbour that would advance the Nasserist goal of Arab unity.)

Gaddafi's fascination with Nasser was not just for his political views, but also his intense charisma. It must have seemed that Nasser's powerful personality had the potential to harness the political might of the ordinary men and women of the Arab world. This was a man on whom Gaddafi could model himself.

Someone of Gaddafi's naturally non-conformist and headstrong nature seems an unlikely candidate for a military career. Nevertheless, it befitted an acolyte of Nasser to use the army as the route to power. Moreover, in a Libya bereft of other strong institutions, there were few options for a man determined to seize control of the state. Therefore, Gaddafi's next step was enrolment at the Military Academy in Benghazi. As well as securing his own position in 1963, Gaddafi encouraged his closest friends from high school in Sebha to join the academy along with him, building up a trusted cadre. Reports suggest that the young Gaddafi did not take well to the punishing discipline of army life and that he was not an outstandingly successful student. Success in the eyes of the army hierarchy was not, however, his goal. Gaddafi had used his time at primary and secondary school to build his networks, and his period in the military represented the culmination of years of carefully constructing the alliances that would best serve his ambitions – a trait that would later ensure his longevity in power. In 1964, he formed the

Central Committee of the Free Officers Movement, embarking on years of underground meetings and furtive political activity, all led by him. All of the Free Officers donated their salaries to the revolutionary kitty, spent hours driving across the country for clandestine meetings and sacrificed their brief holidays from army service to revolutionary activism. During academy holidays, Gaddafi himself toured the country, building up support and gathering intelligence on his countrymen and women. Apparently, he aroused little suspicion from Idris's security agencies: his origins were so humble, and his rhetoric so over the top, that he seems to have been dismissed as an eccentric dreamer.

As part of his military training, Gaddafi was able to secure a four-month placement for training in Britain in 1966. He studied English in Beaconsfield, and then took a course at the Royal School of Signals in Blandford, providing him with high-level skills in military communication that were likely to have been essential when he deposed the government three years later. Reports were that the young Gaddafi, like many inexperienced students who flocked from all over the developing world to study in London, found life in Britain deeply alien and something of a struggle. He was apparently troubled by the racism he saw and by what he perceived as disgusting moral decay. Nevertheless, over the years, his British training took its place as part of the Gaddafi mythology, and seemed to grow in significance, to the point where he has frequently been referred to as a graduate of Sandhurst, a vast exaggeration of the reality.

★

Carefully, slowly and thoughtfully, Gaddafi continued to gather around him the people that he thought he would need to mount a successful revolution. By all accounts, he invested immense amounts of effort in this. Using the undoubted force of his personality, Gaddafi ensured that these men's loyalty was to him – the leader who knew so much about them, who took such a strong interest in their personal lives and welfare, who was a man of such great seriousness and determination – more than it was to an overarching cause. He watched over his networks carefully and, when needed, played people off against one another. This was to be replicated on a grand scale as he settled into the governance of Libya, which would depend on a ruthless, unpredictable policy of dividing and conquering, and of keeping a lid on the power of any one institution.

*

As Gaddafi and his Free Officers hatched their plans, independent Libya was experiencing something of a rollercoaster ride through the travails and excitements of incipient nationhood. Idris al-Senussi, grandson of the Grand Senussi and a Cyrenaican to the core, had been anointed monarch by the UN and was ruling over the federal system agreed on for Libya. Idris was manifestly not the perfect leader, but he had been judged the best of the bunch. Aged sixty-one when he took power, he had been an unenthusiastic nominee, who would have preferred to govern Cyrenaica alone and who had required considerable persuasion to take on the role. A complete contrast to Gaddafi, he refused to allow his picture to go on Libya's new currency and disliked having anything named after him.

Idris was to prove frequently frustrated by the task of governance, and this frustration led him to resort to an increasingly autocratic style of rule. The federal constitution had given the provinces considerable powers, which were counterbalanced not by the central government, but by the personal power of the King and his advisors. This power was exercised often, and mostly to the benefit of Cyrenaican elites. Idris saw little role for popular participation in all of this. Elections took place once, in 1952, but after that political parties were banned and a tight rein was kept over the new society. Sadly, the elections of 1952 were Libyans' first and last experience of a free vote.

This jerry-built monarchy, constructed by UN committees, was utterly foreign to the forms of social organisation that had existed in Libya in the past. Libya had never been ruled by a king. There had been no popular role at all in the constitution of the new state: no local movement or ideology had drawn the nation together, and a Libyan identity was completely lacking. Idris did not seem to anyone to be willing or able to give his

FIRST/LAST FREE ELECTION 1952

people a sense of themselves as proudly independent Libyans, rather than as Cyrenaicans, Tripolitanians or Fezzanis. This sense of shared interests was to come from another source entirely: oil.

When Idris took power in 1951, Libya's main claim to international distinction was that it was certainly among the very poorest nations of the world, and had most of the possible disadvantages a nation could face. Very few of its citizens had any kind of wealth: one of the chief industries was the collection and sale of the piles of scrap metal left behind from the war. Only international aid provided by the Western countries which had created the Libyan monarchy kept the population from starvation. The literacy rate was about 10 per cent, women's rights were almost unheard of, per capita annual income was roughly $25, about 5 per cent of land was usable for agriculture, and society had been rendered profoundly dysfunctional first by a brutal colonisation and then by a ferocious world war. In 1959, however, oil was found, immediately transforming Libya's prospects in the eyes of the world. Development in post-war Europe was gathering steam, transport costs from Libya were very low, and its oil deposits were of extremely high quality. From 1963, crude oil began to be produced and exported in large quantities.

Idris's central government, which had watched carefully over promising early efforts at exploration, now sought the best-quality advice available on how to manage this astonishing new fortune. The 1955 Petroleum Law they drafted was viewed throughout the world as fair, innovative and encouraging towards the smaller, independent oil companies, and it ensured that the government would not be exploited by the oil majors. Government control over the oil industry grew during the 1960s through wise policy-making as the true extent of the profitability of oil became clear. Gaddafi was to be bequeathed an oil industry that was well run and well regulated, a legacy he protected vigilantly and which formed the financial basis of his later revolutionary experiments.

Oil was also the force that led to the prospect of a coherent, unified Libya. To make the oil industry as profitable as possible, and to share the proceeds evenly, it became increasingly obvious that the very loose federal structure would be inadequate. Oil revenues had also shifted most existing power dynamics – importantly, much of the oil was discovered in Cyrenaica, which no longer had so much to fear from Tripolitanian dominance. Oil money meant more jobs and more schools, and the population quickly became more urbanised and sophisticated, loosening traditional regional and tribal identities. The centre grew inexorably stronger, and in 1963 Libya abandoned federalism, adopting a new constitution and a unitary state. In theory, at least, the country was now united.

This was a key moment in the nation's history, and it is important to understand that when Gaddafi took power in 1969, a meaningfully united Libya was merely six years old. It was a shaky, inexperienced nation, seized on by the relentless force that was Gaddafi.

The oil industry was set up carefully and well, but Idris was less wise in his management of the revenues it produced. The task of managing a country that had to all intents and purposes been buried in an avalanche of money was extremely difficult. The inexperienced new government proved unable to regulate or to set up any kind of transparent mechanisms for distributing money. Corruption was rife. Property contracts, information about oil deals, lucrative access for foreigners to the powerful members of the royal entourage – all were up for sale. Patronage and family connections became vital in securing the government positions that would enable access to state funds. From the late 1950s, corruption scandal after corruption scandal rocked the tottering regime, which seemed able to find no way to protect itself from the rapacity of its elites. Idris clearly saw the compelling need for reform, but he was an elderly, frail man, and proved unable to stand up to his self-interested advisors.

Meanwhile, the population was increasingly excited by the Arab nationalism that was sweeping through the region. The monarchy, beholden to the Americans and Europeans, had no effective way of responding to this. It sought to present itself as Arab and Islamic, but was visibly surrounded by and dependent on British and American advisors. The Arab nationalists might have had a vent for their fervour if the King had not got rid of all Libya's political parties. In 1967, Egypt's defeat in the Six Day War, and the subsequent occupation of Sinai by Israel, was a humiliation felt keenly throughout the Arab world. Idris's shaky monarchy was clearly going to find it difficult to survive the tide of anger that rose in Libya. There were anti-Western riots in Tripoli and Benghazi, and workers shut down oil terminals to demonstrate their support for the Arab nations battling Israel.

Frustration with Idris, however, was not limited to the fervent Arab nationalists. His opponents also included more peaceful and pragmatic men working high up in the oil industry and in the government, who were disgusted by the extensive corruption. Many such men wished for reforms that could make Libya a transparent, effective, well-regulated state, and a more peaceful and predictable place in which to live and to do business.

Gaddafi's bloodless revolution was quietly to put an end to the Idris era.  He would be greeted by some Libyans with a sigh of relief at the prospect of much-needed change. Many hoped that the new regime would shape something stronger and fairer out of a Libya characterised by uncontrolled wealth and rampant corruption. Quickly, however, this prospect was to recede, replaced by a police state that would terrify its citizens and squander its money, the vanity project of a leader who soon became a law unto himself.

Over the course of its history, Libya had been invaded, subjugated, colonised, parcelled up by Westerners, then simultaneously blessed and cursed by the sudden discovery of ludicrously profitable rivers of oil – now Gaddafi's confidence and vigour held out the promise to Libyans that they might finally begin to control their own destiny. In reality, Gaddafi was to prove another of the massive cataclysms visited upon the country, another unstoppable force that was yet again to put on hold the emergence of a confident citizenry who would be allowed to shape their nation according to their needs, hopes and desires.

2

# GADDAFI'S REVOLUTIONARY EXPERIMENT

There is no state with a democracy except Libya on the whole planet.

Colonel Gaddafi [1]

In mid-1969, King Idris I of Libya, with 400 suitcases to hold his essentials, departed to spend the summer in Greece and Turkey. Gaddafi and his Free Officers recognised the arrival of a long-anticipated opportunity and began the planning of what they called 'Operation Jerusalem'. On 1 September, they put these plans into action, moving in to occupy airports, police depots, radio stations and government offices throughout Tripoli and Benghazi. Gaddafi addressed the citizens of Libya by radio, proclaiming the end of a corrupt regime, 'the stench of which has sickened and horrified us all'.[2] In the end, the coup was almost completely bloodless, and the new leaders seemed remarkably mild, taking very little violent action against supporters of the monarchy.

Gaddafi's Libya was quickly awarded international recognition. Iraq, Syria, Sudan and Egypt recognised it immediately, and Britain and the United States shortly followed suit. The Egyptians helpfully dispatched experts to advise the completely inexperienced new leadership, almost all of whom were aged under thirty. The general reaction inside Libya was more relief than surprise and the monarchy quietly crumbled. King Idris's regime had lasted longer than many had expected, and there was cautious optimism that this new alternative would dispense with some of the corruption and division that had characterised his years in power.

Idris made some relatively weak and clearly doomed efforts to seek British support, which was discreetly withheld. Idris was frail, old and unmotivated, and the political disaster of Suez made the British reluctant to intervene. Generally, the West was not averse to the prospect of a youthful, energetic military regime and no country took action to oppose Gaddafi. The British evacuated their Libyan military bases in March 1970, the Americans in June. A relative of Idris, Abdullah al-Senussi, plotted to invade and retake Libya from Chad, but his plot was discovered in May 1970, and it did little to undermine the Free Officers' control.

Many in Libya had expected a coup against Idris, but few had successfully predicted its source. I interviewed a Libyan businessman in London for this book, a man who escaped the country in the mid-1970s to pursue a successful career in the energy world. He wished to remain anonymous, so I refer to him by the alias Ahmed. Ahmed told me that there were various candidates who were the subject of rumours about a possible coup. In particular, Abdul Aziz al-Shelhi, a member of a conflict-riven and periodically influential family that had accrued great power under Idris, was thought to be a likely usurper. As we know, it was not the educated and experienced Shelhi who stepped forward, but a completely unknown minor captain from Libya's army. According to Ahmed, 'Suddenly out of the blue came this Gaddafi. No-one took him seriously, they were laughing at him.'

Confronted with the figure of Gaddafi, Libyans largely took him at face value, perceiving him as a young army officer possessed by the spirit of Nasserism and a lust for independence. Few then guessed that this obscure soldier would prove a megalomaniac with a penchant for some of the most bizarre attempts at social engineering the world was to see in the second half of the twentieth century. More prescient than Ahmed was a Libyan butcher he had chatted to in Cairo back in September 1969, who had told him, 'I have heard three slogans – "freedom", "Arab unity" and "socialism". We're in trouble!'

The events of 1969, however, could barely even be termed a revolution. This was more like a coup: a takeover of the state by a group of army officers disillusioned by corruption and passionate about the Arab cause. Revolution in the sense of a complete social upheaval and reconstruction of the state was still three or four years away. During the first years of Gaddafi's rule, he was unquestionably the leader, but the coup had been a group affair, and the opinions of his colleagues on what was formalised as the Revolutionary Command Council (RCC) were important. The more moderate and economically minded RCC members would fight hard in the early years to restrain Gaddafi's more extreme impulses.

The RCC was to be a body of profound importance in Libya's development. Its members – including Major Abdul Salam Jalloud, Major Bashir Hawadi, Captain Mukhtar Abdullah Gerwy, Captain al-Khuwaylidi al-Hamidi, Captain Mohammed Nejm, Captain Ali Awad Hamza, Captain Abu Bakr Yunis Jabr and Captain Omar Abdullah al-Muhayshi – wielded considerable influence both early in the regime and later on. Some worked by Gaddafi's side, while others fled and became implacable enemies of the regime. These men were all from Libya's middle or working classes, and from tribes outside the elites that had been favoured by the Senussi monarchy. They were young, mainly from rural areas, and without university education. They represented a profound cultural break from the wealthy, educated, conservative leaders selected under King Idris. Most were spirited, energetic young men, keen to make their mark, but straightforwardly motivated by the glaring inequalities they saw every day, in contrast to Gaddafi's messianic sense of his own destiny. One, Mohammed Zwai (a schoolmate of Gaddafi's), told Mirella Bianco, 'Libya was a poor country. It was not fame or fortune that we were seeking; we dreamed of liberty and justice and unity and a place in the sun for everybody.'[3]

At first, Gaddafi had to work with the RCC, he had to figure out how government worked, and most of all, he had to safeguard the all-important oil revenues. For these reasons, there was caution in the early years of his rule. The Free Officers were all young and inexperienced, and they needed to learn the ropes when it came to the oil industry. As they were drastically lacking expertise in most areas of economics and management, even their purges had to be somewhat restrained, because Libya could not afford to lose too many men from its small educated elite.

Nonetheless, there were some big changes. Key supporters of the monarchy were removed from power, and the army was purged of Senussi officers. Importantly, the Free Officers also set about establishing an ideological basis for their rule. The coup had been the work of a few middle-ranking army men, and it desperately needed to portray itself as something rather grander. A clear way this could be achieved was to paint the Free Officers' coup as an expression of the people's innate desire for the assertion of Arab nationalism and the challenging of Western dominance.

The population was deeply scarred by its experience of colonisation. Every aspect of life in Libya had been damaged and retarded by the vicious and unproductive experience of Italian rule. Then, the Americans, the French and the English had worked between themselves to concoct what could justifiably be viewed as an illegitimate and certainly an autocratic monarchical system of government. Meanwhile, the refreshing winds of Arab nationalism had swept through the region, encouraging Arab self-confidence and decrying the perceived crimes of Israel. Appealing to the people's sense of wounded patriotism and Arab pride was a political step that could not fail. The new regime framed its rhetoric accordingly, and also took some important actions to back it. In the early 1970s, Gaddafi and the Free Officers closed down British and American oil bases in Libya, took on the oil majors to win fairer prices for Libyan oil, and nationalised a number of oil companies. Western books and musical instruments were thrown on bonfires, churches morphed into mosques, nightclubs closed down, traditional Libyan dress was promoted, sharia law replaced Western law and the months of the Gregorian calendar were renamed. Signs written in the Roman alphabet were removed and replaced with Arabic ones all over the land, an understandable ideological measure but somewhat impractical in a land where nearly half the workforce were foreigners. 'Ladies' and 'Gents' signs were taken off the toilets at Tripoli airport, menus could no longer be obtained in English, and even a statue in Tripoli's marketplace of the Libyan-born Roman emperor Septimius Severus had its Latin inscription ripped off. Italian settlers lost their rights to hold property, and 12,000 of them returned to Italy, leaving behind villas, apartments and thousands of hectares of valuable farmland.

Many of these were popular measures, some of which could fairly be said to have served Libya's interests. Ahmed told me that during the first few years of the regime, 'like many other people at the time, I shared the ideas of Nasser. I was excited, and hopeful, yes. For the first four or five years the country was booming.'

The confident, anti-imperialist actions of these early years were to form the foundation of Gaddafi's legitimacy. To many back then, he seemed like the embodiment of everyone's hopes and dreams for a prouder, stronger Libya. In contrast to the frail, weak, elderly King Idris, Gaddafi was youthful, Bedouin to the core and boundlessly confident. He enthusiastically insinuated himself into all of Libya's key national 'stories' – he was the inheritor of Omar Mukhtar, he was a physically active, virile but meditative Bedouin, he was the underdog, the oppressed, the poor boy made good. He was handsome, he was determined constantly to mingle with the ordinary man and woman and he stood proudly on the world stage, a confident Libyan and Arab to be reckoned with by the world. Undoubtedly, he had an enormous well of charisma on which to draw as leader. It was to take two decades before this well ran dry, to be supplemented by an even more abundant resource of pure ruthlessness and cunning.

By 1973, Gaddafi had begun to settle in, and the way looked clear to launch Libya on the road to something rather more radical. On 16 April, the Colonel delivered a speech in the town of Zuwara that announced the beginning of a Popular Revolution. The speech heralded the real foundation of his enormous, tumultuous political experiment on Libya, and it contained all the seeds of what was to follow. The programme he outlined at Zuwara involved dissolving existing political institutions, suspending the nation's legal system and creating the first incarnation of the nation's popular committees, the community-level citizens' groups that were tasked with running the country. The law had gone, all the familiar parts of government had gone, and they had been replaced with something that was clearly eminently fluid and changeable at the regime's whim. The cloud of chaos that was to hang over Libya for decades to come had descended.

The Zuwara speech also intensified the urgency and the violence associated with the purging of the elites, who Gaddafi saw as blocking the will of the people. A wave of forced resignations and sackings shook Libya's media, government, universities and major enterprises. To replace the purged elites, Gaddafi encouraged thousands of inexperienced young would-be bureaucrats from outside the traditional groups to take up positions in key government agencies. The ranks of the public sector swelled enormously, while efficiency dropped dramatically. Gaddafi's long-standing policy of using public sector employment to manage and control society had been put in place, and administrative chaos was the order of the day. Gaddafi had acted decisively to remove the control of government bureaucracy from its traditional holders, but he had also signalled his intention to use the agencies of the state to promote his political ends, which ultimately would be a costly, destructive policy.

Zuwara was followed by chaos and uncertainty. At the top, there was the conflict between revolutionaries and technocrats that has long been a feature of such politics as Libya can be said to have. The more revolutionary members of the RCC pushed for Libya's riches to be spent on ideological projects that would promote Arab unity. The technocrats, on the other hand, pushed for proper, predictable economic management through the development of strong, independent state bureaucracies, and argued that spending money on unity pacts and interference in foreign conflicts was recklessly wasteful.

This fear of what was being done to Libya was not confined to the uppermost tiers of government. The year 1975 saw discontent with the regime erupt into widespread student demonstrations, prompting the RCC to introduce compulsory military service for young people as a solution to restive student politics. Gaddafi and his closest allies had never much liked university students, viewing with suspicion their tendency to ask too many questions. There were mass arrests of students in April, and reports emerged from Libya that Gaddafi had ordered his most loyal army units to encircle Tripoli, providing a protective wall against a potential coup. In August, this fear was realised: Bashir Hawadi and Omar Abdullah al-Muhayshi launched a coup. Gaddafi survived and the plotters fled. The coup came to nothing,

probably because the rumours of it had been so persistent that Gaddafi had
had many months to erect his defences. Hawadi and Muhayshi's failure
cleared the way for him. His most powerful opposition in the RCC had
self-destructed, meaning he was free to implement his revolutionary vision
and to forge Libya into what quickly became a state ruled by one man. He
purged the army and the government of those who opposed him, and sat
back to consider his options.

★

Libyan people, it seemed, were not very gung-ho about eternal revolution
and productive revolutionary disorder. They wanted jobs, education and
peaceful existences, and had little truck with talk of a revolutionary, Arab,
Islamic, socialist utopia. Gaddafi, intensely frustrated by his lethargic
compatriots, set his mind to the task of reorganising society from the
bottom up. He now had almost limitless funds with which to experiment,
as Libya had become possessed of an enormous fortune, particularly after
the oil boom of 1973. Per capita income in 1969 was $2,000, but by 1979
it had risen to nearly $10,000. What was needed, Gaddafi felt, was to stop
experimenting gingerly with cautious bits of ad hoc reform, and instead
to use Libya's bounty to launch a full-scale ideological overhaul. This
would require an intellectual base, a text that would cement Gaddafi's
image as a visionary revolutionary, putting paid to any notion that he
was in fact merely an ambitious, cunning but under-educated military
dictator. The Green Book, in his eyes at least, would fulfil this need. In
it, Gaddafi sketched out his Third Universal Theory, designed to be an
alternative to Marxism and capitalism. The Green Book's three volumes
contain Gaddafi's thoughts on politics, economics and society, and
provide the text on which his revolutionary experiments were based.
The Green Book was limitless in its ambitions – it suggested that the Libya
it created would be the apex of human political, social and economic
achievement. Its political model was unique, according to the author,
synthesising all the advantages of every political system while eliminating
all their injustices, and grounding the resultant product in Arab, Bedouin

and Islamic tradition. On 2 March 1977, Gaddafi proclaimed people's power in a speech at Sebha, signalling the launching of a refashioned Libya to be based entirely on the revolutionary thought of *The Green Book*, which was to become the source of both the political and the legal system.

I first encountered *The Green Book* on a political delegation to Libya. Boarding a flight from Tripoli to Sirte, I was handed a copy by the flight attendant. Oddly enough, it was a French translation I was given, but I was able to read it in the many long periods of waiting that characterised the trip. At the core of Gaddafi's thinking was a kind of libertarian wildness, which was very clearly in tension with his desire in practice to control every aspect of Libyan life. The strangest of political thinkers, he declared his wish for Libyans to exert total command of their own destinies, freed from the malign interference of politicians and bureaucrats, but at the same time he wanted and needed to retain a frighteningly complete control over every aspect of society.

*The Green Book* celebrated the principle of statelessness, proposing that the men and women of Libya should be freed from the interference of political parties and political representation. Political parties were seen as a canny investment by the rich in a mechanism perfectly designed to manipulate the poor. The adversarial system of Western democracy also meant that politicians on opposing sides bickered like children, rather than spending their time working for the national good. Government by elected representatives was seen as highly exploitative. Gaddafi saw no reason for people to hand over important decision-making powers to an elected representative, rather than maintaining a real say for themselves in what happened to the country. The elected member was, he declared, the 'monopoliser of the people's sovereignty'. Moreover, the inescapable truth, according to the Colonel, was that elections meant many people's wishes were ignored: it was quite possible that 49 per cent of a local population would have voted against any given elected representative. Governance by someone who had won only 51 per cent was, according to *The Green Book*, the 'essence of dictatorship'. (This is certainly among the many points on which I, as chairman of the Commons All-Party Group for the promotion

of first-past-the-post, differ in my political views from the Colonel.) To
Gaddafi, representative government meant that

> the people are the prey fought over by the predators: instruments of
> government compete in their power struggle for the votes of the people
> they in turn neglect and exploit, while the people move silently towards
> the ballot box, like the beads in a rosary, to cast their votes in the same
> way that they throw rubbish in dustbins.

The better solution, Gaddafi felt, was that the power of the individual
should be preserved. *The Green Book* proposed a means via which this
could be achieved, and formed the blueprint for Libya's unique system of
government, implemented in March 1977. Local congresses are held, which
choose working committees. These local working committees then meet
at a district level, and district working committees feed up to the national
level. There is thus a pyramidal structure. At the top are the General
People's Congress (the legislative branch, composed of working committees
from the district level) and the General People's Committee (equivalent to
a cabinet), the members of which are the secretaries of committees for
areas of government including health, education and women's affairs. The
intended result is that government works from the bottom up, not from
the top down.

Gaddafi's attraction to statelessness was also rooted in his Bedouin
origins. Traditional Bedouins were stateless nomads, and many certainly
proudly retain this nomadic inheritance as an aspect of their modern self-
image. The Bedouin tribal unit worked on the principles of unanimity and
consensus, and was without formal structures of social organisation. Though
the Turks and the Italians had commanded swathes of Libyan territory, they
had not really managed to impose a strong or a meaningful modern state
over the Libyan territories they claimed to rule. The concept of a state had
little resonance within the Libyan imagination. The one successful local
political movement of the nineteenth and twentieth centuries, the Senussi,
had structured itself in a way that mirrored tribal organisation, and was
grounded strongly in a tribal ethos. Tribal culture and tribal ways had a

moral, political and personal appeal to Gaddafi, who was the product of a traditional, rural childhood in the desert. He co-opted this heritage with great enthusiasm, and presented his *Green Book* as a refashioning of it into a viable modern politics.

The new Libya, a realisation of the political vision of *The Green Book*, was said by Gaddafi to allow, as far as possible, the chance for citizens to manage their own lives, as their Bedouin ancestors had once done. He termed this new form of state a *jamahiriyya:* a state that would be governed through the consultation and participation of the people. The full title of the new republic was *al-Jamahiriyya al-'Arabiyya al-Libiyya al-Sha'abiyya al-Ishtirakiyya al-'Uzma*: the Great Socialist People's Libyan Arab *Jamahiriyya*. It was proclaimed the ultimate in cutting-edge democracy, a system under which citizens would have a unique level of control over their lives.

According to Gaddafi, however, this control was so exhilarating and so complete that Libyans should not require any other form of organisation. No form of political activity was permitted, because attendance at the basic people's congresses should fill every conceivable political need. Neatly, Gaddafi had managed to design something that promised power to the people, from the bottom up, but that in reality delivered power to the Colonel, from the top down. Trade unions, sports clubs, women's groups, political parties, professional associations – all were declared not only unnecessary, but an evil repression of the people by the interests of the powerful.

In practice, of course, the system of government by committee was very different than it looked on paper. Committee secretaries were supposed to be appointed by the General People's Congress, but in reality they were chosen by the regime. The General People's Committee was supposedly the highest level of power in the nation, but it was denied any responsibility for the military, the budget, the oil sector, the police, the army or foreign policy. From day one, the committee system of government was limited, and very obviously stage managed from above.

What to do about the law had been a prickly problem for Gaddafi. It was difficult to create a grand, ongoing revolutionary experiment in which the people would be eternally set against the institutions of the state in a condition of glorious flux, when the law was inconveniently interrupting by setting out defined boundaries and rights. He had dispensed with the monarchical legal system back in 1969, replacing it with sharia law. Sharia law, or Islamic religious law, does not often get good press in the West, but it undoubtedly gave the Libyan people consistent and clear rights, including the right to private property.

The inconvenience this posed to Gaddafi was solved by the simple solution of replacing sharia law with *The Green Book*. It declared that constitutions and 'man-made laws' were unnatural and dictatorial, and that legal decisions must be placed into the hands of the people. The mullahs and their supporters were outraged and protested accordingly, but Gaddafi insisted that sharia law could not deal with the conflicts of a modern society. Not only was the law itself thus thrown out the window, but the private practice of law was banned in May 1980 (along with all professional occupations). There were to be no laws – only *The Green Book*, and no lawyers – only revolutionary zealots who were appointed to the new revolutionary courts to deal out punishments that were often harsh and violent. These courts made it significantly easier for the regime to carry out the numerous executions of political dissidents that characterised the 1980s, and certainly induced a general reluctance among the population to seek out legal remedies.

Socialism was also a major influence on Gaddafi's thinking, and *The Green Book* is highly egalitarian. It is marked by a profound distrust of hierarchies and the belief that bureaucratic elites merely form a bar to people's ability to control their lives. This egalitarianism certainly translated into a real commitment to creating a more equal society. In his first years in power, Gaddafi redistributed land, provided low-cost housing, expanded free education, provided interest-free loans and raised the minimum wage. Some elements of the programme were sensible and fair, such as the construction of affordable housing. Others had the ring of madness, particularly those that were implemented following the publication of the second volume of *The Green Book*, which put forward the Colonel's economic philosophy. From the late 1970s through to the mid-1980s, such policy initiatives as the elimination of savings accounts, the random and spontaneous reallocation of property title and the complete eradication of small businesses wreaked havoc on life in Libya (of which more in Chapter 11).

Gaddafi's redistribution of wealth certainly sprang in part from his beliefs about how the world should be organised. At the same time, such generosity from above was also a very good way to keep the people on side. The populist distribution of wealth, in a manner that ensured the total dependence of most Libyans on the largesse of the state, was an excellent means of safeguarding his position in power. Libyans were prisoners of Gaddafi, but Gaddafi was also a prisoner of the people: he had made an implicit bargain, in which oil revenues would be funnelled constantly down to the populace, while the development of a normal market system and a robust economy was put permanently on hold.

Gaddafi's relationship with Islam has been idiosyncratic to say the least. The early Gaddafi was renowned for his purity, piety and austerity, and repeatedly declared Arab failures to be failures of religious belief. Visiting world leaders were frequently subjected to attempts to convert them. On coming to power, the Free Officers banned alcohol, closed down nightclubs and churches and introduced sharia law. In a conservative, religious society like Libya, it was always clear that religion would be an indispensable source of legitimacy for the new leaders. As he settled into power, however, Gaddafi became jealous and fearful of the loyalties Islam commanded in the Libyan people and the *ulama* (the Muslim clergy) ultimately came to be seen as enemies. In May 1975 he prohibited the *ulama* from commenting on politics, telling them to stick to prayers alone. He began to assert people's ability to interpret the Koran for themselves, rejecting the spiritual guidance of the clergy. The clergy, however, proved a less compliant enemy than others Gaddafi encountered. Angered by such policies as the conscription of female soldiers, many bravely denounced Gaddafi from the mosques of Libya. In particular, the Mufti of Tripoli, Sheikh Mohammed al-Bushti, managed to enrage Gaddafi with his principled defence of traditional Islam. In 1980, Bushti disappeared after making a speech in favour of the Muslim Brotherhood, an Islamic group that came to Libya from Egypt, and which Gaddafi feared greatly as a potential source of opposition. Reports emerged that the Mufti had been tortured and murdered. Over subsequent years, Gaddafi attempted to paint him as a Saudi agent.

In 1984, Gaddafi ordered the tomb of the founder of the Senussi sect, Sayyid Mohammed bin Ali al-Senussi, which was a hugely popular pilgrimage site for believers, to be removed from Libya. Islam in Libya was to belong to Gaddafi alone, and the late 1970s and 1980s saw a concerted and a successful battle against the defenders of the old ways.

*The Green Book* was a radical text, and its implementation required some radical action. This was the task of the revolutionary committees, created by Gaddafi in 1977. Ostensibly, the revolutionary committees were designed to realise *The Green Book*'s vision and to reinvigorate the revolution, in the style of the Chinese Red Guards. Those with the appropriate passion and the right level of vim and vigour were encouraged to come forward to become members. To many, however, this sounded more like a recipe for a police state than a prescription for popular liberation, and this was indeed how it panned out. The Libya scholar Lisa Anderson has written that the revolutionary committees 'soon grew into a paramilitary force of between 4,000 and 5,000 enthusiasts and thugs'.[4] The revolutionary committees had started out with a motivational function but quickly assumed a sinister security role, evolving into a surveillance instrument that turned citizen against citizen. By 1979, it was generally accepted that these new revolutionary committees had overtaken the People's Congress as the topmost level of authority in Libya.

The story of Gaddafi's creation of his *jamahiriyya*, therefore, is the story of *The Green Book*, but it is also the story of the parallel creation of a shadowy, sinister security apparatus and a network of informal, hidden power. *The Green Book* would trumpet the virtues of the ultimate authority of the people, but it would be those working behind the scenes, outside the authority of the pyramidal structures of popular power, who would make the real decisions. From the beginning, Gaddafi's rule was defined by the existence of two power structures. On the one side were the formal, publicly recognised institutions, drawn from the pyramidal committee system. On the other side was a small circle of the Colonel's intimates, who, along with their leader, took all major decisions and exerted ruthless control over the rest of society, including the army, the police, the media, the General People's Committee (GPC) and the people's committees. This second, informal sector was protected by the dreaded revolutionary committees.

Gaddafi's own power was firmly located in this informal sector. In 1979 he resigned from the GPC, and from then on was to declare himself merely a 'guide' to the nation, without formal power. This was then a convenient ruse to a large extent, allowing others to take the blame for every poor decision and paving the way for Gaddafi to portray himself as stepping in sagely to proffer advice when things went wrong. In latter years, however, the notion of Gaddafi as a guide has seemed less ridiculous. The Gaddafi of the twenty-first century is a different prospect to the firebrand radical of the 1980s and 1990s, and he has been increasingly willing to defer to the expertise of his often highly capable ministers.

Mike O'Brien was the Foreign Office minister charged with negotiating Britain's rapprochement with Libya in 2002. He had many opportunities to witness the workings of the Gaddafi regime, and told me that in his view,

> there is a set of parameters, set out in *The Green Book*. Provided the ministers stay inside the parameters, they could disagree and express differences. They didn't seem self-conscious about doing so. I had expected they would all be in fear of the leader, but it wasn't like that. I think it's difficult to know what's in Gaddafi's mind. I think Gaddafi sees himself as a 'philosopher-king', who weighs in when he disagrees with things . . . Gaddafi sets the big broad principles, but the ministers are allowed to do a lot of the detail.

I agree with O'Brien that Gaddafi keeps his ministers on a loose rein these days. Nevertheless, few fail to see through the fiction of him as a benevolent, detached 'guide'. The form of his autocratic control has been refined and tempered over the decades of his rule, but the substance remains. Gaddafi sets the direction in which Libya must travel, and, as ever, he is willing to step in and change this at his whim.

★

*The Green Book*, then, is crucial to understanding Gaddafi's leadership of Libya. It was the blueprint for an increasingly unhinged series of radical policies that turned life in Libya upside down during the 1980s. It provides a unique insight into the mind of the dictator – a rambling, inconsistent, but also simplistic and blunt view of the world. *The Green Book* was an indispensable tool of power; it gave Gaddafi the pretext to repeatedly turn society on its head, and it was also an ideological stick with which to beat those he wished to be rid of. It set in place a whole new political system that in theory gave the people all the power but in practice was a hollow shell, which could not hide the all too obvious fact that Libya's destiny was in the hands of one man alone. *The Green Book*'s section on politics tellingly ends with a thought that seems to contradict all that has preceded it about the glorious potential of the popular committee system: 'Theoretically, this is genuine democracy, but in reality, the strong always rule: that is to say those who are strongest in society hold the reins of government.' This seems the most truthful moment of the book.

When we look at Gaddafi's long years in power, it seems that *The Green Book* ultimately inspired most of what led his people to fear and dread him – the purges, the chaos, the disappearances, the 'spontaneous' policy decisions that ruined thousands of lives – but very little of what had led them in the early days to invest a level of hope and belief in his leadership. The Gaddafi of the 1970s was a charismatic man, a handsome man, a young man, and a credible symbol for a longed-for reawakening of Libya's self-belief. He asserted Libya's rights against Britain and the US in a meaningful way that many of his compatriots supported. (The educated few in Tripoli and Benghazi were likely to have been as bemused by the rough naïvety of his politics as any onlookers in London or Washington, but the deprived masses probably saw much of themselves in him and could place a genuine faith in his egalitarian promises.)

The publication of *The Green Book* marked the end of all this. It signified his descent into a revolutionary madness and his determined intention to take the Libyans with him. Soon, his charisma and people's belief in him had evaporated, and from the early 1980s onwards, his posturing on the world stage as an authentic Bedouin, an opponent of neo-imperialism and a defender of Arab values had become hollow and distasteful. It was his incredible cunning, his ruthless craving for complete power, and his populist channelling of money into Libyan homes that was to keep him at the helm, not his revolutionary philosophies.

# GUNS AND MONEY

Yasser Arafat famously described Gaddafi as 'the soldier of revolutionary phrases'. This *bon mot* nicely captures the Colonel's taste for bombastic, menacing, lengthy speeches. Yet is it also somewhat unfair, as Gaddafi has often put his money where his mouth is. Many other dictators have spouted similarly stark, simplistic and confused views of world politics, but few have had his opportunities to spend huge amounts of cash pursuing the realisation of his views. Through the 1970s and 1980s, Libya was a saviour to many extra-state groups, whether terrorists, liberationists, anarchists or secessionists. As the glossy black oil flowed out of Libya, money flowed into dubious bank accounts in every corner of the world, from Manila to Dublin to Chicago to Beirut.

In pursuing their foreign objectives, Libyans contributed cash and weapons, but also training. *Time* reported in 1986 that Libya was playing host to twenty training camps, where thousands of rebels from numerous different countries joined together to receive training in the techniques of terror.[1] Tripoli became renowned as a sort of international university of terror, and most of the states battling secessionist or revolutionary movements during the 1970s and 1980s cited the involvement of 'Libyan-trained' men. So extensive was Gaddafi's association with the terrorist organisations of the world that in 1977, President Ford's administration was said to have ranked Libya fourth on its list of enemies of the United States, behind the Soviet Union, China and North Korea, but ahead of Cuba.

By setting himself up as a financier to such a broad range of organisations, Gaddafi extended his influence over world affairs, inserting the Libyans as players in a massive variety of conflicts. Directing money to revolutionaries, dissidents and terrorists meant Gaddafi was able to harass former colonial powers, to promote Islam, to support small nations in their independence struggles and to undermine regimes he considered politically undesirable. To those who criticised him for ignoring the conventional avenues of diplomacy, Gaddafi often responded that those avenues had been created by imperialists for their own benefit. As is so often the case with Gaddafi, there was an irritating kernel of truth in the arguments he used to justify his erratic and violent behaviour.

Many commentators compare Libya to the US and the Soviet Union in its determination to interfere in the affairs of other countries. This seems to me to be over-stating things, at least in the case of Libya. Gaddafi certainly shaped Libya into a force to be reckoned with, but there was little evidence that he did this according to a well-thought-out grand plan. His sponsorship of extra-state groups was random and ill informed. Little attempt was made to research the aims and credentials of the groups that trooped through Libya in search of funds. The journalist Donald Trelford described this bluntly as 'the awful naïvety of a man who "supports just causes everywhere" – i.e. passes round the plastic explosive to any rag-bag revolutionary movement that visits his tent'.[2] Daniel Pipes, the controversial scholar of Islam in world politics, has pointed out that whereas the Saudis used oil money to develop their influence logically, carefully and peacefully, Gaddafi focused energetically on funding movements that pursued turmoil, revolution and violence.[3] The result of his indiscriminate distribution of cash was that he ended up associated with violent, mercenary groups with dubious aims, as well as with a smaller selection of the most influential and admired liberation movements of the twentieth century. The randomness of Gaddafi's support robbed him of credibility and made most governments of the world increasingly reluctant to deal with him. His association with such a bizarre breadth of movements contributed much to his image as an erratic, mercurial leader who lacks a strong moral or intellectual base from which to judge world affairs.

It is true, though, that Gaddafi's desire to mould world events according to his ideological vision echoed Soviet and American desires. His superpower-esque behaviour brought him a degree of support in the Arab world, where he was viewed by many ordinary people as admirable in his determination to play the same game as the Americans. At home, though, emotions were mixed. Gaddafi may have bought Libya a reputation as a player to be reckoned with, but it remains a tragedy that so much of the nation's money was spent on uncertain and mainly unsavoury and violent organisations, whose success or failure had little impact on the lives of ordinary Libyans. As oil revenues dropped throughout the 1980s and as Gaddafi's revolutionary economics stifled the economy, no-one within his administration was able to confront the dictatorial Leader to plead restraint: the Colonel continued to inject enormous sums into the pursuit of unrealistic goals abroad.

★

In 1986, Gaddafi told a *US News & World Report* interviewer that he was just like George Washington and Abraham Lincoln in his struggle to promote freedom for Arab nations. He told his interviewer, 'What you view as terrorism is the Palestinian struggle for liberation against the Israelis.'[4] At the heart of Gaddafi's mission as leader has been his desire for justice for Palestine, and the willingness to pursue this violently and without compromise. While other Muslim and Arab nations moved towards diplomacy and negotiation, Gaddafi blasted forth streams of anti-Semitic rhetoric and threatened to assassinate moderate Arab leaders who were willing to talk to the Israelis. Over the course of the late 1960s and early 1970s, Syria, Jordan, Egypt and Lebanon all accepted UN Resolution 242, which called for the withdrawal of Israel from the occupied territories, an end to violence and an acknowledgement of the sovereignty of all states in the region. Gaddafi vociferously condemned them for doing this and called for their governments to be overthrown.

The embrace of terror by numerous Palestinian groups from the early 1970s pointed the way to a new role for Libya. At this time, it was becoming obvious to the Palestinians that conventional conflict with the Israelis would bring impossibly high costs, both financially and in human terms. Instead, many moved decisively towards the use of violent guerrilla operations against civilians, inside and outside Israel. Hijackings, bombings and machine-gun massacres were not cheap, however, and the terrorists of the world were engaged in a constant search for steady finance. Gaddafi immediately spotted a use for Libya's growing oil wealth, one which was to benefit the more extreme Palestinian groups immensely, and which would also be extended to hundreds of other movements worldwide.

In June 1972, after just under three years in power, Gaddafi announced publicly his intention to help Palestinians and any other anti-Western revolutionaries. The *Washington Post* quoted him as calling for any Arab wishing to join a Palestinian movement to go and register at a Libyan embassy and await an invitation to take part in the combat training Libya would provide.

Perhaps the best-known face of the Palestinian cause is still Yasser Arafat, the founder of the liberation movement Fatah and one-time chairman of the Palestine Liberation Organization (PLO). Within his lifetime, Arafat moved from being regarded by the West as a vicious terrorist to receiving the 1994 Nobel Peace Prize alongside the Israeli leaders Shimon Peres and Yitzhak Rabin. Arafat and Fatah received support from most Arab states at some stage. Gaddafi's predecessor, King Idris, had sent money, and Gaddafi continued to do so immediately after taking power. Yet the relationship between Fatah and Libya quickly broke down. Gaddafi was wary of Arafat's strong commitment to Marxism and preferred the more extreme violence adopted by other Palestinian groups. For his part, Arafat often seems to have found Gaddafi's bellicose naïvety irritating and dangerous. There are numerous anecdotes of acerbic exchanges between the two. Patrick Seale, the biographer of the terrorist Abu Nidal, has written that Gaddafi sent Arafat a telegram during the Israeli siege of Beirut in 1982, urging the Palestinian leader to commit suicide rather than let Israel expel him from Lebanon. Arafat responded that he and his men were ready to make this sacrifice as soon as Gaddafi agreed to join them.[5]

By the early 1980s, relations between Gaddafi and Fatah were generally very poor, and Libyan support was going chiefly to rival groups. Gaddafi was closely associated with the Popular Front for the Liberation of Palestine (PFLP), the Popular Front for the Liberation of Palestine – General Command (which was later to be suspected of involvement in the Lockerbie bombing), the Popular Struggle Front, and the Abu Nidal Organization (ANO), among others. He was thought to be a personal friend of the notorious Ilich Ramírez Sánchez, known as Carlos the Jackal, a Venezuelan who became a revolutionary and a close associate of the PFLP. It was rumoured that in the mid- to late 1970s Carlos kept a permanent suite in a seaside hotel a few miles from Tripoli.

Libyan money quickly made its presence felt in the burgeoning world of international terrorism. Gaddafi gave money and rhetorical backing to Black September, the militant liberation group responsible for the massacre at the 1972 Munich Olympics, in which eleven Israeli athletes and a West German police officer were killed. In a typically provocative action, Libya volunteered to receive the bodies of the five terrorists killed in the operation and hailed them as heroes at public funerals carried out in Tripoli.

Another of Gaddafi's early Palestinian adventures was a massacre at Rome airport in 1973, carried out by an organisation known as the National Arab Youth for the Liberation of Palestine (NAYLP). NAYLP terrorists hurled two thermite bombs into a Pan American Airlines plane, killing thirty-two and wounding eighteen. Martin Sicker has written that when the terrorists surrendered in Kuwait, where they had fled in a hijacked plane, they told the authorities there that Gaddafi had directly ordered the attack in Rome. They also said that Gaddafi had asked them to assassinate the then US Secretary of State, Henry Kissinger.[6]

The early 1980s saw a collapse in oil prices, and Libyan revenues dropped considerably. Gaddafi was also reported to be under extreme pressure domestically, with stronger opposition to his regime and growing unhappiness at the enforced escalation of revolutionary fervour and the tyranny of *The Green Book*. Added to this was the pressure of steadily increasing US sanctions. Yet Libyan support to the Palestinians continued to be generous: it was reported that in 1981, Gaddafi spent $100 million in funding to Palestinian movements.[7] In 1985, he was accused of supporting the hijacking by the Palestine Liberation Front of the *Achille Lauro* cruise ship. This incident had shocked the world, as reports emerged of the Palestinian leader, Abu Abbas, throwing Leon Klinghoffer, a wheelchair-bound Jewish American, into the sea while his wife looked on.

Much of Gaddafi's support for terror was financial, but his relationship with the notorious Palestinian terrorist Abu Nidal went beyond just sending cash and weapons: Nidal is judged by some to have become a crucial part of the functioning of the Libyan state. Nidal formed his own organisation, referred to as the Abu Nidal Organization, after divisions within the PLO led to a split with Arafat's Fatah faction (in 1974, Fatah is thought to have passed a death sentence on Nidal *in absentia*). It is estimated that Nidal's random, frenzied attacks killed more than 900 civilians over the course of his career. His relationship with Gaddafi began properly in about 1985 (although the two had had a brief flirtation in the late 1970s). In the early 1980s, Nidal worked mainly out of Syria, but became disillusioned by the limits Damascus placed on him and by the Syrian leadership's desire to maintain a diplomatic distance from his unsavoury activities.

No such distance was to characterise the relationship he developed with Gaddafi. Patrick Seale feels that the two men had a close affinity, writing that they 'had much in common – a neurotic suspicion of the outside world, an inferiority complex – but they also shared the belief that they were men of great destiny'.[8] Nidal moved into a luxurious Tripoli residence from about 1985 and began working closely with Gaddafi to promote the Palestinian groups the two men favoured, and to target opponents of Libya. In 1987, he was allowed to set up an extensive terrorist training facility in the desert, just 100 miles from Tripoli. From this base, Nidal trained the men who would carry out his vicious attacks, but his role in Libya went beyond this. Seale reports that by the late 1980s, the terrorist had virtually complete control of Libya's intelligence department.

Nidal worked with Gaddafi on some truly horrific acts of violence. It has been reported that in the wake of the US bombing of Tripoli in 1986, Gaddafi requested his protégé to carry out revenge attacks. These are said to have included the April 1986 kidnap and murder of Leigh Douglas and

Phillip Padfield, two British schoolteachers working in Lebanon. Nidal's most widely recollected atrocity, however, is his attack on El Al's ticket counters in Rome and Vienna in 1985, which killed 18 and wounded 138. It is widely believed that these attacks were executed with the help of Libyan intelligence, and again the terrorists involved were hailed as heroes by the Libyan media.

Nidal was famous for his extreme cruelty. Seale describes how members of his own organisation suspected of treachery would be buried alive, fed through a tube for a few days, and then, when it was felt that guilt had been established, killed by a bullet fired down the feeding tube. Libya was the site of some of Nidal's worst atrocities against members of his own movement – in 1987–8, Seale records that 165 members of the ANO were murdered at the organisation's Libyan training camp. These were chiefly very young Palestinian men who had been sent to fight with Libya in Chad but who Nidal felt were conspiring against his leadership. Gaddafi's personal human rights record, especially during the 1980s, was despicable, and it was blackened further by the *carte blanche* Nidal was given to carry out the paranoid killings of young men.

The politics of Palestine moved forward dramatically in the 1990s – with the negotiation in 1993 of self-rule in the Gaza Strip and parts of the West Bank – and there was less of a part to play for virulent rejectionists like the Gaddafi of the 1970s and 1980s. By this time, Libya had anyway officially renounced terrorism and launched a diplomatic offensive to come in from the cold of Lockerbie sanctions. The Palestinians, however, will not forget Gaddafi's unwavering dedication to promoting their cause; nor will the Israelis be likely to forget his enthusiastic sponsorship of the extremist groups that killed so many of their citizens.

★

Libyan money aided some of the deadliest terrorist acts witnessed in late twentieth-century Europe. Terrorist organisations that profited from friendship with Libya included the Spanish Basque separatist group ETA, which has waged a campaign of violence that since 1968 has claimed the lives of at least 820 Spanish citizens; the Italian Red Brigade, a communist terrorist group linked to the PLO; the French Action Directe, a libertarian communist group that carried out assassinations and violent attacks between 1979 and 1986; the German Baader-Meinhof gang, a militant left-wing terrorist group; and the communist terrorist movement Forças Populares 25 de Abril in Portugal. Further afield, Gaddafi also gave generous amounts to the Armenian Secret Army for the Liberation of Armenia, a Marxist-Leninist group formed in 1975 with the aim of forcing Turkey to publicly admit to the 1915 genocide of 1.5 million Armenians. Its brutal attack on the Turkish Airlines counter at Orly airport in Paris in 1983 left eight dead and fifty-five wounded.

Although much of Gaddafi's most extreme rhetoric has been directed at the US and Britain, it is perhaps France which has had the most deeply troubled relationship with independent Libya. The two nations spent much of the 1980s for all intents and purposes at war in Chad, where each sponsored different factions, always on opposing sides (discussed further in Chapter 5). Although in the late 1980s Gaddafi's support for terror had appeared to be on the wane, it was at this point that the French suffered a horrific terrorist attack, sometimes referred to in Britain as the 'French Lockerbie'. UTA Flight 772 from Brazzaville in the Republic of Congo to Paris, via N'Djamena, the capital of Chad, was blown up in mid-air on 19 September 1989, killing all 156 passengers and 14 crew on board. Testimony from a Congolese man who said he had helped smuggle a bomb onto the flight led to six Libyans being charged with the attack. Among them was Abdullah al-Senussi, Gaddafi's own brother-in-law. The six men, all senior members of the Libyan government, were said to have masterminded the attack in revenge for French assistance to the Chadians, who were resisting Libyan expansionism.

The celebrated French judge Jean-Louis Bruguière, nicknamed 'the sheriff' and renowned for his success in prosecuting anti-terror cases, pursued the UTA case vigorously and also pushed for Gaddafi himself to be held accountable. The six suspects were not handed over to France, but in 1999, a French court tried and convicted them *in absentia*. Britain, of course, had suffered a remarkably similar attack over Lockerbie in December 1988, which is discussed in Chapter 8. Notably, as with Lockerbie, Libyan guilt in the UTA bombing has since been questioned. A 2001 book, *Manipulations africaines*, written by a French journalist, Pierre Péan, accused Bruguière of highlighting the case against Libya while ignoring evidence that might have implicated Lebanon, Syria and Iran.[9]

One of Gaddafi's favourite European states was Romania, where he developed a close friendship with the Communist dictator Nicolae Ceauşescu. Ceauşescu's rule was authoritarian and repressive, and he was notorious for the extremes of his personality cult, referring to himself as 'Conducător' ('Leader') and 'Geniul din Carpaţi' ('The Genius of the Carpathians'). According to *Red Horizons*, a memoir of the regime written by the defector Ion Mihai Pacepa (Ceauşescu's chief intelligence officer and one of the most senior Eastern bloc defectors of the entire Cold War), Ceauşescu was fascinated by Gaddafi: both had come to power young – Ceauşescu aged forty-seven, Gaddafi twenty-seven – both had wild ambitions to forge their small nations into leaders of the developing world, and Gaddafi had plenty of money to aid Ceauşescu in realising his ambitions for Romania.[10] The two first met in Tripoli, where Ceauşescu made great show of being terribly impressed by Gaddafi and, in a flamboyant gesture, 'spontaneously' sent a plane back to Bucharest to collect a gift for him, an original manuscript of the first Romanian translation of the Koran. With the friendship cemented by this well-chosen gift, Gaddafi went on to send thousands of Libyan students to Romanian universities; Romania benefited from generous arrangements for the supply of oil; and Romanian agricultural experts prospered hugely through Gaddafi's invitation to participate in his desert irrigation projects. On a more personal level, Gaddafi was said to have developed a passion for the sport of hunting through his friendship with Ceauşescu.

Alongside this relatively wholesome economic activity sat an extensive and sinister security co-operation. Pacepa reported that Libya ran an enormous bank of international passports, many of which it confiscated from foreigners working there. Romanian intelligence men were able to use some of these in their own security operations, while Libyans benefited from the sophisticated counterfeiting techniques Romanians taught them, which enabled them to fake invaluable American passports.

The two leaders also co-operated on weapons-building, including, Pacepa claimed, the development of bacteriological weapons. One joint venture was the development of a tank, designed using stolen NATO plans for a West German model, which was named Ceauşescu-Gaddafi, shortened to Cega, after the two leaders. Pacepa caused enormous embarrassment to the Ceauşescu regime by defecting to the US in 1978. This was reflected in the $4 million bounty placed on his head – $2 million from the Romanian government, $1 million from Yasser Arafat and, unsurprisingly, $1 million from Gaddafi. It has been claimed in the Western media that Gaddafi sent Carlos the Jackal to pursue Pacepa.[11]

The IRA was Gaddafi's main focus in the British Isles (as is discussed in Chapter 4), but he is also known to have given money to the National Union of Mineworkers (NUM) during the 1984–5 miners' strike. This strike brought the most extensive labour unrest seen in Britain since the General Strike of 1926, as the NUM battled the National Coal Board and Margaret Thatcher's government over the future of the British mining industry. It was a pitched, bloody conflict in which ten people died and during which deep-seated social divisions became apparent. Gaddafi's part in this conflict was to be a public relations disaster for the NUM: any boost given by Libyan money was dwarfed by the damage done to the miners by the association with Gaddafi, then at the height of his reign as the West's Public Enemy No. 1. By late 1984, the NUM president, Arthur Scargill, was desperate for funds to continue the strike. A British Pakistani, Mohammed Altaf Abbasi, a fan of Gaddafi who was said to run a 'Green Book centre' in the north of England, came forward with the idea that the NUM should contact Libya. Scargill was amenable to the suggestion, and sent Roger Windsor, the NUM chief executive, off to Tripoli. Like all visitors to the Colonel, Windsor was kept hanging around for several days, but eventually was able to meet him, and left Libya with the promise of cash in the region of £160,000. Windsor's visit was the subject of considerable publicity in Libya: he was shown on Libyan television greeting Gaddafi by kissing him on both cheeks, an image that was not to play well at home.

The NUM's shady involvement with Libya was revealed to the British public in a Sunday Times scoop in October 1984.[12] The details were embarrassing in the extreme, especially the revelation that Scargill had disguised himself as 'Mr Smith' in order to travel to Paris to meet a Libyan the paper termed 'Gaddafi's bagman'. Only six months previously, the British government had suspended bilateral relations with Libya after Libyan diplomats murdered PC Yvonne Fletcher. Growing public disapproval of Scargill's leadership thus dramatically escalated with the news of the Libyan entanglement. As was the case with so many of Gaddafi's causes in the West, the Colonel had brought terrible embarrassment upon the unwise recipients of his generosity, while pleasing himself by yet again putting Libyan money to good effect in needling the Western governments he loathed.

★

South and Central America, where the US fought hard to discourage communism in its own backyard, presented particularly tantalising opportunities for Gaddafi. Sponsoring revolutionary movements there represented a means to hit the US where it really hurt. For Gaddafi, his work in the Americas went beyond promoting causes that he felt were ideologically sound: Latin American movements could in his view contribute actively to Libya's self-defence by weakening the strength and will of the US. And so, through the 1970s and 1980s, Gaddafi put his money, weapons and inflammatory rhetoric behind many movements in the region.

Fidel Castro has outlasted Gaddafi as an enemy of the US, if not as a head of state: Cuba continues to suffer US ire, while nowadays Gaddafi enjoys photo opportunities with Barack Obama. Back in the days when both were among the most reviled enemies of the US, they maintained a friendship that seemed purpose built to rile the Americans. In March 1977, Castro travelled to Libya to meet Gaddafi, taking the podium as guest of honour at that year's General People's Congress. Thumbing their noses at the West, the two issued a joint statement supporting the Palestinian cause and endorsing liberation struggles throughout Latin America and Africa. Although Gaddafi was never a communist, and had differed with Castro in the past, he was hugely impressed by Cuban defiance of the US, and also grateful for Castro's commitment to the Palestinian cause. Cuba was also, in Gaddafi's eyes, a force for good in Africa: he was appreciative of the role it played as another counterweight to US influence on the continent, in particular in the Angolan and Ethiopian civil wars. Gaddafi's distant friendships have usually been more successful, and in the case of Cuba and Libya, there were few major ructions between the two. In 1998 Castro was able to place the Gaddafi International Prize for Human Rights on his mantelpiece, alongside his Golden Hammer and Sickle Medal from North Korea.

Gaddafi also irked the US in Nicaragua, a troublesome Central American state that was to prove an enormous embarrassment to the Reagan administration. In 1979, the Sandinista National Liberation Front, a left-wing revolutionary movement, had deposed a disastrously corrupt American-supported dictatorship. The Sandinistas were the type of populist movement the Americans most loathed. The Reagan government imposed a trade embargo on the new regime and began channelling money to anti-Sandinista rebels known as the Contras. In 1986, the scandal known as the Iran–Contra affair rocked the US: it came to light that the Reagan administration had agreed to sell arms to Iran in return for the release of US hostages held in Tehran, with a percentage of the profits to be siphoned off and sent to the Nicaraguan Contras. Struggling with this Nicaraguan quagmire, the Americans were incensed to discover Gaddafi's enthusiastic overtures to the Sandinistas: in 1980, for example, reports emerged that he had presented the Sandinista government with $100 million in aid. Martin Sicker quoted Sergio Ramírez, a Sandinista leader, proclaiming that solidarity between Libya and the front 'was always manifest and has been made more fraternal since the triumph of our revolution'.[13] In this instance it was Gaddafi giving money to the government, and Reagan funding a violent insurrection, but the US still portrayed Gaddafi's involvement as 'terrorist', asserting that Managua, the capital of Nicaragua, was a hotbed of terrorist plotting, where Libyans came to share their knowledge and expertise with Palestinians, Cubans and Iranians, as well as with the locals.

Gaddafi's influence was felt in most countries of the region. In 1982, Costa Rica complained that young people were being smuggled out of

the country to attend military training camps in Libya. *Time* reported
that Gaddafi was funding Colombia's M-19 guerrilla movement, which
mounted a violent coup in Bogotá in 1985.[14] On the Caribbean island
of St Lucia, Gaddafi was said by the Prime Minister, John Compton, to
have spent $1 million sponsoring dissident groups, including the provision
of bomb-making classes. Movements in Guatemala and El Salvador also
benefited from his assistance.

Gaddafi also felt it important to influence events in the US itself, although
his efforts there were particularly clumsy and counterproductive. He separated
the US people from their government and maintained rather optimistically
that he could be popular with one, if not with the other. For this reason,
the money spent in the US was designed both to irk the government and
to portray a positive picture of Libya. From the mid-1970s, Gaddafi sent
cash to universities, labour unions and a range of political organisations.
He was particularly keen to target black Americans, and also funded Native
American organisations. In the early 1970s, he sent $300,000 to the Black
Panthers, but is said to have suspended funding after hearing reports of
members drinking alcohol and behaving in a less than exemplary Muslim
fashion. In September 1979, Gaddafi was presented with a brass Martin
Luther King medallion by the Reverend Hosea Williams of the Southern
Christian Leadership Conference, of which King was chairman at the time
of his death. Gaddafi was also said to have close links with Jesse Jackson and
his organisations. It was widely reported that Jackson had enthusiastically
sought business opportunities for the American black community in Libya.
As late as 1996, Gaddafi was defying US sanctions by attempting to give his
annual human rights award and a $250,000 cash prize to the black separatist
Muslim leader Louis Farrakhan. Promises had also been made to Farrakhan
of up to $1 billion in financial aid to his group, the Nation of Islam.

One of Gaddafi's strangest encounters with American culture was
his entanglement with a Christian cult called the Children of God. The
Children of God were led by David Berg, a preacher who used the alias
of Moses David, or Mo. Mo communicated with his followers through
his 'Mo letters', which set out his philosophies and his instructions for
their realisation. The Children of God first approached the Libyans in

1970, and a correspondence developed between Mo and Gaddafi. After they were threatened with arrest in the US, the Children took refuge in a number of locations, including Libya. The cult was notorious for the belief that converts should be sought by all possible means, including sex. A member of the group told *Time* magazine in 1977 that 'there is nothing wrong with a sexy conversion. We believe sex is a human necessity, and in certain cases we may go to bed with someone to show people God's love.'[15] Conservative clerics in Libya unsurprisingly disapproved of Gaddafi's liaison with the Children of God, and the cult was never encouraged too enthusiastically. The episode does illustrate, however, Gaddafi's general willingness to engage with the most bizarre of organisations on their own terms, with minimal concern for the effects this kind of dalliance had on his international reputation.

Perhaps Gaddafi's most public victim in the US was Billy Carter, the failed businessman who was the brother of the President, Jimmy Carter. Gaddafi identified Carter as a useful potential 'way in' to the White House. In particular, he hoped that he would be useful in persuading the Americans to allow him to buy some transport planes. Initial contact was made via Libya's ambassador to Italy, Jibril Shalouf, who expended considerable time and effort on cultivating Carter and his business associates. Carter was spectacularly open to Libyan advances: he hosted a visit from Libyan dancers to the state of Georgia in 1979, he founded the Libyan Arab Friendship Society and he paid visits to Tripoli in 1978 and 1979. Carter worked on behalf of a US company looking to buy Libyan oil and accepted a loan from Libya of $220,000. These close connections to an increasingly dubious regime attracted official attention, and prompted a federal inquiry into the nature of Carter's relationship with Libya. Carter told the inquiry that he had never promoted Libyan causes in the White House. The political damage to his brother, however, was considerable. A month before Jimmy Carter lost the 1980 election the inquiry published its findings, which criticised the President for not dissociating himself more strongly from his brother's questionable business relations.

★

Type 'Gaddafi' into an internet search engine, and a good few of the sites that come up will relate, surprisingly, to cricket. This is because in the Pakistani city of Lahore, the stadium which hosts international cricket matches is named after Gaddafi, in gratitude for the aid he sent to West Pakistan in its 1971 civil war with East Pakistan (now Bangladesh). The resonance of the Gaddafi name in the popular culture of cricket-obsessed south Asia suggests the extent of his involvement in the continent.

Asia, of course, is home to hundreds of millions of Muslims and a number of Islamic states, notably Pakistan, Malaysia and Indonesia. It is no surprise that Gaddafi saw it as a crucial locale for his influence-building work in the 1970s and 1980s. Help went, as usual, to a broad spectrum of causes, ranging from the terrorist Japanese Red Army (allowed to land a hijacked flight in Tripoli in 1973) through to aid for relatively moderate governments such as Pakistan, Malaysia and Sri Lanka.

One of Gaddafi's better-documented Asian excursions was into the politics of the Philippines during the 1970s. This south-east Asian nation has a large Muslim population, known as the Moros, who live mainly in the southern islands. From the early 1970s, the Moros began to organise to demand independence, forming the Moro National Liberation Front (MNLF), which launched terrorist attacks and also engaged in full-scale conventional conflict with the Filipino army. For the MNLF, Libya became a crucial source of weapons and money and Gaddafi a valued friend.

Aided by Libyan money, the MNLF's activities became increasingly disruptive and costly for the Philippines over the 1970s. In 1977 President Marcos took the decision to grant a degree of independence to the Moros, and asked Libya to act as intermediary in his negotiations with them. It was agreed that Tripoli would be the scene of these negotiations. To represent his government, Marcos sent one of the few characters in international relations likely to match Gaddafi in ostentatious weirdness: his wife, Imelda. She and Gaddafi joined together to make what was known as the Tripoli Agreement, which gave a degree of autonomy to thirteen Muslim provinces. This agreement ultimately broke down, and in subsequent years Gaddafi backed off from his work in the Philippines, alienated from the MNLF by what he saw as their factionalism and their susceptibility to

Maoism and communism, and perhaps daunted by the complexity and intractability of the conflict and the serious problems it was causing to other Muslim governments in Asia.

In his associations with the Marcos duo, Gaddafi had again displayed his unerring instinct for suspect friendships with villains. When Imelda Marcos had to post $5 million for bail on racketeering charges brought against her in 1988 by the US government (on which she was later acquitted), she said, 'The first one to come to my rescue was Gaddafi, who said he was willing to post bail for me even if it were ten times higher.' Notably, Saddam Hussein also offered to help out. Marcos's account of her meeting with Gaddafi in 1977 suggests that there had been a certain spark between the two:

> Gaddafi said to me, 'You're a good woman, why don't you become a Muslim?' I said I didn't know Islam. He said Islam was kind, so I said, 'Then don't let Mindanao [home to most of the Moros] separate from the Philippines.' He said Islam was generous, so I said, 'Then give us oil at a low, friendship price.' I ended up getting eight concessions, including cheap oil.[16]

Libyan influence was also felt in Indonesia, where Gaddafi was linked to the Free Aceh Movement (known in Indonesia as GAM – Gerekan Aceh Merdeka). GAM was a separatist movement that fought a guerrilla war against the Indonesian state between 1976 and 2005, claiming many thousands of lives. It was widely reported that GAM soldiers, including key commanders, received training in Libya[17] and that Libya sent them money and weapons. Libya was also suspected of contributing funds that supported the 1981 hijack of an Indonesian flight by another group of Islamic fundamentalists.

Through such activities, Gaddafi thoroughly irked President Suharto, who ruled Indonesia between 1967 and 1998. The reinvented, moderate 21st-century Gaddafi, however, has been a different proposition. By the early 2000s he was extending guarantees of Libyan co-operation to the Indonesian government, and pledging to help them put an end to GAM's activities. With Lockerbie sanctions suspended, the then Indonesian President, Megawati Sukarnoputri, was the first international leader to pay a visit to Tripoli, where in 2003 she put to Gaddafi her request for assistance in the clampdown on GAM. Gaddafi promised Megawati that he would search out Acehnese rebels still resident in Libya.

In Thailand, Muslims in the south of the country have long been comparatively impoverished and disadvantaged, and have been conducting an insurgency that has troubled the Buddhist majority nation for decades. Gaddafi offered Thai Muslim militants considerable financial aid and military training. His financial aid is said to have peaked in the late 1970s, but when the conflict in southern Thailand reignited in the early years of the 2000s, rumours again circulated of Libyan involvement. A Thai general, Pallop Pinmanee, told the BBC in 2005 that twenty militant leaders were among the numerous alumni of Libya's terrorist training camps, where they had been trained in bomb-making and combat techniques.[18] The Thai government, however, denied that there was solid evidence to support the general's claim.

Gaddafi has also taken a great deal of interest in Malaysia, where Muslim ethnic Malays have existed in an often delicate harmony with ethnically Chinese and Indian Malaysians. Libya's relationship with Malaysia is among its more benign alliances and has seemed less subject to the temperamental, sudden changes of heart that have plagued most of Gaddafi's international friendships.

From the 1970s, Malaysia entered into enthusiastic alliances with the oil powers of the Middle East, using its status as a small, relatively poor Muslim nation to attract loans and alliances from the Libyans and the Saudis. Libyan influence in Malaysia centred on the religious side of things. Libya's Islamic Call Society, founded in 1972 to fund the building of mosques and the development of worthy Islamic projects, was an active player on the Malaysian scene. Gaddafi's money helped to build and finance PERKIM, the Malaysian government's Islamic missionary arm. The Libyans tried to promote a more radical Islam in Malaysia, and their efforts were noted by a 1978 correspondent to the *Far Eastern Economic Review*, who commented on the presence in Malaysia of Libyan preachers promoting an unusually strict practice of Islam. The writer of the letter noted that these men 'harangued Malay girls to abandon the Malay sarong as well as Western dress and adopt the Arab veil and caftan . . . The sight of large numbers of young women adopting the veil and relinquishing the freedom they had enjoyed was horrifying.'[19] While the relationship between Libya and Malaysia has mostly been friendly, the author Shanti Nair has pointed out that the Malaysian Special Branch nonetheless kept a very close eye on the Libyans resident there in the late 1970s and 1980s, scrutinising their support of a range of movements and monitoring the nature of their missionary activities.[20]

Many of Libya's expensive and vigorous investments in the promotion of Islam yielded few tangible results. In the case of Malaysia, at least, consistent support for Prime Minister Mahathir's Islamic nationalist regime did bring benefits to Gaddafi. After Tripoli and Benghazi were bombed by the US in 1986, Malaysia was one of the few countries to offer a ringing condemnation of the attack and to express convincing support for Libya. Just a month after the attacks, Gaddafi sent a special envoy to Kuala Lumpur to thank the Malays for their support. The unusually cordial relationship endured through the subsequent decades. In 2002, Mahathir led a large Malaysian visit to Libya, on which he was taken on an aerial tour of Gaddafi's Great Man-made River project. In 2005, Mahathir, by now retired, was awarded the Gaddafi International Prize for Human Rights, previously bestowed on Fidel Castro and Nelson Mandela, among others. In his acceptance speech he praised Libya for being a nation that had neither colonised nor oppressed any other.

★

Gaddafi's sponsorship of extra-state groups was pursued most vigorously during the 1970s, thereafter gradually diminishing, until by the late 1980s it was much less of a focus. Gaddafi himself told the *Observer* journalist Donald Trelford, 'By the passage of time, everyone changes, through experience. In the 1970s, we supported liberal movements without knowing which were terrorists and which were not. In the 1980s, we began to differentiate between terrorists and those with legitimate political aspirations.'[21]

Seeking to come in from the cold after the Lockerbie sanctions, Gaddafi renounced his career as a supporter of terror: in 1993 Abu Nidal was asked to find a home outside Libya, and in May a statement was made officially renouncing terrorism. Gaddafi has since found a new respectability, meeting with the likes of Tony Blair and Condoleezza Rice in his desert tent.

As I await the chance to see a new Conservative government in Britain, I wonder what lessons about Gaddafi the party's foreign policy team should draw from his sponsorship of terrorism worldwide. It seems to me that the lessons are few, except to realise Gaddafi's own very profound limitations. Gaddafi has been a failure far more often than he has been a success. He has wasted billions of dollars on what seems largely to have been a vanity project, stemming from his own desire to seem important in the world. He may have made Libya a thorn in the side of the big powers, but he has never made himself respected, and rarely has anyone asked for his advice without also wanting his money. He has never been capable of vision, statesmanship, strategy or diplomacy in pursuing his aims; instead, he has thrown money around wantonly and with frequent fits of pique. It is something of a tragedy to consider what the billions spent on a hotchpotch of liberation movements, many of which brought so little to the world, could have done for the Libyan people in the hands of a wiser leader. We need to deal with Gaddafi, we need to engage with Libya, but we also need to realise the reality: Gaddafi is an international showman, not a world power.

# 4

# THE IRA'S TRIPOLI CONNECTION

Many people I have talked to while writing this book have seen Gaddafi as a distant figure, entertaining and shocking them via the pages of their morning newspapers, but having little to do with us here in Britain. This is a grave misconception: along with the atrocity at Lockerbie and the murder of PC Fletcher, Libya also helped the IRA to terrorise the British population for decades, and Libyan weapons were at the heart of some of the IRA's most lethal attacks. As Britain moves to build bridges with Libya, it will be crucial, in my opinion, to have an open and honest discussion of this.

The IRA was a tantalising prospect for Gaddafi, as he worked hard through the 1970s and early 1980s to develop an international image for himself as a warrior fighting the forces of neo-colonialism. In Gaddafi's eyes, Britain sat alongside the United States as an oppressor of the developing world – the British had led the way in the Suez crisis, they had betrayed the Palestinians, and they had even briefly held authority over Libya itself. Britain was a target that could not be ignored. The IRA, moreover, was just the kind of organisation favoured by the Libyans at the time – violent, extreme and desperate for support from any source. By channelling money and weapons to be used in IRA assaults on Britain, Gaddafi could further his commitment to supporting the self-proclaimed liberation movements of the world, he could harass the British and he could, as an added bonus, prove that Libyan influence on world affairs transcended the boundaries of religion.

Gaddafi's friendship with the IRA began just three years after he took power in Libya. In August 1972, Joe Cahill and Denis McInerney, senior members of the IRA's Army Council, were asked to meet with the Libyans. The two men flew to Poland to meet Libyan intelligence agents, and then visited Tripoli itself. Cahill recollects in his memoir that he was asked to give the Colonel a shopping list of his movement's demands for weapons and training. His impression of Gaddafi was of a man sincerely motivated by the desire to help those he saw as fighting for freedom:

> Gaddafi said he did not understand why we did not speak in Irish, and [asked] why did we speak in English, the language of our enemies . . . My impression was that the man was very genuine. Libyans had obtained their freedom and they wanted to help other countries which were struggling for their freedom. He did tell me that he was interested in other liberation movements throughout the world. He said he believed the IRA were sincere, they were genuine, they were dedicated people who were committed to bringing about the reunification of their country.[1]

Initial discussions pleased both parties, and Gaddafi declared, 'We are making war on Great Britain, and if the Irish revolutionaries want to liberate Ireland we will back them to the hilt.'[2] The Provisional IRA embraced the opportunity to profit from Libyan support. Three agents were sent over to take up residence in Tripoli, renting villas and settling into the odd world that was revolutionary Libya. By 1975, it is thought that around $3.5 million of Libyan money had found its way into IRA bank accounts. Various IRA men regularly travelled to Libya to join the multicultural community of terrorists congregating there to learn the techniques of bomb-making and subversion. One of the IRA men who took this training was Thomas McMahon, later the mastermind of the horrific 1979 bombing that killed Lord Mountbatten of Burma and several of his family and friends who were holidaying on board his yacht.

The early Libya–IRA connection was soon derailed, however, by a spectacularly clumsy plot to ship arms to Ireland. In March 1973, the Republic of Ireland's navy intercepted a ship called the SS *Claudia*, commissioned by the IRA to transport a stash of weapons and explosives from Libya. Cahill was on board, and was tried and convicted for the attempt to smuggle weapons. At his trial, he told the court defiantly that 'if I am guilty of any crime, it is that I did not succeed in getting the contents of the *Claudia* into the hands of the freedom fighters of this country'. After the debacle of the *Claudia*, relations between Libya and the IRA cooled considerably: the ease with which this operation had been penetrated aroused angst and suspicion on both sides.

Nevertheless, Gaddafi continued to voice support for the IRA and its actions. After a rash of IRA bombs devastated London in 1976, he declared in the Libyan paper *al-Fajr al-Jadid* that the 'bombs which are convulsing Britain and breaking its spirit are the bombs of the Libyan people . . . We have sent bombs to the Irish revolutionaries so that Britain will pay the price of her past deeds after we have liquidated her presence from our land.'[3]

But Gaddafi's fondness for the IRA did not preclude him from entertaining its enemies. The Ulster Defence Association (UDA), one of the IRA's key unionist opponents, had watched the developing relationship between their enemies and Libya with grave concern. They decided to meet with Gaddafi in order to present their side of the story, and in 1974 a UDA delegation was received in Libya. The UDA were able to meet senior Libyan ministers, as well as Gaddafi himself. They reported back that the Libyans had been polite and sympathetic, but had not shown a very sophisticated understanding of the Irish conflict.

Early contact with Libya had its impact on the subsequent development of the IRA. The Irish journalist Ed Moloney records, in what is thought to be the best history of the IRA, that the organisation's fling with Libya was not confined to weapons and money alone: IRA leaders including Gerry Adams and Ivor Bell were also impressed by Libya's revolutionary experiments with new forms of democracy.[4] Moloney writes that in the 1970s the IRA considered replicating Libya's pyramidal system of popular committees in restructuring its own organisation. Later, at the instigation

of Adams and Bell, the IRA did set up a Revolutionary Council, designed
to ensure that its leadership was tied closely to rank and file members.
According to Moloney, it was modelled on Libya's Revolutionary
Command Council, the organisation that oversaw the people's committees.

Most strikingly, Adams and Bell led a project to develop a 'Green Book'
for the IRA, which Moloney feels must have been linked to Gaddafi's
own *Green Book*, his attempt to construct a philosophical justification of his
rule. The IRA's version, however, was somewhat different: it contained
information about the organisation's politics and aims, but also focused
strongly on techniques for withstanding interrogation.

★

The true impact of Libya's partnership with the IRA, however, was only
to be felt much later on. The Libyans and the IRA revived their early
friendship during the 1980s, and the second stage of this relationship had
by far the more devastating effects. A number of explanations have been
posed for the renewal of the Libyan connection, which seems to have
been instigated by Tripoli. It may have been that Gaddafi was impressed
by the IRA hunger strikes of the early 1980s, and especially by the widely
publicised death of Bobby Sands, who starved himself to death in 1981.
Also, the relationship with Britain had soured dramatically. Diplomatic
relations between the two countries had been suspended following the
murder in 1984 of PC Yvonne Fletcher, policing a protest by Libyan
dissidents outside Libya's embassy in London. The Libyans claimed that
Britain had sponsored the dissident protesters and was plotting with those
who wanted to overthrow Gaddafi's regime. What Gaddafi saw as Margaret
Thatcher's perfidy was, of course, reinforced in 1986 when she allowed the
Americans to launch their brutal raid on Tripoli from British territory. All
of this gave Gaddafi plenty of motivation to rekindle the friendship with
his IRA allies of old.

At the heart of the new partnership was the IRA leader Tom Murphy,
a pig farmer whose land straddles the border between Northern Ireland
and the Republic. He was described in the *Irish Independent* as 'a ruthless

IRA leader, a former chief of staff of the IRA and the man who personally masterminded the importation of hundreds of tons of lethal weapons from Libya'.[5] According to Toby Harnden's account of the IRA in South Armagh, *Bandit Country*, Murphy had been to Libya for terrorist training in the mid-1970s, making him the ideal candidate to work with Gaddafi's agents later on.[6]

Murphy's Libyan contact was a man called Nasser Ashur, who was ostensibly in the UK because Gaddafi had sent him to London to rebuild the relationship with the British in the wake of the shooting of PC Fletcher. Ashur was an elegant businessman, fluent in English and reportedly fond of Italian shoes. He had a taste for unusual gifts, and his IRA connections were said to have presented him with presents that included an Alsatian puppy, a double bed, a clock and crates of olive oil. Money spent on such gifts for the Libyan agent was well invested. Ashur offered the IRA a deal they could not refuse: according to an interview Moloney conducted with an unnamed senior IRA leader, Ashur offered $10 million and 300 tons of weaponry, with the stipulation that all of it was to be used to damage the Thatcher government. This remarkable quantity of weapons had the potential to completely reinvigorate the IRA's activities, greatly reducing the need for the leadership to travel around constantly soliciting money. The practicalities would, however, be challenging. Delivering such sizeable quantities of arms required considerable subterfuge.

An agent was hired to supervise the transfer of the weapons by sea. He carefully planned circuitous routes that would attract the least possible attention. IRA-commissioned boats would take a meandering path to Malta, from where they would meet Libyan vessels at sea, transferring the precious crates of weapons from boat to boat. The weapons would then to be delivered to Clogga Strand, an isolated Irish beach, and from there on to secret stashes throughout Ireland.

The first four deliveries were successful. In August 1985, Murphy took delivery of 300 boxes of Libyan arms, including AK-47 rifles, pistols, Semtex explosive, grenades and machine guns. A tractor was needed to haul the enormous arsenal to shore. Another shipment followed that October, and the third in early 1986. The fourth, sent in 1986 on a Swedish ship called the *Villa*, included a ton of Semtex. Semtex imported from Libya was to play a part in numerous lethal IRA attacks: Harnden wrote that 'since late 1986, virtually every bomb, rocket and mortar made by the IRA has incorporated Semtex brought into Ireland on board the *Villa*'.[7] Semtex is a particularly valuable component of the terrorist arsenal: it is impossible to detect, highly malleable and perfect for the kinds of booby-trap bombs popular with the IRA.

The fifth shipment, attempted in 1987, went spectacularly wrong: perhaps the IRA were betrayed by a mole, or perhaps they were just too ambitious. Gaddafi had certainly never been discreet or covert about his intentions with the IRA. In 1986, the British media was full of Libyan government statements in which Gaddafi declared his intention to resume funding the IRA. The *Irish Times* reported that his son Saadi had declared at a conference that the Libyans planned to open an office for the IRA in Tripoli. In 1987, Gaddafi told Donald Trelford that he had resumed selling arms to the IRA after the US bombed Tripoli in 1986, motivated by his deep hatred for Thatcher and Reagan.[8] Both Geoffrey Howe, Foreign Secretary in the Thatcher government between 1983 and 1989, and Charles Powell, Thatcher's private secretary from 1983 to 1990, told me that the government was very much aware that the Libyans were regularly supplying weapons and money to the IRA. It is likely that IRA connections with Libya were being watched very closely indeed.

The cargo of weapons transported in the doomed fifth shipment was too big to be transferred from a Libyan to an IRA ship at sea, and was instead loaded straight onto the IRA's vessel at Tripoli docks. It is possible that British intelligence in Libya realised something was up and alerted the authorities. The *Eksund*, originally a Panamanian ship, was allowed to set sail with its deadly cargo, but those on board reported being tracked by planes throughout much of the journey to Ireland. In November 1987, the *Eksund* was intercepted by the French navy. On board were 150 tons of Libyan weapons, including Kalashnikovs, surface-to-air missiles and a range of explosives.

In the wake of the *Eksund*'s interception, there was shock around the world at the scale of Libyan assistance to the IRA. The Republic of Ireland was particularly incensed, given that the cache was to have been delivered onto its territory, as earlier deliveries had been. The Irish politician Maurice Manning, calling for a complete suspension of diplomatic relations between Ireland and Libya, told the Dáil in 1987:

> The basic point is that the evidence is very clear that the Libyan government are engaged in the export of terrorism. The evidence is clear that the Libyan government have no respect for the sovereign rights of other countries. The evidence is clear that we are seen as a pawn in the relationship between Libya and Britain and the US. If Libya can destabilise or embarrass those countries, then we are a very useful pawn in all of that. This is the basic situation in which we find ourselves with Libya. That country continues to export arms to this country on a scale so potentially destructive that it baffles imagination and description.[9]

By the early 1990s, Gaddafi had begun to distance himself from the violent excesses of the 1970s and 1980s. As part of his quest for better relations with the West, in June 1993 he met with British Foreign Office officials in Geneva to provide them with a list of the weapons Libya had sent to the IRA. This was valuable intelligence in helping to establish what weapons the IRA might still have had at its disposal. Today the Libyans are claiming, to the embarrassment of those involved, that as a result of this co-operation they were promised that British politicians would let their former IRA connections lie.

The Conservative MP Teddy Taylor, a former journalist distinguished as one of the relatively few Tories to have a successful political career representing a Scottish seat, took a strong interest in Britain's relationship with Libya. He travelled to Tripoli in 1991 to meet Gaddafi and to discuss the murder of PC Fletcher. Taylor published a note sent to him by Gaddafi at the time that read:

> With regard to relations with the IRA, and similar organisations, Libya has frequently declared, and I herewith confirm, its condemnation of terrorist activities whose victims are innocent people, and on this basis Libya believes

the so-called IRA is not worth for us to have any contacts with, or to give
it any support or backing. And that applies to any organisation that uses
terrorism as a means to further its aims.[10]

Although changing times forced him to let it go, Gaddafi's friendship
with the IRA had been a boon to Libya: a convenient way to irk the
British, a channel for Gaddafi's vehement hatred of Thatcher and, later, a
bargaining tool. Journalist Liam Clarke commented in 2004:

> The IRA's weapons deal with Libya worked out well for both. The IRA
> was kept in business as a result. The weaponry helped sway hardliners to
> back the leadership's move towards politics and secured Murphy's power
> base.
>
> Gaddafi later won brownie points in the West by giving the British
> government an inventory of what he supplied to the IRA. Murphy and the
> IRA are still using the same guns to buy political influence by demanding
> concessions in return for decommissioning them. And that's not counting
> the concessions they won when the guns were in use.[11]

For the victims of IRA attacks, this is naturally difficult to stomach. The
British IRA victims, moreover, have had no recognition of the suffering
inflicted on them via Gaddafi-funded explosives, and have never been
paid any compensation. In contrast, the victims' families whose lives were
ruined by the Lockerbie, UTA and La Belle disco bombings have all been
compensated by Libya, as has the Fletcher family, and as have the American
victims of the IRA. It seems that the British government has thus far found
it politically expedient to leave these families well alone in their search for
an apology for and a meaningful recognition of their horrific experiences
at the hands of Libya.

Hope is not lost, however, as Jason McCue, a partner of the London
law firm $H_2O$, is currently spearheading a legal fight for justice, pursuing
avenues through the US courts and lobbying the British government.
The release in August 2009 of Abdelbaset al-Megrahi, the man convicted
of the Lockerbie bombing, has given fresh impetus to his efforts. Prior

to this date, the Foreign Office and the Prime Minister had openly told McCue that the government would not be supporting the IRA victims' fight for compensation from Libya, owing to commercial interests and valuable intelligence co-operation. The public furore over Megrahi's release, however, has led to a mammoth about-turn. Gordon Brown has now promised the establishment of a dedicated Foreign Office team to assist the IRA victims in their drive for compensation, as well as meetings with Libyan officials for the victims, with support from the British ambassador.

Given my own interest in Libya, I have also worked closely with members of Northern Ireland's Democratic Unionist Party to press for compensation for the families of victims of IRA attacks involving Libyan-supplied explosives. I have tried as far as possible to publicise their case, being interviewed on BBC Radio Ulster alongside Gerry Adams and speaking with journalists as often as I can. It is my fervent hope that the Libyans will come to recognise the urgent need to resolve this sad and sorry chapter in their history in a fair and honourable way. Their ill-conceived work with the IRA damaged thousands of lives, and this needs to be acknowledged before the relationship can move forward.

Unfortunately, however, it has become clear that the Libyan camp are increasingly offended by the revisiting of issues they consider to be closed. They fear that publicly embarrassing and financially costly claims for compensation may extend indefinitely into the future, whereas their hope had been that in shaking hands with Tony Blair in the Libyan desert in 2004 and again in 2007, Gaddafi had closed the door on Libya's iniquitous past. Unfortunately, in a free and democratic country with a robust press, this is not only undesirable but also plainly unrealistic. Victims will wish to hold Gaddafi and Libya to account, and journalists will inevitably and rightly help them push politicians to do so.

In a sense, the IRA connection bookends the Britain–Libya relationship. From the beginning, it held us back in developing strong connections. Senior politicians told me that it was always obvious that British business could have made a great deal of money in Libya, but that this quickly became impossible due to the obvious IRA links. Lord Owen, for example, who as David Owen was Foreign Secretary between 1977 and 1979 and later the leader of the breakaway Social Democratic Party, told me that when he was Foreign Secretary, 'the early feeling that [Gaddafi] was playing footsie with the IRA' meant that little effort was put into developing links with him and promoting partnerships between the two countries. Nowadays, the Libyans are unenthusiastic about efforts to finally close the door on their IRA links by properly compensating victims. The relationship is thus still held back, and it will continue to be until resolution is achieved. To this end, a cross-party delegation of MPs visited Libya in October 2009 to press the case for compensation for the victims of IRA atrocities. Despite my party nominating me as their representative for this delegation, my participation was blocked. I am still unsure whether this was due to pressure from Libya or from the Foreign Office.

As this case moves forward, it is likely that the British public will be reminded dramatically of the days when Libya was a pariah state, and of the direct effects this had on some of our nation's ordinary citizens. It is no-one's intention to return to those days, nor can we realistically expect to dwell forever on the crimes of the past. It is very clear that friendship is the way forward: the better relations seen in recent years have made the likelihood of any future Libyan enmity remote. We must not, however, forget the suffering of the families of the British people killed by weapons sent from Libya.

# ARAB AND AFRICAN DREAMS

Since he was a boy, Gaddafi had dreamed of a grand Arab unity, conjuring up a future in which the Arab world joined together, under his leadership, to face up to the West. Taking power in Libya was for him just one step in a larger plan: to subsume Libya into a greater entity that would bring Arabs together to remedy historical injustice. Ideally, in joining together, Gaddafi hoped that Libya's revolution would also be exported to his Arab and his African neighbours, so that they too could reap the benefits of his system of 'popular democracy'. This dream of a unified group of states pursuing a 'third way' was to animate Gaddafi's international activities through much of the 1970s and 1980s. Along the way would be war, acrimony and disaster, but only occasional success. In general, while many of Gaddafi's neighbours were attracted by Libyan riches, few warmed to the prospect of standing alongside Libya in permanent union, or of having their national political life transformed according to the Gaddafi model.

In many of Gaddafi's plans to unify the region, there was a grain of good sense – often, standing together more firmly might have brought African and Arab nations more success in international relations – but his plans were scuppered by the failure to think them out properly and by Libya's stunning inability to execute them consistently. His ideas for co-operation came undone through his bullying behaviour, his unreliability and his duplicity. During the 1970s and 1980s, most of his potential allies came to distrust him deeply, in part because he was almost unbelievably two faced, often negotiating pacts on unity with governments while simultaneously channelling money to their opponents.

From the early 1970s, Gaddafi launched a more radical policy of working with the masses as well as with regimes. In practice, this meant that he regularly addressed himself to the people of other states via Radio Tripoli, calling on them to rise up and create a Libyan-style revolutionary state. Arab and African leaders, many heading poverty-stricken, unstable, conflict-riven states, deeply resented this destabilising interference, and many came to dread Libyan influence in their internal affairs.

★

Seizing power at a time of growing Arab nationalism, Gaddafi then believed passionately in the unity of the Arab world. He viewed its separation into different regions and countries as a devious ruse by Western colonisers to weaken the Arab people. Gamal Abdel Nasser was Gaddafi's greatest hero, and Gaddafi viewed himself as the Egyptian leader's ideological heir. Nasser wrote in 1955 that 'it seems to me that within the Arab circle there is a role, wandering aimlessly in search of a hero'.[1] To Gaddafi, Nasser's most fervent disciple, this was an inspiring call to action; in his eyes, he could be the hero to take on the Arabist role.

The other dimension to Gaddafi's quest for Arab unity has been his fervent belief in the injustice done to Palestine, and his deep commitment to winning back Palestinian territories from Israel by force. Gaddafi's search has been animated by a profound hatred of Israel and the belief that it would only be by the Arab world coming together that Palestine could be freed.

By clinging so vigorously to the cause of Arab unity, Gaddafi was to prove a discomfiting anachronism in the Arab world. It could be said that he had come to power twenty years too late, after the powerful dreams of the Nassers, the Nehrus and the Sukarnos of the idealistic post-colonial landscape had subsided into a grittier, more pragmatic engagement with the realities of international politics. It had become impossible for most Arab states to ignore the many differences and competing interests that existed between them. As other Arab leaders were coming to terms with this, and pursuing their national interests as best they could, Gaddafi's oil riches allowed him to continue to play the ideologue. Periodically, other nations would join him in his ambitious plans for Arab power blocs, usually motivated by money or security, but in general Gaddafi was seen as a naïve, populist irritant in his continuing pursuit of grand schemes for Arab unity.

The Libyan quest for Arab unity began with Egypt. Libya and Egypt are next-door neighbours, and this is perhaps Libya's most important foreign relationship. The interests of the two countries are inextricably intertwined, and Hosni Mubarak, the Egyptian President, like his predecessors occupies the unenviable position of being unable to ignore Gaddafi: a powerful, wealthy leader who provides employment to many thousands of his nation's citizens. Historically, the relationship between the two states has been something like a bad marriage: each depends on the other, but the love went years ago – at times there has been outright hostility, at times a kind of tired acceptance.

On taking power in 1969, Gaddafi immediately declared his hope that Libya would be united with Egypt, and that this would be the beginning of a grander unity across the Arab world. In 1969, Nasser, Gaddafi and President Nimeiri of Sudan met to discuss merging the three countries together into one glorious revolutionary state. In 1970, Syria announced that it also wished to join the union. It may seem odd that the much more democratic and stable state of Egypt should wish to join with Libya, but for the Egyptians, the union promised financial salvation: at the time, Libya's annual per capita income was fourteen times larger than that of perpetually struggling Egypt.

Cracks soon began to appear, however. After Nasser died from a heart attack in 1970, his rather more pragmatic successor, Anwar Sadat, began talking of a 'federation' instead of a union. Libya pressed hard for a quick implementation of the planned union, while the other partners nervously called for caution. Nevertheless, by April 1971 three of the parties – Libya, Egypt and Syria – had agreed on a Federation of Arab Republics, with Sadat as President. Egypt and Syria immediately reaped financial benefit – Gaddafi paid £1.16 million to Egypt and committed £1.5 million to Syria.

In September 1972, Sadat and Gaddafi signed an official charter of union between Egypt and Libya.

Sadat was keen for Egypt to profit from Libyan wealth, but by 1973, he had become frightened by the strength and unpredictability of Gaddafi's overtures. By this time, Gaddafi had adopted the policy that was ultimately to render him deeply unpopular with most of his fellow leaders: his attempt to export Libyan revolution straight to the international masses. In early 1973, he told a press conference that Egypt needed to mount a proper cultural revolution like that in Libya. In June, he ordered Libyans to undertake a holy march across the border into Egypt, to present Sadat with a demand for immediate unity that would impress the Egyptians as a plea straight from the Libyan people. The Egyptians were deeply alarmed by the bizarre plan, and stopped the procession of 30,000 Libyans at the border. They politely allowed a small group of delegates to meet Sadat, but the episode was important as one of the earlier indicators of Gaddafi's tendency towards bizarre, spontaneous and alarming actions. When Sadat's September 1973 deadline for inaugurating the federation passed by with no action from either side, it seemed that the death knell of the Federation of Arab Republics had been sounded.

A horrific plane crash in 1973 soured relations between Egypt and Libya still further. Libyan Arab Airlines (LAA) Flight 114, from Tripoli to Cairo, was shot down by the Israeli Defence Forces on 21 February. Of the 113 passengers and crew on board, just five survived. The plane had become lost in a sandstorm, wandering accidentally across the Egyptian border into Israeli airspace. The French LAA pilot allegedly failed to comply with instructions issued by Israeli fighter planes, which fired on him and forced him to execute a failed emergency landing. Gaddafi was enraged by the incident. He felt that the Egyptians had completely failed to provide any assistance to the Libyan aircraft, which might have expected some sort of protective intervention, given that the incident took place right on the Egyptian border with Israeli-occupied Sinai.

The loss of Flight 114 led directly to one of Gaddafi's most flamboyant but fortunately unsuccessful anti-Israeli plots: his 1973 attempt to blow up the famous British liner *Queen Elizabeth 2* (QE2). The QE2 had been chartered by a group of American Jews to sail from Southampton to Haifa to join celebrations for the twenty-fifth anniversary of Israel's foundation. Gaddafi issued a clandestine order to an Egyptian submarine moored in the Gulf of Tripoli at the time to launch an attack against the *QE2* as she motored towards Israel. The alarmed submariner checked the order with the Egyptians before executing it, and Sadat rushed to put a stop to the plan. The consequences had Gaddafi been successful are unthinkable: he would have engineered a situation in which an Egyptian submarine had bombed a quintessential British icon, killing numerous Israelis. The resultant discord in the Middle East is horrible to contemplate.

When the Egyptians went to war against Israel in 1973, it was rumoured that Gaddafi heard the news via his radio. Given the erratic, eccentric diplomatic routes pursued by Gaddafi, it was no surprise that the Egyptians had shut him out of their plans, but this was to put any projects for unity straight into the deep freeze. The Yom Kippur War outraged Gaddafi, partly because he had had no part in its planning, and partly because it concluded with the Egyptians agreeing to peace talks with the Israelis, against Gaddafi's oft-declared policy that the only way forward was to eliminate the state of Israel completely. Gaddafi felt that having begun a war, no possibility of peace should have been entertained: the war should have been fought to the death so that the Palestinians could reclaim their land. Egypt, the home of Gaddafi's greatest hero, had in his eyes betrayed the entire Arab world. The rosy visions of unions and federations between Egypt and Libya that had been such a feature of Gaddafi's early years of rule had now passed into history.

In the wake of the Yom Kippur war, Libya's relations with Egypt deteriorated dramatically, particularly when Gaddafi began calling on the Egyptian people to overthrow Sadat. The growing hatred between the two was increasingly obvious to the world: Sadat famously described Gaddafi in 1975 as '100 per cent sick' and repeatedly asserted that the Colonel was trying to destroy Egypt by encouraging its internal enemies.

Continuing hostility turned into out-and-out war in July 1977. Sadat had begun truly to fear the unstable, belligerent Gaddafi, with his enormous cache of Soviet-supplied weapons, while Gaddafi saw the Egyptians as setting back the cause of the Palestinians to an unbearable degree through their willingness to work with the United States and Israel. The Egyptians were particularly alarmed by Libya's willingness to allow the Soviets to use their border territories to monitor Egyptian military installations. Unfortunately for Libya, the war demonstrated Egypt's unquestionable military superiority. Nor were Libya's Soviet allies forthcoming with additional military aid and support. The conflict lasted just a week before the two sides agreed that a peace should be brokered by Kuwait, Algeria, the Arab League and Yasser Arafat.

After the war, the enmity between Libya and Egypt solidified, particularly when Sadat signed the 1978 Camp David Accords (for which he shared the Nobel Peace Prize with the Israeli Prime Minister, Menachem Begin). The accords set out plans for peace in the Middle East and included an agreement for Palestinian autonomy in the West Bank and the Gaza Strip. Many Arab states, with Libya at the forefront, labelled this a betrayal and condemned Sadat's willingness to negotiate with Israel as a blatantly self-interested act designed to keep US aid flowing into Egypt. Libya led the Arab world in arguing for the exclusion of Egypt from regional forums, and did considerable damage to its international interests. Partly due to Libyan activism, Egypt was excluded from the Arab League between 1979 and 1989. Libya's enthusiastic denunciation of Egypt during the late 1970s represented perhaps its most successful achievement in foreign policy: there was considerable support for Libya's position, and many countries joined together against Egypt at Libya's urging.

Travel between Libya and Egypt was highly restricted for much of the late 1970s and 1980s, and many of the hundreds of thousands of Egyptian workers in Libya returned home (although around 30,000 remained). Periodically, the Egyptians who remained in Libya were subjected to sudden and devastating expulsions.

Given that plans with Egypt came unstuck so quickly, Gaddafi early on turned his attention elsewhere in the Middle East. Syria was a likely target, as it shared many interests with the Libyans. The Syrians also had a close relationship with the Soviets, they virulently opposed Egyptian negotiations with Israel and they maintained close relations with many of the same

Palestinian groups favoured by Gaddafi. Like Libya, the Syrians had flirted with pacts of union in the past as a way of strengthening a relatively weak country: in 1958 Syria had embarked on a full merger with Nasser's Egypt. This union was only briefly successful, with the Syrians quickly seceding back to independence. Syria was nonetheless keen to try again, and by 1980, Gaddafi and the Syrian President, Hafez al-Assad, had agreed a plan to unite Libya with Syria, with the sweetener that Libya would pay off a $1 billion Syrian debt to the Soviet Union.

As with others among Gaddafi's proposed partners, Assad quickly realised the volatility of the man he was dealing with. He rapidly backtracked from full union, and revised plans for a union into a fuzzier agreement on sharing a 'revolutionary leadership'. Little further concrete action was taken. Syria has been a relatively loyal friend to the Libyans, however, and in 1985 vague talk of unification was still to be heard. Libya sent generous financial aid to Syria through the 1980s, and the two generally pursued similar interests.

Gaddafi found few such loyal friends in the rest of the Middle East, where highly conservative regimes tended to be alarmed by his unpredictability and subversion. His support for Iran in its war against the Arab state of Iraq alienated many of his fellow Arab nations, in particular the Saudis. Despite this support, and despite Libyan enthusiasm for friendship with Iran (including a rejected offer to negotiate on Iran's behalf with the US during the 1979–81 hostage crisis), relations with the revolutionary government in Tehran were not particularly good either. The Iranians held the disappearance of the revered Shia leader Musa al-Sadr (of which more below) against Gaddafi for many years.

Saudi Arabia had even less in common with Gaddafi's regime than most. The Saudis frowned on Gaddafi's coup against King Idris, the ruler of a fellow Arab monarchy, and Saudi Arabia was the last Arab state to give official recognition to Gaddafi's government. The Saudis worked assiduously and quietly to cultivate a peaceful world conducive to the profitable and undisrupted sale of their oil, and pursued a close relationship with the US. They had enormous prestige throughout the Muslim world as the guardians of Islam's holiest sites, as highly conservative practitioners and defenders of the faith, and as generous sponsors of Muslim states. Gaddafi resented the prestige accumulated by the Saudis and often proclaimed to the world that Saudi Arabia was a corrupt, decadent monarchy in need of revolutionary reinvigoration. He regularly criticised the Saudi rulers as lackeys of the US and called on the Arab world to launch a jihad, or holy war, to wrest control of Mecca from them. As well as urging the Saudi people to rise up against their king, Gaddafi was rumoured to have been involved in some more practical plots, including the bombing of the Saudi embassy in Sudan in March 1973 and, in 1977, an attempted air force mutiny.

Jordan fared as badly as the Saudis with Libya. Gaddafi was automatically opposed to King Hussein's regime on the grounds that it was a wealthy, conservative monarchy. Moreover, the Jordanians had encountered terrible difficulties with the Palestinians. In the wake of the Six Day War with Israel in 1967, Palestinian militants poured over the border to take refuge in Jordan. Their presence in such large numbers was seen by the monarchy as a clear threat to its sovereignty, and so King Hussein sent the Jordanian army into battle against the militants, who included Arafat and much of the PLO. The Palestinians and the PLO were expelled in what became known to Muslims throughout the world as the 'Black September' of 1970. Gaddafi labelled this an unforgivable treachery and spent the succeeding years riling the Jordanian regime at every opportunity.

The complex politics of Lebanon – with its competing Sunni and Shia Muslim factions, its large Christian minority and the constant interference of foreign powers including Syria, the US and Israel – represented a tantalising prospect for Libyan involvement. Gaddafi sent money to a wide range of militant political parties and Muslim militias there, adding fuel to the fire of the civil war that decimated the nation between 1975 and 1990. Many Lebanese people reserve particular loathing for Gaddafi over his alleged role in the mysterious disappearance of a renowned moderate Shia leader. Imam Musa al-Sadr was the political leader of the Lebanese Shias and is credited with having made them a potent force in national politics. He travelled to Tripoli to meet Gaddafi in August 1978, possibly to discuss Libyan funding for his organisation. Neither he nor his two travelling companions were ever seen again. Some believe the Libyans had him murdered, others that he may still be alive in a Libyan jail. Gaddafi claims that Sadr left Tripoli for

Rome back in 1978, and that it is among the piazzas and cafés of the Italian capital that the Lebanese should be seeking him, not in Libya. Gaddafi has not set foot in Lebanon since Sadr disappeared, fearing that either legal or extra-legal action might be taken against him. Just as we British have pushed Gaddafi to take responsibility for funding the IRA and in the murder of PC Fletcher, the Lebanese have continued to demand that the Libyans reveal Sadr's fate. In August 2008, Lebanon took the step of officially charging Gaddafi with conspiracy to kidnap and false imprisonment.

★

As Egypt, Syria and others knocked him back, Gaddafi turned his attention westward, keenly pursuing unity pacts with the countries in the Maghreb region of north-west Africa. Algeria, Libya's enormous neighbour to the west, is the most powerful state in north Africa, and is one of the few regimes that could be said to have a really strong influence in Tripoli. When relations with Egypt went bad, Libya was left without any powerful friends, something of a quandary for a very new state with a tiny population. Algeria was a viable replacement, a powerful umbrella for the Libyans to shelter under when needed. In 1975, Libya and Algeria signed the Hassi Messaoud defensive alliance, designed as a bulwark against Moroccan expansionism. The relationship was not always smooth: for example, Libya was deeply alarmed by its exclusion from Algeria's 1983 Treaty of Concord with Tunisia. Libya often resented Algerian influence and leadership – for example refusing to resolve contentious border issues – but has in general submitted to Algerian imperatives. The world was surprised when Gaddafi took the step of allowing Libya's territorial dispute with Chad to go to the International Court of Justice in 1987, and even more surprised when he accepted its decision against Libya. Many feel that it was at the urging of Algeria that he went down this peaceful path.

Other states in the region, lacking Algeria's power and might, suffered more disruptive relationships with their unpredictable neighbour. One of Gaddafi's earliest targets for a pact of union with Libya was Tunisia, ruled by the pro-Western President Bourguiba. Bourguiba felt Libya had far more in common with its Maghrebi neighbours than with Egypt or the nations of the Middle East, and in the beginning actively sought out Gaddafi's attentions. Tunisia and Libya certainly had strong shared economic interests: Libyans enjoyed and continue to enjoy holidaying and shopping in Tunisia, while the Tunisians profit hugely from Libyan business and from the money sent home by their citizens with lucrative jobs in Libya. There were also, however, tremendous differences: Bourguiba was a stable ruler who sought to promote Tunisian development, if necessary via productive alliances with the West. Gaddafi was an entirely different proposition, as his treatment of the Tunisians was to prove.

On 12 January 1974, Libya and Tunisia announced that they would join together to form the Arab Islamic Republic, in what became known as the Jerba union. Tunisia quickly backed away, however, as the union was greeted with outrage at home, being viewed as an unparalleled disaster by many Tunisian politicians, including Hédi Nouira, Bourguiba's Prime Minister. Gaddafi did not easily forgive the Tunisians for rejecting unity with Libya, and began an energetic campaign of subversion. By 1976, the Tunisians were denouncing Libyan attempts to depose their government. Gaddafi was said to be extending ongoing support and encouragement to the Progressive National Front for the Liberation of Tunisia, which was trying to topple Bourguiba. In 1980, expatriate Tunisians trained and financed by Libya were implicated in a ludicrously unsuccessful military attack on the mining town of Gafsa in Tunisia. In 1985, Gaddafi suddenly expelled 32,000 Tunisian workers from Libya in the hope of bringing Bourguiba's shaky regime down. Only Algerian intervention stopped Tunisia and Libya from embarking on a border war at this point.

The stable, pro-Western social reformist Bourguiba was something of an unlikely partner for Gaddafi, but Morocco under King Hassan was perhaps an even more surprising proposition for union with Libya. Gaddafi's pet hatred is monarchies, which he views as in particularly dire need of Libyan-style revolutions. The Saudis, the Jordanians and the Moroccans have all been targets of diatribes on the inherent corruption and decadence of monarchical government. In the case of Morocco, there was also the irksome issue of the Western Sahara region, engaged in a full-scale battle for its independence with the Moroccan government. Gaddafi had put enormous although inconsistent effort into promoting the efforts of Polisario, the Western Saharan independence movement. Throughout most of the 1970s, Libyan money had been a boon to Polisario, and the cause of considerable angst to the Moroccan leader. (Libya's support for Polisario was also in part aimed at keeping the Algerians, strong supporters of the movement, happy.) In retaliation, Morocco provided a home to Libyan opponents of Gaddafi's regime, notably the National Front for the Salvation of Libya (known as the National Front), which mounted a dramatic failed coup against Gaddafi in May 1984.

Gaddafi's capacity to change direction suddenly and dramatically, however, was never to be under-estimated. Suddenly, it seemed that both Hassan and Gaddafi had something to gain from a union, regardless of past enmities, and both were willing to take the somewhat cynical step of setting these enmities aside. Both regimes were worried by increasingly strong union between Algeria, Tunisia and Mauritania, and dreaded being sidelined by a powerful grouping of their neighbours. For the Moroccans, Gaddafi also offered jobs and money. The early 1980s had brought severe economic strain to Morocco and, as a result, political unrest in the form of student protests and rioting. Libya, always in need of foreign labour, could offer prosperous employment that might help placate dissatisfied Moroccan youth, as well as oil at generous prices that could free up some of the Moroccan budget. Union with Libya, firmly entrenched in the minds of many ordinary Arab citizens as a radical defender of Islam, might also help King Hassan bolster his Islamist credentials with the many Moroccans who felt he was too pro-Western and too close to the Americans. Another condition of the union was that Gaddafi would cease funding Polisario, hopefully providing the Moroccans with some respite from this ongoing conflict.

For Gaddafi, friendship with Morocco could provide a bit of respectability at a time when his international stock was low and his regime intensely isolated. The Moroccans, known as conservative friends of the Americans, could do much to restore Libya's reputation in the world. Gaddafi, too, was plagued by internal opposition, and union with Morocco offered some prospect of restraining international dissidence. A union would mean an end to the inconvenient hospitality that Morocco offered his opponents. Libya was also perpetually short of good healthcare, and closer co-operation with Morocco could bring more doctors and nurses into the country, as well as access to Moroccan pharmaceuticals. Gaddafi could conveniently and probably sincerely dress all of this up in the ideological justification of his long-held dream of Arab unity.

Accordingly, in August 1984, the two leaders signed the Oujda Treaty, calling for an unlikely unification between Libya, formerly Polisario's greatest supporter, and Morocco, friend to America and one of the most conservative regimes in Africa. The union was labelled the Arab–African Union. It was not, as with others of Gaddafi's mooted unions, merely a piece of paper. Real co-operation did occur, including the establishment of a new political institution: a federal legislative assembly, to which each country sent thirty delegates. The assembly had secretariats in Tripoli and Rabat, and maintained a number of functioning committees.

An immediate benefit of the union for Gaddafi was the handing over of prominent members of the National Front. His great enemy, Captain Omar Abdullah al-Muhayshi, an original member of the Revolutionary Command Council, was among them. He had been a vocal, articulate and effective opposition leader, and his capture was a great relief to Gaddafi. It is assumed that the unfortunate Muhayshi was executed.

Cordial relations between Libya and Morocco lasted only two years, which is perhaps even longer than might have been expected between two such dramatically different countries. The Arab–African Union was brought undone by a number of factors. The Moroccans valued their alliance with the US, and Gaddafi's erratic behaviour became very embarrassing, particularly as the Reagan regime drastically increased the pressure on Gaddafi, linking him to international terrorism and proclaiming him a major enemy of the Americans. King Hassan had promised his American allies that Gaddafi's union with the Moroccans would modify his behaviour, but it seemed that in fact the opposite was occurring – Yvonne Fletcher was shot dead by Libyan diplomats in London in 1984, and Gaddafi was linked to a growing number of acts of international terrorism. The Moroccans therefore put less and less effort into protecting the alliance and indeed seemed deliberately to irritate the Libyans. In March 1986, they hosted CIA director William Casey at ceremonies to celebrate Hassan's twenty-fifth anniversary in power, a provocative gesture given the extremely tense state of Libyan–US relations at the time. Hassan's meeting with the Israeli Prime Minister, Shimon Peres, was denounced by Gaddafi as treasonous, prompting the King to declare his determination to protect Morocco's sovereignty against Libyan interference. On 29 August, the moribund union was terminated: King Hassan declared it officially over in statements to the Moroccan media.

The union with Morocco had been one of Gaddafi's more successful, and rare in that it had involved substantial co-operation. Yet it was no exception to the increasingly obvious rule: Gaddafi's wealth could lure regional partners, but his unpredictable personality and the international political costs of association with him made it impossible for him to keep them. The pact with Morocco was to be one of his last experiments in unity – regard for him in the Middle East and north Africa was at possibly a historic low by the mid-1980s. Today, most politicians in the Arab world continue to enjoy the common Gaddafi joke related by the journalist Robert Fisk:

> Gaddafi, President Mubarak of Egypt and Saddam Hussein [are] driving across the desert only to find their path blocked by a lion. Saddam, author of the 'mother of all battles', cannot persuade the lion to move. Nor can Mubarak, leader of the largest Arab nation. But when Gaddafi lifts the leathery ear and mutters into it, the lion races off across the desert. 'What did you tell him?' Mubarak and Saddam chorus.
>
> 'I offered him', Gaddafi replies, 'unity with Libya.'[2]

★

It would be polite to describe Gaddafi's history in Africa as chequered, perhaps more accurate to label it an utter disaster. He injected tremendous amounts of money into Africa and achieved very little, either for Libya or for the nations he targeted. Scholars of far greater knowledge and ability than me have tied themselves in terrible knots trying to figure out exactly what Gaddafi wanted to achieve in his adventures in the Sahelian and sub-Saharan regions of Africa, constructing tortuous arguments over whether the Colonel was motivated by self-interest or by his ideology. There seems to me to be little point imposing a logic on his African doings that does not in fact exist. Gaddafi acted from a random, chaotic, unpredictable jumble of naked self-interest and ideological goals. It seems likely that often he himself would not have been able to see where the one ended and the other began. He wanted to counteract Western and Israeli influence, he wanted to promote independence movements, he wanted to promote Islam, and he certainly wanted to make sure he did not lose control at home in Libya. But these objectives clashed and became confused, and one or other of them was always available to justify any course of action that suggested itself. Gaddafi, with his dreadfully short attention span, could always change tack suddenly and devastatingly, putting one or other of his enormously broad foreign policy objectives to work to lend respectability to the whim of the day.

It is to be expected that Libya should play a role in African affairs – it is the fourth largest country in the continent and one of the most prosperous. Libyans share culture and history with many of their neighbours. The borders made rigid by colonial powers were historically far more fluid: the people of Fezzan share history and culture with Chad, Niger and Sudan; the Tripolitanians traditionally interacted extensively with the Maghreb nations to the west of Libya – Algeria, Tunisia and Morocco; those living in Cyrenaica shared trade and culture with Egypt. Libya's close ties to its neighbours are not just a matter of history: the oil-rich nation has required more labour than its people have been able to provide, and its neighbours have profited from this. Remittances from lucrative work in Libya have benefited many economies in the region.

Gaddafi worked hard to extend Libya's influence in Africa to the south, forging alliances with a broad spectrum of regimes throughout the continent. As he intended, this alarmed the US and Egypt, who saw him as a profoundly destabilising force in Africa, a reliable source of weapons and cash for most of their enemies in the continent. Nor were they unjustified in this opinion: much of Gaddafi's African activity was indeed flamboyantly designed to act against Western and Egyptian interests.

Africa initially appealed to Gaddafi as a highly promising front in his battle to isolate Israel. As Egypt and other Arab countries moved closer to the US and backed off from conflict with Israel in the wake of the Yom Kippur War, Gaddafi looked to Africa for support against the Israelis. In doing this, he was to inflict considerable damage on Israel's African position. The Israelis had carefully cultivated African nations, whose chronic need for aid made them good potential allies against the hostility of Arab and Muslim states in international political forums. In 1970 all the Arab countries combined had fewer diplomatic missions in Africa than Israel alone.

Gaddafi's campaign to remedy this imbalance was launched in 1973. The aim was to persuade as many African states as possible to break off diplomatic relations with the Israelis. Like the Israelis, and indeed the Americans and the Soviets, he gave generously to the nations willing to fall into line. Burundi was invited to open a Libyan embassy in April 1973 and broke its ties with Israel just a month later. Gaddafi claimed with some justification that it was Libyan influence that persuaded Chad, Congo, Niger, Ethiopia, Nigeria, Zambia and Mali to suspend their relationship with Israel the same year. Libya vigorously lobbied the Organisation of African Unity (OAU), urging all member states to abandon ties with Israel. Following the Yom Kippur War, all but four OAU member states cut off diplomatic ties with the Israelis, representing a real victory in the Libyan campaign to scale back Israel's African influence.

Gaddafi was also virulent in his opposition of Christianity in Africa, believing that it was the religion of colonial powers and should be rejected in favour of Islam. He tried hard to persuade non-Muslim leaders to convert, with some notable successes. In 1973, President Bongo of Gabon became a Muslim after a visit to Libya, one of the more opportunistic conversions the world has seen in recent times. Bongo was not renowned for his piety as a Muslim, but profited greatly from the flow of Libyan oil money that followed his embrace of Islam.

Jean-Bedel Bokassa, ruler of the Central African Republic from 1965 until 1979, also converted to Islam after meeting with Gaddafi. Bokassa has been described as one of the most corrupt and vain of the world's dictators. He was rumoured to throw disobedient servants to his pet crocodiles and lions, and kept a harem of mistresses. An obituary in *The Independent* described him as 'a military dictator of low intelligence but some cunning who took a poor country and over thirteen years exploited its few assets relentlessly for his own grotesque advantage, ultimately leaving it in a state of anarchy and ruin'.[3] This unlikely convert embraced Islam in Tripoli in September 1976. In December of the same year, however, he renounced his new religion and returned to Catholicism. Some felt this was because he had proclaimed himself Emperor, renaming his country the Central African Empire, and wanted to hold his grandiose coronation ceremony in an attractive Catholic cathedral, others put it down to characteristic Libyan tardiness in the payment of promised aid.

One of Gaddafi's most unsuccessful and embarrassing African entanglements was in Uganda. His enthusiastic support for Idi Amin's murderous, xenophobic regime left him looking both amoral and ineffective in the eyes of the world. In 1972, Amin famously expelled 80,000 south Asians from Uganda. This was a move that brought tremendous benefits to Britain, which gave refuge to many of the capable and talented individuals who fled the regime, but which caused enormous trauma and suffering at the time. It was the sort of flamboyant yet blunt manoeuvre that Gaddafi (who himself frequently ordered similar mass expulsions of foreign workers) thoroughly approved of.

Amin visited Libya in 1972, and the two leaders got along famously. Trade and military co-operation between the two nations was vigorously promoted, and Uganda joined the Libyans in pursuing an intensely anti-Israeli foreign policy. In July 1976, Israel launched a dramatic and successful raid to rescue hostages taken to Uganda by the Palestinian hijackers of an Air France flight. The hijackers had been allowed to land at Entebbe, Uganda's main airport. Gaddafi declared his support for Amin, and co-sponsored a UN resolution condemning the Israeli 'attack' on Entebbe.

Amin's brutal regime began to crumble in the late 1970s, and in 1979 the Tanzanian President, Julius Nyerere (having suffered repeated Ugandan incursions into his territory), sent an army to overthrow the dictator, with the blessing of most of the world. Amin had very few friends left, but the faithful Gaddafi airlifted around 2,000 Libyan troops to Kampala. As they arrived, it became clear that the Ugandan army had disintegrated and fled; only the unfortunate Libyan soldiers remained to be roundly humiliated. Four hundred were killed and the rest rounded up and sent back to Libya. Libya was establishing a reputation (to be cemented in its war with Chad) as a state with a tremendous, expensive military arsenal, but a completely incompetent army led by commanders devoid of strategic ability.

Gaddafi also expended a huge amount of money and effort in Sudan. The President, Jaafar Nimeiri, was in many ways Gaddafi's double – both came to power in 1969, both were from poor families (Nimeiri was the son of a postman), both loved football and both modelled their revolutions on the overthrow of the monarchy in Egypt. Like Gaddafi, Nimeiri was capricious, unpredictable and violent, but he differed in that he was to become a much more fervent advocate of Islam. He introduced sharia law to Sudan in 1983, reportedly pouring $5 million worth of alcohol into the Nile. Nimeiri also lacked Gaddafi's longevity, being toppled in a coup in 1985 (although he reappeared in 2000 to contest elections, coming second to the current President, Omar al-Bashir).

Despite their many similarities, the two men were rarely friends: Nimeiri spent much of his career defending himself against Gaddafi-sponsored plots and pursuing alliances with the US and Egypt, which he hoped would protect his regime against Libyan animosity. Nimeiri declared of Gaddafi that 'he has a split personality – both parts evil'. In the immediate aftermath of the Libyan and the Sudanese revolutions, however, relations were excellent. Sudan proposed joining Egypt and Libya in Gaddafi's mooted union of Arab states, and Gaddafi was a boon to Nimeiri – helping to foil an attempted coup against him in 1971, and capturing two of its leaders and returning them to Sudan, where they were hanged.

Things turned sour quickly, as Gaddafi became angered by his fellow leader's willingness to work with the West. By 1975, Gaddafi was sponsoring Sudanese mercenaries to work against Nimeiri. Nimeiri crushed this resistance, and it is rumoured that many of the captured rebels were

tortured. Another coup attempt, in July 1976, was said by Nimeiri to
have been financed by Libya. This led him to sign a defence agreement
with Saudi Arabia, one of the nations most despised by Gaddafi. Sudan
also attracted Gaddafi's ire by agreeing to play host to Libyan dissidents.
On 7 October 1981, the National Front announced its formation to the
world from Khartoum, greatly provoking Gaddafi. Not surprisingly, Sudan
increasingly aligned itself with Egypt and the West, spooked by Libya's
erratic and violent hostility. Libyan enmity, however, was not without its
benefits. Sudan's status as one of Libya's main enemies on the continent
proved rather lucrative: the worse its relations got with Libya, the more US
aid it attracted, as the Americans keenly supported any African state willing
to declare against Gaddafi.

Gaddafi has made, and continues to make, unsavoury friendships in
Africa, but his record is not entirely to be criticised. In his search for friends
and influence, he extended life-saving aid throughout the 1970s and 1980s
to many of the smallest and poorest nations of Africa. Gaddafi has certainly
saved many sub-Saharan Africans during times of drought and famine.
Libyan aid has benefited Niger, Mali, Uganda, Togo, Burundi, the Central
African Republic and Gabon, among others.

Gaddafi also gave generously to some of the most important liberation
movements of the twentieth century. He funded the groups fighting Ian
Smith's white minority regime in Rhodesia (now Zimbabwe) and he was
hailed by Nelson Mandela as one of the greatest supporters of the African
National Congress's struggle against apartheid in South Africa. Mandela
told a Libyan audience in 1997:

> The people of Libya shared the trenches with us in our struggle for freedom.
> You were in the front ranks of those whose selfless and practical support
> helped assure a victory that was as much yours as it is ours. We are therefore
> deeply moved to be amongst freedom fighters for whom the freedom of
> others was as precious as their own.[4]

To his credit, Gaddafi was, as Mandela suggested, one of the most
vociferous and active opponents of apartheid, but his approach was tainted

by an unpalatable anti-Semitism. He proclaimed to the world that apartheid was identical to Zionism, and enthusiastically promoted a 1975 resolution in the United Nations General Assembly (Resolution 3379) to this effect. Twenty-eight African nations supported this resolution (five opposed it and twelve abstained). The Israeli ambassador to the UN, Chaim Herzog, tore a copy of it in half as he described it as being 'devoid of any moral or legal value'.

Gaddafi's generosity was also undermined by the fact that he seemed to give to anyone and everyone. Money and arms were sent off to a huge assortment of ideologically disparate groups: in the mid-1970s, Gaddafi was supporting liberation movements in Eritrea, Rhodesia, Portuguese Guinea (now Guinea-Bissau), South Africa, Morocco and Chad, among others. The support given to rebels and liberation movements was erratic and largely without logic. He often changed sides, for example supporting the mainly Muslim Eritreans in their war for independence from Ethiopia, but then switching to support mainly Christian Ethiopia when Mengistu Haile Mariam's military junta came to power.

It is no surprise to find that in general African leaders quickly became wary of and exhausted by Gaddafi. In the early 1980s, he was accused separately by Nigeria, Tunisia, Uganda, Niger, Mali, Mauritius, Senegal and Gambia of plotting against their governments. It is symptomatic of the low regard in which Gaddafi was held that a planned OAU summit, due to be held in Tripoli in 1982, was cancelled, mainly due to disapproval of Libyan subversion throughout the continent. If the summit had been held in Tripoli, Gaddafi would automatically have been the chairman for 1983, and most leaders felt this to be an unbearable prospect. The summit did not take place until a year later, in Addis Ababa under Ethiopian chairmanship. Gaddafi attended but left early, unable to stomach the humiliation of his status as the first leader in the history of the organisation to be denied the chairmanship.

★

It is important to realise that Gaddafi's entanglement in Chad is one of the great tragedies of his rule in Libya. We hear so much in the West about the toll taken by Libyan-sponsored terrorism against Western victims, but the war against Chad claimed many more lives. This lengthy, profitless, expensive conflict brought no benefit to either party and represented a terrific squandering of resources and opportunity. Ahmed, my Libyan businessman friend, was moved to tears as he talked of the enormous cost of this conflict: in human terms, in financial terms and in terms of the status of Libya, which was deeply humiliated by the outcome.

Chad is one of the poorest countries in the world. As a colony of the French in the early twentieth century, it was grossly under-developed, valued very little for its major resources: cheap cotton and cheap labour. Gaining independence in 1960, Chad unsurprisingly suffered woeful post-colonial fortunes, an educated, politically skilled elite being pretty much non-existent in the new nation. Decades of civil war followed, with only brief interludes of peace. The north and the south appear to be almost irreconcilable, and the competing aims of the French and the Libyans have for much of Chad's history determined who has come out on top.

Libya's involvement in Chad had a certain logic. Libyans and Chadians had traded with each other for centuries, and members of Libya's nineteenth-century religious and political Senussi movement set up outposts in northern and central Chad. The borders drawn up by the French and the Italians did not necessarily reflect the situation on the ground. The Tebu, a nomadic black Muslim tribe, have always moved back and forth between their lands in Chad and in Libya. Arabs from territory that is now Libyan and Sudanese moved to Chad, but retained strong cultural ties to their homelands.

After independence, Chadian politics developed along worrying lines, almost entirely determined by ethnic loyalties. Conflict erupted almost immediately, and Libyans were involved from early on. Chad's first government was led by François Tombalbaye, who was strongly backed by the French and aligned with southern Chadians, who were mainly animist or Christian. Tombalbaye's government was deeply unpopular in the mainly Muslim regions of central and northern Chad. Various opposition movements sprang up to fight him, a number of which united in 1966 to form the Front de Libération Nationale du Tchad, or Frolinat.

Gaddafi's predecessor, King Idris, offered token support to Frolinat, allowing it to work with Chadian students in Libya and stating agreement with the group's aims, but stopping short of sending weapons or suspending relations with the official Chad government. Gaddafi judged Idris's approach grossly inadequate. For him, instability, poverty and division in Chad meant that it was a country perfect for the export of his own ideologies: Chad could become another *jamahiriyya*, it could become a dependent friend to Libya, and it could help him to extend his influence over the rest of Africa. From the early 1970s, Gaddafi provided Frolinat with comfortable offices in Tripoli, weapons and sophisticated military training. In 1972, it was given official recognition by Libya as the government of Chad.

In retaliation, Tombalbaye publicly invited Gaddafi's opponents to set up bases in Chad. Chad and Libya teetered on the brink of war as a result. This time, it was averted: with the mediation of the President of Niger, Hamami Diori, the two parties reached an accommodation, Gaddafi threw Frolinat out of Tripoli and Tombalbaye withdrew all Chad's diplomatic links with Israel at Gaddafi's behest. In December 1972, a friendship treaty was established, and Libya sent money to help Tombalbaye.

The full details of the peace between Libya and Chad at this time are somewhat murky, but it seems that Tombalbaye gave Libya tacit permission to maintain its presence in the region of Chad known as the Aouzou Strip. The Libyans set up a military base there, gave Libyan citizenship to its residents, and showed it on all official maps as a part of Libya: they were to occupy it until 1994.

The Aouzou Strip was at the heart of the Libyan–Chadian conflict. Flying over it, it is difficult to understand how so many lives could have been sacrificed for such an unpromising tract of land: the strip consists of 40,000 square miles of arid, barren nothingness. As usual, the answer lies underground. It is thought that there are uranium reserves waiting beneath the surface to enrich the government that develops the capacity to exploit them. Uranium reserves might also prove useful for Gaddafi in his ongoing but very unsuccessful search to develop a Libyan nuclear capability. This makes Gaddafi's involvement even more distasteful in my eyes: already massively rich in natural resources, Libya sacrificed thousands of lives to deprive Chad of a much more modest and difficult to exploit source of energy wealth.

Taking control of the Aouzou Strip was also about remedying historical injustices. From Gaddafi's point of view, Chadian control of the region was a profoundly unfair legacy of imperialism. The Franco-Italian treaty of 1935 awarded the Aouzou Strip to Libya, but this was revoked in negotiations following the end of World War II, when it was reassigned by the French to Chad. This was an act clearly governed by self-interest, given that Chad was still under French rule at the time. As Africa's territory was carved up, assigned and reassigned during the late 1950s, the Aouzou Strip ended up remaining with Chad. King Idris accepted this state of affairs, but Gaddafi the anti-colonial crusader refused to follow suit.

By 1978, a full-scale civil war was underway in Chad, as the new military regime under General Félix Malloum (who had deposed Tombalbaye in 1975), with its power base again in the south, fought the growing forces of Frolinat, based in the north. Malloum had refused to continue with Tombalbaye's accommodating tolerance of the Libyan occupation of the Aouzou Strip. This led Gaddafi to devote considerable energies to cultivating Malloum's enemy, Goukouni Oueddei, a rebel Tebu who had emerged as Frolinat's latest leader. In 1978, Gaddafi declared to the world that Chad was now effectively divided into French and Libyan spheres of influence (the French supported Malloum, the Libyans Oueddei).

Meanwhile, one of Gaddafi's sworn enemies was becoming increasingly influential in Chadian affairs: Hissène Habré. Habré led a breakaway faction of Frolinat that questioned Libyan motives in its support for Chad. In March 1979, Gaddafi's protégé Oueddei led Frolinat in the taking of N'Djamena, Chad's capital. Habré's faction contested this and civil war continued, this time with Habré's breakaway forces fighting Goukouni's Frolinat. Goukouni appealed for more Libyan aid, which provided the perfect excuse for Gaddafi to send in the troops. He dispatched 7,000 soldiers from the Libyan army and 7,000 members of the Islamic Legion, an organisation of Arab and Muslim African mercenaries established by Gaddafi to promote Libyan interests in Africa, to occupy Chad. Gaddafi's force marched across Chad to rout Habré's troops, one of the few convincing Libyan victories of the war. In a situation where the lines between military aid and self-interested intervention were thoroughly blurred, Gaddafi could also declare that his strengthened presence in Chad was at the invitation of President Oueddei.

Gaddafi has never proven himself capable of fashioning a subtle approach; his has always been the blunt, blind enthusiasm of an ideologue uninterested in reading others or reading situations. True to form, in 1981 he ignored the delicacy of Libya's position as an invading force in Chad to begin discussing the possibility of merging the two countries. The shaky Goukouni regime could not cope with the ensuing public outrage: Habré's forces were reinvigorated by this alarming prospect, and the OAU vociferously condemned the proposal, aghast at the prospect of greatly increased Arab influence in Africa. Goukouni asked the Libyans to withdraw from Chad, and Gaddafi agreed. His reasons for agreeing so readily have been much debated: perhaps it was his desire to build Libyan influence in the OAU, or perhaps the complete lack of international or African support for his presence in Chad. Meanwhile, the much-weakened Goukouni had taken refuge in Paris. Into the OAU-policed vacuum stormed Gaddafi's implacable enemy, Habré, now backed up by American and French support.

Things were not quiet for long. Libya sent troops to help Goukouni restore his position, taking control of the north. France sent troops to support Habré in the south, and drew a 'Red Line' that divided Chad in half. This time, the forces ranged against Gaddafi in his Chadian mission were daunting. The Americans, under Ronald Reagan's presidency, were resolute in their determination to scale back the Colonel's ambitions, and had sent fighter jets, military aid and money to help the French prop up Habré.

In a situation of considerable tension, the French attempted to come to terms with the Libyans. An agreement was reached in September 1984 that both would withdraw their troops. Gaddafi, however, reneged: while the French moved out of southern Chad, the Libyan forces stayed right where they were in the north. Despite photographic evidence of their presence, Gaddafi denied to the world that there were any Libyan troops in Chad: President Mitterrand recognised Gaddafi's dishonesty, but was unwilling to order French soldiers to return to the Chadian mire.

In 1986, Goukouni reopened hostilities by launching an attack over the

Red Line, with Libyan support. Habré, backed by French and American weapons, money and logistical support, mounted a retaliatory ground attack in January 1987, moving north and successfully ambushing the Libyans in two bloody encounters. The events of 1986–7 were truly devastating for Libya. By March 1987, it was said that 3,600 Libyan soldiers had died, with 1,165 injured. Chad had lost just thirty-five men and, under the triumphant Habré, had driven the Libyans almost completely out of the country. The Chadians were unable, however, to recapture the Aouzou Strip, although another 1,700 Libyans died in battles over the area in August 1987. By September it was thought that Gaddafi had lost 7,500 men (one tenth of his army) and more than $1 billion in equipment. The war was for all intents and purposes over, although skirmishes continued between Habré and Gaddafi until Habré was deposed in a 1991 coup by one of his generals, Idris Déby, who was unsurprisingly supported by Libya.

One of the most unpleasant aspects of Libya's role in Chad was its use of mercenaries. Many of those killed in Chad in 1987 were foreigners. Geoff Simons writes in his history of Libya that 1,700 Druze militiamen from Lebanon were among the dead, having been hired out at between $500 and $2,300 per month, with $50,000 going to their families if they were killed.[5] Rumours have persisted that impoverished foreign labourers in Tripoli from sub-Saharan Africa and from Palestine were press-ganged into the war, shipped off to fight in Chad without even knowing their destination.

Under Déby, Libya and Chad have enjoyed cordial relations. Libya has supplied Chad with weapons, and the two agreed to take the question of the Aouzou Strip to the International Court of Justice (ICJ). In 1992, the ICJ awarded sovereignty over the area to Chad, voting sixteen to one against Libya. On 31 May 1994, Déby and Gaddafi signed an agreement that formally ceded control of the Aouzou Strip to Chad, and a treaty of friendship was signed in Tripoli. Many were shocked that Gaddafi had accepted the ICJ verdict so willingly: the world had yet to become fully accustomed to the remodelled, peaceful, institution-building Gaddafi who was to emerge in the 1990s.

★

The end of the war in Chad was a sobering moment for Gaddafi. The Chadians had received generous help from the French and the Americans, desperate to put an end to this Libyan 'sphere of influence'. The fact still remained that Libya, which had spent billions on costly Soviet weaponry, had shown to the world that it was militarily extremely weak, defeated by one of the poorest nations of the world. The complete failure to respond to the American bombing of Tripoli and Benghazi in April 1986 reinforced this picture of weakness. About the best that could be said of Libya's army was that it was remarkably good at airlifting tanks and troops. Unfortunately, this airlifted military might seemed invariably to be immediately trounced once it hit the ground. Gaddafi's ambitious vision for himself as a regional hegemon, using Libya's vast fortunes and expensive army to influence other states, would need to be adjusted to new realities.

The story of Gaddafi's search for influence makes for a confusing and bizarre wander through the politics of Africa and the Middle East during the 1970s and 1980s. Gaddafi was driven by such an enormous range of motives – exporting Libyan revolution, promoting Islam, working for Arab unity, restoring Palestinian territories, opposing and undoing the deeds of Western colonialism – that his interventions had no meaningful pattern. Nor did he achieve much success. His pacts and unions crumbled, he often backed the loser, and he fell out badly with most of the states with which he dealt closely. By the end of the 1980s, he had lost all credibility, repeatedly proving himself incapable of constructing sustained relationships involving trust or real empathy towards the problems of his partners. There was little respect for him left in the region, except, perhaps, for a grudging admiration for his willingness to speak bluntly and to say the things no-one else would incur the political cost of saying. His fellow leaders enjoyed watching him serve up blunt truths to the Americans and the British, but it would be a long time before anyone once more saw him as a credible regional player.

6

# DEATH IN ST JAMES'S SQUARE

We cannot, and will not, permit foreign countries to export their internal disputes to the streets of London in this way.

Geoffrey Howe, Foreign Secretary, 1 May 1984

On 17 April 1984, 25-year-old Police Constable Yvonne Fletcher, from Semley, near Shaftesbury, was shot dead in the course of her routine duties in central London. Fletcher had been posted alongside her fiancé, Michael Liddle, outside the Libyan diplomatic mission in St James's Square, London, policing a small protest mounted by Libyan dissidents. She was a dedicated officer, excited by the prospect of a promising career with the Metropolitan Police. Fletcher was famous for her stature: she was tiny, at about 5 feet 3 inches, and special exception had been made to the normal rules to allow her to join the force. This young woman had defied regulations to forge her career, but her potential was to go unfulfilled. She was denied not only this career, but also the rich and happy family life stretching out in front of her.

Walking to my office in the House of Commons a quarter of a century later, on a warm day in May 2009, I watched young police officers supervising another protest, this time held by British Tamils. Mostly, these men and women do their job bravely and effectively. Occasionally, they get it wrong. But whatever happens, I feel passionately that they deserve to be able to trust us, the politicians who are the face of the state that sends them out to do such a dangerous job. It is for this reason that I have raised this case whenever and wherever I am able, pushing hard for the truth to be aired. PC Fletcher's murder is a shameful stain on the histories of both Britain and Libya, and it needs to be resolved. More than anyone, I want Libya and Britain to move closer together, forging an honest and a productive relationship. I think, however, that this needs to be done on the basis of a clean slate: we need to talk through the crimes of the past, and then to move on to a happier future.

The circumstances of Fletcher's murder illustrate the distance between the Gaddafi of 2010 and the Gaddafi of 1984. Now, Gaddafi meets with heads of state from all over Europe and the West, and has been allowed to put many of Libya's most heinous crimes behind him. He cultivates Western leaders assiduously, if somewhat idiosyncratically. In 1984, Gaddafi's world was an entirely different place. Then, he saw it as dominated by former colonial powers who were queuing up to support those who wished to depose him, hoping to replace him with a more pliable government. This Gaddafi of the early 1980s was perhaps at the height of his career of violence; he had spent much of the 1970s funnelling money and weapons to some of the most noxious terrorist groups in the world. His most detested and feared enemies, however, were Libyans. He dreaded the potential of the Libyan opposition working against him abroad and was willing to take any action to halt their activities, no matter how hard the criticism of the rest of the world would rain down on his regime as a consequence.

★

The murder of Yvonne Fletcher by a Libyan diplomat shooting from inside an official London mission was not something anyone would have predicted. The Libyans themselves had certainly never intended to murder a British police officer: it was their compatriots protesting against Gaddafi's cruelties who were supposed to be silenced that day. On the other hand, the violent breakdown of the British–Libyan relationship was far from a surprise. Over the preceding five years, Colonel Gaddafi had willingly and deliberately chosen to turn the capital cities of the West into the setting of a murderous struggle to consolidate his regime. Indeed, to act in this way suited Gaddafi ideally. Assassinating his opponents abroad opened up the very useful possibility that Britain and the United States could be implicated in the violence that ensued and then portrayed to Libyans at home as enthusiastic supporters of those who wished to bring down his *jamahiriyya*.

To understand Fletcher's death, we also need to understand what was happening in Libya in the years leading up to it. Gaddafi had spent the early 1970s consolidating his rule and the mid-1970s concocting a revolutionary ideology and devising plans to radicalise Libya. Part of this was the establishment of his revolutionary committees, which recruited citizens keen to re-educate their compatriots in appropriate revolutionary ardour. Predictably, the revolutionary committees turned into a shadowy, much-feared security apparatus that quickly became the most powerful institution in the country. From the late 1970s, Libya was to be the site of an ongoing struggle between revolutionary ideologues and the moderate men of learning and expertise who wished to develop the country into a functional, modern state. In the early 1980s, it was the revolutionary side of affairs that predominated, and the sycophantic men who were forging successful political careers via the revolutionary committees who were ahead.

Gaddafi's project of revolutionary radicalisation was not confined to Libya's borders. One of Libya's greatest needs was to develop its poor skills base, and the only way to achieve this quickly enough was to send Libyans abroad to be educated, and to improve their skills by working in foreign cities for foreign companies. There was therefore a growing population of bright, ambitious Libyans living outside Libya. On the one hand these students represented a treasure trove, a repository of skills that would ensure Libya's national growth and, hopefully, diversification away from being just an oil state. On the other hand, the universities of Britain and the US were in Gaddafi's view a potential snakepit, their liberal environments promoting the politicisation of students and their exploration of activism and dissent. It seemed to him that Libya's embassies needed to play a role in ensuring that the treasure trove viewpoint won out over the snakepit. For this reason, Libya's embassies were given a revolutionary makeover. No longer were they to wear the conservative, traditional badge of 'embassy'; instead, in 1979 they were restyled as 'people's bureaus', which would promote an appropriate revolutionary consciousness to Libyans abroad, but also to foreigners. This was not just a stylistic makeover. Libyan people's bureaus became the instruments of the revolutionary committees at home, and went on to become sites of intrigue and violence. They played a crucial role in Gaddafi's policy of eliminating the people he termed 'stray dogs': Libyans abroad who did not toe the party line. In 1979, for example, the FBI monitored the activities of four Libyan diplomats posted in Washington who were suspected of being assassins on a mission to murder Libyan dissidents in the US. The FBI found evidence that included a hit list recording the names of students who were to be murdered. The four Libyans were expelled from the country, but in a strange foreshadowing of events in London in 1984, they fled into the grounds of the people's bureau, claimed diplomatic immunity and refused to leave for a week.

Gaddafi chose a crack team to head up the promotion of revolutionary committees abroad. One of the most interesting figures involved was Musa Kusa, long a close advisor to Gaddafi and currently Libya's foreign minister. Kusa undertook his undergraduate studies in sociology at Michigan State University, reportedly submitting a biographical essay on Gaddafi as his master's thesis. By 1980, his career had progressed to the point where he was appointed chief of the London people's bureau. His time in London was brief, however: nicknamed 'the envoy of death', he was expelled from the UK after less than a year in post, after calling publicly for the murder of two Libyan dissidents. Kusa was also reported to have threatened to finance the IRA if Britain refused to hand dissidents to Libya (no empty threat, as Chapter 4 of this book has shown). After his expulsion, he went on to head the Libyan External Security Organisation, and has been one of Gaddafi's most trusted aides. His history as a chief architect of the 'stray dogs' campaigns has made the skin of many a Western politician forced to deal with him crawl uncomfortably.

Also arriving in London in 1980 to promote the influence of the revolutionary committee camp was Omar Sodani, a talented and ambitious 28-year-old medical doctor and a protégé of Gaddafi. Sodani has been described as originating from a similar background to Gaddafi, born in Fezzan to illiterate parents living in the desert. He was one of the most fervent of those who worked for the revolutionary committees, and was rumoured to have overseen executions while active in student politics in Libya.[1] Sodani led the push to discipline Libyan students in Britain, organising them and promoting to them the cause of the revolutionary committees. Regular meetings were held at which students were mobilised against dissidents. Sodani is thought to be one of the men who mounted the takeover of the people's bureau, and thus one of those inside when PC Fletcher died. After her murder, he was prominent among the suspects sought by the Metropolitan Police for interview. It was widely rumoured that he had been executed by the Libyans following his return, but reports that emerged in the early 2000s suggested that he was still alive.

As Kusa, Sodani and others promoted the radicalisation of Libya's embassies and the 'stray dogs' campaign, the period from 1980 through to 1984 unsurprisingly became one of great diplomatic strain between Libya and Western countries. The Libyans flagrantly and publicly murdered dissidents in a number of major cities. Hotels and cafés in Rome, Paris and Bonn bore witness to bloody, public killings perpetrated by Libyan gunmen. Typically, Gaddafi would follow the murders by claiming diplomatic immunity for the perpetrators and harassing Western nationals working in Libya. Libya became notorious for its abuse of diplomatic immunity and privileges such as diplomatic bags, which could not be opened by host countries' customs organisations. Many suspected Libya of using these bags to smuggle weapons. Relations with Britain were tense, as the Libyans' actions in London became increasingly erratic and at times, horrifically violent. In April 1980, a Libyan journalist, Mohammed Mustafa Ramadan, was murdered outside a London mosque. This was followed two weeks later by the death of a lawyer, Mahmoud Nafa, shot by a hitman on the doorstep of his office. In November, Britons were appalled when the two children of a dissident family living in Portsmouth were poisoned. In May 1984, the Foreign Secretary, Sir Geoffrey Howe, neatly summarised to the

House of Commons the state of affairs between the two countries in the period leading up to Fletcher's murder:

> During this period, Her Majesty's Government took firm action against those Libyans who infringed our laws. In June 1980, Mr Musa Kusa, the newly accredited secretary-general of the Libyan people's bureau, stated publicly his approval of the killing of Libyan dissidents in the United Kingdom. On the following day, my predecessor required him to leave the country forthwith. With the co-operation of the Home Secretary, three other Libyans were also expelled.
>
> In November 1980 the two children of a Libyan dissident were poisoned in Portsmouth. As a result of that crime, four Libyans – none of whom had any diplomatic status – were convicted and sentenced to long terms in prison. In purported retaliation, the Libyans expelled three members of the British embassy staff in Tripoli and an attempt was made to burn down the embassy building.
>
> Throughout the next three years, the behaviour of the Libyans remained unpredictable and sometimes very difficult. On many occasions, the Libyans made hostile threats in characteristically intemperate language. There were, however, no further incidents of comparable gravity to those of 1980.[2]

For Gaddafi in 2010, these wild events on the streets of Britain in the early 1980s are long past, one of many shocking episodes in a long career of repression and violence. Those caught up in these episodes, however, continue to be haunted by them. In September 2009, I met Ramsay Nafa, the son of Mahmoud Nafa. Mahmoud Nafa had been a moderate man, every inch the intellectual. He had somewhat naïvely hoped that he could point out the wrongs of the Libyan regime so that the regime could deal with them peacefully. Nafa, like others of those murdered at the time, had published anonymous articles critical of Gaddafi. Ramsay was six when his father died, his younger sister just three:

> It was April 1980. I was six, I would have been seven that year. I remember, leading up to it, that there was a lot of tension, a lot of stress. My mum

told me before it all happened that she would always check under the car for a bomb. I remember seeing my dad the day before he was murdered. I remember being at school that morning, I saw my mum with two other people, Special Branch or something. I was taken to a bright yellow car and driven home. I don't know if anyone told me what happened, but I worked out what had happened. My sister was three, her only memory of my father is him washing his hands, how spotlessly clean they were.

He was not a violent man. He was not a man who went in for extremism. He was a qualified lawyer. He was an intellectual who had asked for police protection, but had been denied it. He had worked on publishing English translations of the Arab world's business and trade laws. He didn't believe the regime was in the best interests of Libya, he didn't believe Libya was going in the right direction, as far as rational thought was concerned, as far as development as a nation, maturing and moving forward with institutions that could be relied on and seen as fair and unbiased. The Revolutionary Council was a throwback to Stalin, a throwback to the French Revolution, to the rule of the mob.

The hitman who shot Mahmoud Nafa was sentenced to twenty years in prison by a British court. He told the court that he had only been in Britain two days and that he had got the gun on the black market. The story was an obvious lie, but because he had pleaded guilty, few questions were asked about his orders and motivations. As was to be the case in so many subsequent incidents of Libyan iniquity, the chain of command leading to the top was resolutely ignored.

Ramsay Nafa is now in his thirties, a British citizen with a young family, carving out a high-flying career in global finance. Yet he remains bereft at the loss of his father so young, robbed so violently and so completely of this vital relationship. Like the Fletcher family and the Lockerbie relatives, he desperately wants the truth behind his father's murder acknowledged. In the main, however, he has been ignored by a Foreign Office juggling the competing demands of a revitalised Libyan relationship with the desire for justice expressed by higher-profile victims of the Gaddafi state. As the son of a Libyan family, Ramsay worries that his case will not be among those the British government sees fit to support. Yet, as a British citizen whose father was killed on a London street, he is as entitled as anyone else to our support. It is my hope that the Foreign Office will press Libya for answers on this, and for an appropriate compensation payment for the Nafas that would acknowledge the random, senseless violence inflicted on this family.

I have always taken a great deal of pride and interest in London's worldwide fame as a refuge for the politically persecuted of the world. It was no surprise to me to find Libya among the rainbow of nations boasting exiles meeting regularly in the cafés, bars and homes of our capital city. In the years leading up to PC Fletcher's death, Gaddafi too was well aware that Libyan dissidence was thriving in London. Libyan security agents reported back to their masters on the activities of the regime's opponents, and Gaddafi was frightened by what was going on here. The most prominent dissident group at this time was the recently formed National Front for the Salvation of Libya, which had publicly announced itself to the world from its headquarters at Khartoum in October 1981. The National Front was formed by Mohammed Yusuf al-Magariaf, previously Libya's ambassador to India and an original member of the Revolutionary Command Council. Magariaf's National Front lobbied for a democratic constitution, a free press and for free and fair elections. It used radio stations, newsletters and guerrilla soldiers in its worldwide campaign to topple Gaddafi. Gaddafi was particularly concerned about National Front activities in Britain, where dissident literature and cassette recordings were filtering through Libyan social networks and reportedly even making their way into Libya itself.

The first demonstration organised by the National Front in London took place on 3 September 1983 outside the elegant Georgian premises of the Libyan people's bureau in St James's Square, London. That protest was sabotaged by the blasting of tape recordings of Gaddafi's speeches at deafening volume into the square from inside the bureau. Undaunted, National Front members and other dissident groups protested against the persecution of students in Libya, as well as the terrible costs to Libya's development of the bloody and exorbitant war Gaddafi was pursuing against Chad.

The National Front was not the only Libyan opposition organisation working in the West. Al-Burkan (The Volcano) was a more extreme dissident group, which carried out assassinations of Libyan officials working outside the *jamahiriyya*. On 21 January 1984, a few months before Fletcher's death, Libya's ambassador to Italy was murdered in Rome. Al-Burkan claimed responsibility for the attack. It is likely that the assassination of one of Gaddafi's own intensified the pressure on the people's bureau in London, ratcheting up efforts to quash opposition activities there.

By 1984, a situation of heated conflict had arisen among Libyans in Britain, with Gaddafi's agents and their supporters regularly clashing with opponents of the regime. Each had agents planted in the other's organisations, and tensions ran high. In early February, orders were issued from Tripoli for revolutionary committee men and their supporters to seize full control of the people's bureau in London. Control of the bureau thus passed into the hands of a group said mainly to be composed of radical, Gaddafi-supporting students. To the British authorities, Libya's unorthodox new diplomatic representatives in London were largely an unknown quantity. Following the revolutionary takeover, Britain's relations with the embassy were said by officials to be stuck in a kind of limbo: no diplomatic status was given to the students who had taken over at the people's bureau, and messages had been sent to Tripoli to ask the Libyan authorities to clarify their status. In practice, however, it seemed that the Foreign Office and other branches of government did interact with the new bureau to carry out the routine business of foreign affairs. The new Libyan staff, however, were far from conciliatory in their approach. They publicly declared that their aims in taking over the embassy were to confront Britain over its hostility to Libya, its role in Lebanon and its support for Libyan dissidents.

The violent consequences of the change of hands at the London people's bureau were quickly felt. On the night of 10 March, the Libyans bombed four sites across the capital: two west London newsagents stocking dissident publications, a Mayfair nightclub and the Omar Khayyam restaurant in Regent Street. All were sites associated with Libyan opposition in the UK. Fortunately, nobody was killed in these attacks, although three people were seriously injured and twenty suffered minor injuries. The next day, two Libyan students in Manchester joined in the campaign of violence, planting a bomb outside a block of flats. It was rumoured, although vehemently denied by Geoffrey Howe at the Foreign Office, that one of the bombers arrested had claimed diplomatic immunity, thus linking these bombings directly to Libya's new people's bureau of student renegades. The Libyans vigorously protested the arrest of suspects in the bombings, demanding an official apology and decrying what they described as racism in the British media.

On 15 April 1984, Libyan dissidents received the news that two students of Tripoli University had been publicly hanged back home in Libya. They decided in response to mount an anti-Gaddafi demonstration outside the London people's bureau on 17 April. News of this reached the people's bureau staff by the sixteenth, and they immediately summoned Gaddafi supporters throughout the UK to mount a counterdemonstration. On the morning of the seventeenth, the protest went ahead, and Yvonne Fletcher was fatally enmeshed in the violence of a dictatorial ruler who seemed increasingly out of control.

The tragedy of Fletcher's death was compounded by the immediate sense that it might have been avoided. After all, most of the parties involved had feared the consequences of the 17 April demonstration. Members of the people's bureau had approached the Foreign Office and warned them that 'the Libyans would not be responsible for its consequences' if the demonstration were allowed to go ahead. The British ambassador in Tripoli had been issued with a midnight summons and, in no uncertain terms, had been given the same warning. Howe suggested that this sort of belligerence from the Libyans was a regular occurrence and was usually nothing but bluster.[3] Others felt that the Libyans could not have given us a clearer warning that night of the need to exercise the utmost caution in policing the demonstration. Considering the bombings that had rocked London and Manchester just a month before, it has been suggested that the warnings ought to have been taken more seriously, and that more should have been done to safeguard everyone in St James's Square on 17 April. It was also later revealed that a telegram ordering the people's bureau to use violence against demonstrators had been intercepted at the GCHQ listening centre in Cheltenham, but had not been translated in time for action to be taken. *The Times* and the *Daily Telegraph* went so far as to describe the attack on

Fletcher and the escape of her murderers as a humiliating national defeat. Denis Healey, then shadow Foreign Secretary for the Labour opposition, attacked Howe in the strongest terms:

> The response of the Foreign Secretary on 11 March was to make it clear that terrorism by any foreign group is totally unacceptable and any repetitions of incidents of this kind are bound to have a serious effect on our relations. The Foreign Secretary has often been described as having a laid-back style, but I suggest that this response to the bombings in London and Manchester was positively horizontal. According to the Foreign Secretary's account, a few weeks later he was warned by our embassy in Tripoli and the Libyan bureau in London that violence was likely to attend the demonstration before Easter. The police were told, but the implication of the Foreign Secretary's statement is that they were warned not to take those warnings seriously. The police were allowed to police the demonstration with an unarmed policewoman who stood during the demonstration with her back to the bureau.[4]

Fletcher's shooting at first glance seemed a case that would be easy to solve. After all, the suspects were few, and after the shooting, they were sitting ducks, holed up inside the people's bureau. The situation, however, was more complicated than that. Andy Buchanan, a guardsman working at St James's Palace on the day Fletcher died, related his experiences to the BBC:

> I was a guardsman mounting Royal Guard on that day. We were doing guard mount in the forecourt of Buckingham Palace and heard the shots fired. I was senior soldier on St James's Palace detachment. It is the only time in sixteen years as a guardsman that I was issued ammunition.
>
> The police we spoke to were really angry and in a very sombre mood, and no wonder really. They were saying even then that they thought that whoever had done it was going to get away with it.[5]

This early intuition that the gunmen would 'get away with it' was spot on. The police were outraged at the killing of one of their own, but no blueprint existed for them or for the politicians overseeing negotiations to manage a truly bizarre situation. Storming in and making an arrest on the spot was clearly a difficult option. It was reported that the police high command was, nonetheless, in favour of doing just that. Not surprisingly, the Foreign Office was less keen. The rules of international diplomacy, after all, gave immunity to embassy staff. When police operatives ordered the thirty Libyan employees to leave the bureau, they refused, clinging vigorously to the protection offered by the extra-territorial status of the embassy and diplomatic immunity.

Meanwhile, police erected blue barriers to fence off the scene and began to do what work they could to gather evidence. The Met's 'Blue Berets', described in *The Guardian* as 'the sharpshooters and weaponry experts of the D11 section', manned the barriers, armed with machine guns and backed by members of the anti-terrorist squad.[6] Edgar Maybanks, the deputy assistant commissioner of Scotland Yard, took over the first floor of the advertising agency D'Arcy MacManus Masius, situated next to the bureau. Activity inside the bureau was monitored closely from the commandeered office, the movements of those inside tracked throughout what became an eleven-day siege.

As the police grew increasingly frustrated, politicians and diplomats worked behind the scenes, desperately figuring out what, if anything might be done. An emergency committee, christened Cobra, was formed under the leadership of the Home Secretary, Leon Brittan. It reported directly to the Prime Minister. Diplomatic links between Britain and Libya were immediately and publicly suspended, but the problem of what to do with the thirty bureau staff, at least one of whom was a vicious assassin, loomed large. While the police urged strong action, the Foreign Office thought with grave concern of the fate of diplomats in Tripoli. The Libyans had immediately surrounded the embassy there and taken staff hostage following the news of the siege in London. Later, the building was attacked and set alight, although it did not burn to the ground. Threats issued forth from the Libyan government against not just the embassy staff, but also the 10,000-odd British citizens living and working in Libya.

After six days of the siege, Colonel Rahman Shaibi, a senior official working in Libya's security agency, was dispatched to London to manage negotiations. Eventually, it was agreed that the Libyan staff sheltering in the bureau would be taken to Heathrow, questioned and allowed to return to Libya. On the morning of 27 April, neutral negotiators and two Libyans entered the bureau, and half an hour later a white van arrived to collect the diplomats and their luggage. The Libyans were led out to the van in nervous-looking groups of five. When they landed in Tripoli after the journey from Heathrow, the bureau staff received a heroes' welcome. With the Italians acting as protective power, Britain's embassy staff in Tripoli were officially expelled and returned safely home. A police search of the London people's bureau conducted immediately after the staff left found guns, ammunition and explosives, possibly smuggled in using Libya's diplomatic bags. Libya claimed that all of this evidence was planted, and announced somewhat dubiously that they too had found weapons concealed in the British embassy in Tripoli.

To stunned citizens watching all of this, the Libyans' escape seemed shocking. After all, we had had the culprit virtually in our hands. The Libyan people's bureau had recently been overtaken by renegades, their status as national representatives was manifestly questionable, so it was doubtful whether those lurking inside even qualified for diplomatic protection. To many, Britain's response seemed weak. The politicians, however, had our embassy staff to think of and, to some extent, firm action was taken. The suspension of diplomatic relations between Britain and Libya was no small step. Britain had only done this three times hitherto since 1945: against Albania, Uganda and Argentina, in each case in a political situation approaching full-scale military conflict. Geoffrey Howe tried to emphasise that the suspension of diplomatic relations was a strong response, telling the House of Commons:

> I recognise very plainly the anger that every British citizen must feel
> in the present case. I share that sense of anger. That is one good reason
> why decisions of this kind should be taken only after a full and proper
> appreciation of the interests of our country and our citizens around the

world. This explains why the severance of diplomatic relations is such an exceptional event. No British government have done this previously in response to abuse of immunity.

The House may be interested to compare our reactions to Libyan provocation with those of some other countries in a similar plight. The United States embassy in Tripoli was burnt down in December 1979, yet it was not until 1981 that diplomatic relations were suspended. Even then they were not broken.

The French embassy in Tripoli was burnt down in 1980. Libyan and French troops to this day confront each other in Chad. Yet diplomatic relations continue. In the case of more than one country the Libyans have taken hostages who have been exchanged for convicted Libyan prisoners without provoking a break in diplomatic relations. The British response in the present case has been stronger than that of any other country in comparable circumstances.[7]

Nevertheless, in the weeks, months and years following Yvonne Fletcher's murder, many felt that something stronger had been required, and that diplomatic protection had been manipulated all too easily to protect Libyan gunmen. There were public calls for an overhaul of the very concept of diplomatic immunity, with some suggesting that the 1961 Vienna Convention on Diplomatic Relations should be rewritten to scale back the much-abused protection it offered. This feeling was aired numerous times over succeeding years. In 1999, Geoffrey Robertson, the renowned QC and human rights advocate, wrote that the Fletcher case had illustrated the damage that could be wreaked by the Vienna Convention. He wrote of it: 'It was drafted by government lawyers under orders to puff diplomats up with as much power as possible, so they bestowed upon them not just immunity but impunity, covering every crime and misdemeanour committed during foreign service, whether or not in the course of duty.'[8]

I was keen to speak with the members of my own Conservative Party, then in government, who had felt the full force of public pressure to take action on the Fletcher case and to re-examine the foundations of diplomatic immunity. On a rainy May morning in 2009, I interviewed Lord Howe,

Britain's longest-serving living Foreign Secretary (famed for his 1990 resignation speech which brought Margaret Thatcher's government down, in which he described being sent to the wicket with a broken bat in his negotiations on Europe), to talk with him about the Fletcher case. We met early in the House of Lords café, overlooking a brown, muddy Thames. There was no coffee yet available, and the sound of enthusiastic vacuuming meant I was continually craning towards this grand old gentleman of British politics to catch what he was saying. It was strange to meet in these prosaic surroundings with the 82-year-old Howe, and to consider the contrast between an old man on this grey London morning and the powerful politician who had traversed the world on government planes, conducting business ranging from the handover of Hong Kong to one of the earliest diplomatic visits from Cold War Britain to Poland.

Howe was on such a flight when he received the news of Yvonne Fletcher's death from journalists travelling with his entourage from Korea, where a ceremony had been held at Gloster Valley to commemorate British soldiers killed there in 1951. Immediately the news had come in, it was clear that this would be a seminal event for British–Libyan relations. For Howe, Fletcher's death and the subsequent struggle to devise a response to the bizarre circumstances of her murder was to lead to some hard thinking about the very concept of diplomatic immunity. Howe had clearly been put under considerable pressure during the debate over the Libyans' cynical exploitation of diplomatic immunity. He emphasised to me, though, that he had never for a second wanted to review the Vienna Convention, and told me that he regarded it as essential protection to British diplomats, particularly those working in countries like Libya where the governing regime has a history of unpredictability and violence. Instead, his government had put into practice a policy of stern action against governments exploiting diplomatic immunity. In subsequent years, firmer steps were taken in all kinds of cases involving crimes by diplomats, ranging from drug offences to unpaid parking fines.

I was awed by Howe's crystal-clear recall of the complex set of arguments being discussed at the time. I admired his approach to a situation that had clearly been stressful and in which the government had been heavily criticised. As a lawyer with enviable analytical skill, he had been able to identify the principles at stake and firmly defend them. Yet a lingering doubt remained for me following this interview. Had everything possible been done to hold onto the suspect when we had him in our grasp? Could negotiations have been spun out for longer, could arrangements have been made to conduct more extensive interviews with the men and women who escaped back to Libya? It is difficult, a quarter of a century later, to answer any of these questions. The safety of our diplomatic staff in Tripoli was clearly a heavy responsibility to carry: no matter how vigorously Howe was accused of bowing to Libyan blackmail, this was truly a duty of the utmost seriousness. The only real option for me is to ensure that I and my colleagues bear in mind the horrors of 17 April 1984. We must take all the steps we can to bring the gunman or gunmen who killed Fletcher to justice.

★

While we British struggled to put together a response to this unprecedented situation, the citizens of Libya received a distorted version of events via their televisions and radios, which proclaimed that the British government had attempted to storm their embassy and had mounted a vicious and unprovoked attack on a group of diplomats. The British siege of the people's bureau was denounced as another episode of racist aggression. Again, Gaddafi played as much as he could on Libyans' sensitivities in relation to their brutal colonial past, a theme he has always relied on in shoring up his regime.

In this instance, it seemed like quite a lot of shoring up was needed. Yvonne Fletcher's murder was the most damaging episode for Gaddafi in a vicious struggle against his opponents. Many thought it showed him in an unhinged state of desperation. Allowing 'diplomats' to open fire on protestors in central London was qualitatively something quite different from the more usual targeted assassinations or planted bombs. Was it a raging, wounded, caged tiger that had allowed this to happen? There is considerable evidence that Gaddafi was under attack in this period. Five months before Fletcher's death, in November 1983, there had been an assassination attempt against him at his Tripoli residence and headquarters, Bab el-Aziziyya. In the wake of this, twenty-seven soldiers were executed. In 1984, Gaddaf al-Damm, a Gaddafi aide spearheading the campaign against Libyan opposition abroad, was seriously injured by a car bomb. It has been suggested that the years 1980–83 saw a number of other coup attempts of which little news reached the West. Gaddafi's fear of such plots is likely to have been intensified by the fact that things were difficult economically, creating discontent over declining standards of living that might aid his opponents. Oil prices had plummeted, so that oil revenue had fallen from $20 billion in 1980 to about $7 billion in 1984.

The National Front seemed to feel that the extreme events at the people's bureau meant Gaddafi was vulnerable. They decided the time was right to take advantage of this, and to swing their carefully developed networks of spies and soldiers into action. The National Front leader, Ahmad al-Hawwas, a former officer in the Libyan army, had established a significant group of supporters within the army. These men worked inside the Bab el-Aziziyya barracks and were perfectly positioned for an action against Gaddafi. Hawwas, however, was betrayed. Libyan intelligence was tipped off and intercepted him as he tried to enter the country at the border with Tunisia. He was killed and his armed cell was attacked and disbanded before it was mobilised. The failed coup furnished the pretext for a mass round-up of opposition in Libya, and it has been claimed that 5,000 alleged opponents of the regime were jailed. Many were publicly hanged, not only in Benghazi and Tripoli, but in small towns across Libya. Gaddafi accused Britain, the US and Sudan of training his National Front attackers, and protested his continuing 'persecution' by the West. He and the Libyan media enthusiastically manufactured rhetoric condemning 'stray dogs', and it seemed, really, that business was chaotically as usual. As had been the case in the past, the Libyan opposition was shown to have been disorganised and easily infiltrated. It is hard really to know how serious the threat to Gaddafi was at this time. All we can say for sure is that he survived it convincingly, successfully riding out yet another attempt to rescue Libya from his clutches.

The Fletcher affair, however, was to cause him considerable problems.

It marked the start of an antagonistic, tense and at times violent period of relations between Libya and Britain. Enraged by the expulsion of his diplomats from London, Gaddafi became obsessive in his hatred of Thatcher and the UK, and pushed ahead with plans to escalate Libya's help to the IRA, as is described in Chapter 4. Two years later, in 1986, Britain decided to support the US in its decision to bomb Tripoli. The murder of PC Fletcher was cited by Margaret Thatcher as an example of the ongoing Libyan violence that justified Britain's help to the American bombers. She told the House of Commons, 'This country too is among the many that have suffered from Libyan terrorism. We shall not forget the tragic murder of WPC Fletcher by shots fired from the Libyan people's bureau in London just two years ago tomorrow.'[9]

★

Libyan determination to maintain hostilities with Britain faded somewhat in the light of her troubles during the 1980s. The protracted war against Chad was decisively lost in 1987, which left Gaddafi weak in political, military and economic senses. The invasion of Iraq by the Americans and their allies in 1991 was said to have caused Libya grave concern: like Saddam Hussein, Gaddafi headed an unpopular regime the invasion of which might possibly be sustained without too much dissent from the Arab world. Sensing the winds of change in international politics, the Libyans made overtures of peace. They began to scale back and to deny their support for the IRA. In early 1991, the Conservative MP Teddy Taylor visited Gaddafi in Libya. He suggested that Libya should express its contrition by offering a donation to a police charity set up in Yvonne Fletcher's memory. A donation of £250,000 was made, but this was vociferously decried in the British press as 'blood money'. The donation disgusted the British, the British reaction disgusted Gaddafi. This particular gesture did little to improve bilateral relations, but it is indicative of Gaddafi's relatively early but somewhat sporadic desire to mend fences with Britain.

Early overtures, however, were to be derailed by events of the early 1990s. In 1991, Libya was implicated in the 1988 bombing of Pan Am Flight 103 over Lockerbie, the UN imposed sanctions, and a decade of painful and near-complete exclusion from world affairs was to follow. Some negotiation on the Fletcher situation continued, as the Fletcher family attempted to drive the case forward. Queenie Fletcher, Yvonne's mother, made her first trip abroad to Libya in 1994. She told *The Guardian*: 'Before I went to Libya I thought of Gaddafi as quite a frightening man . . . But he seemed quite frightened himself, and very ordinary. He said how sorry he was about Yvonne, and I said how sorry I was that he had lost his daughter in the US raid on Tripoli.'[10] Little real progress was made, however, until things moved forward in relation to Lockerbie. By the end of the 1990s, Libya was looking desperately for a way out of the Lockerbie situation, and was finding some success. Negotiations were underway for a trial of the two Libyans accused of the bombing (discussed later in this book), and a general thawing towards Libya was evident. Fletcher's death could not be ignored in this process of rapprochement. On 7 July 1999, Libya agreed to take 'general responsibility' for Fletcher's death, and financial compensation was paid to the Fletcher family. The Foreign Secretary, Robin Cook, announced the resumption of full diplomatic relations, an ambassador and his staff were dispatched to Tripoli, and British Airways began flying to the Libyan capital twice weekly, nicely symbolising the new lines of communication and exchange that began to open from this time.

Yet 'general responsibility' was hardly enough to satisfy Fletcher's family or colleagues. The resumption of diplomatic relations was against the wishes of the Metropolitan Police Federation (MPF), the organisation that represents rank and file police officers, and which has campaigned vigorously to bring the man who killed one of their own to justice. The MPF declared that relations should not be restored until Fletcher's killer was identified and convicted. Geoffrey Robertson wrote in July 1999 that Cook had a duty stridently to demand the handover of the killers, pointing out that the legacy of the post-World War II Nuremberg trials was the inviolable principle that crimes are committed by individuals, not states.[11] Michael Winner, the film director and chairman of the Police Memorial Trust, set up after Fletcher's death, has described Libya's failure to hand over the killer as 'disgraceful', feels that 'they know perfectly well who

Yvonne Fletcher was shot by' and has accused the Libyans of 'laughing in the face of justice'.[12]

The resumption of diplomatic ties in 1999 at least meant that the Met was able to reopen investigations into the case. In November that year Tam Dalyell, the then Labour MP for Linlithgow, who has been a persistent advocate for the Fletcher family and the Lockerbie victims, put a parliamentary question to the Home Office, asking them to declare to the Commons what progress had been made. Charles Clarke responded that the Metropolitan Police had 'made clear . . . that they intend to pursue this investigation vigorously and expect full co-operation from the Libyan authorities'. In 2002, the Met travelled to Libya to interview key suspects. This expedition, however, was widely judged a failure, as Gaddafi was said to have withheld access to crucial witnesses whom our police officers desperately wished to interview.

In 2004, Tony Blair held historic talks with Gaddafi in the Libyan desert, which heralded an unprecedented new warmth in Britain's relations with Libya. Again, many of the victims of Libya's attacks over the years viewed this as a betrayal of those who had died. The MPF declared that Libya had 'blood on its hands' and demanded that Fletcher's murderer be handed over before Blair's talks were allowed to begin. The warmer diplomatic relations initiated by Blair, however, led to another burst of co-operation from the Libyans. The Met was able to make a second trip to Libya to take up the investigations there again. Public statements at this time became less cautious; senior people all but admitted to knowing exactly who the killer was. The Metropolitan Police commissioner, John Stevens, told the media, 'We have good reason to know who pulled the trigger as perhaps they [the Libyans] do. We are absolutely determined to bring this person to justice.' Like all the others, however, this trip produced no tangible results for the police. In 2007, the investigation appeared to be underway yet again. This time, the Libyans were said to have co-operated obligingly during the Met's seven-week stay. It was reported in the media that British officers had come face to face with a suspect, and that a number of promising statements had been recorded. The 2007 visit, it was claimed, had had the personal support of Gaddafi.

All this got everyone's hopes up, but two years later we did not seem any closer to justice until some unexpected events in 2009 intervened with stunning effect. Upon the release in September of the man convicted of the Lockerbie bombing, Abdelbaset al-Megrahi, from his Glasgow prison cell, pressure on the government escalated considerably. Suddenly, the press was focused on every aspect of British–Libyan relations, and I and many others were given the chance to make our feelings known in regard to the need to push much harder for the Met to be given the chance to bring their investigations in Libya to a conclusion. Shockingly, it was revealed at the time of Megrahi's release that in 2006 the Foreign Office had promised Libya that the British government would never seek to get PC Fletcher's murderer tried in Britain. This was a shady piece of realpolitik, and one that left many rather disillusioned. If such pragmatic and, in my view, unprincipled compromises are to be made, at the very least we should be able to expect that they are not kept secret from the British people.

As it stands, the case remains bafflingly obscure, and it leads one to wonder if the persistent rumours that the regime had the killer executed decades ago may be true. A quarter of a century on, the identity of the killer still seems to be in doubt, a strange situation given that there were, after all, only thirty or so people inside the bureau. *The Guardian* has reported that the suspects of interest are Abdel-Gader Tuhami, a student reputed to have been trained as an assassin; Moustafa Mgirbi, a military intelligence officer; and Ali Jalid, the people's bureau press officer.[13]

Clearly, however, proper legal proceedings are required to wrest this case out of the uncertain domains of media and politics, and to start to establish transparently and convincingly what evidence there is against individual men. Subsequent chapters of this book will sketch out my argument that the trial of the two Libyan Lockerbie suspects had terrible shortcomings. It did at least, however, provide a forum in which some of the legal evidence was laid out before the public. Those with a stake in the Fletcher case have not even been given this. And, as was the case in the many years before the Lockerbie suspects were brought to trial, conspiracy theories have abounded in this legal vacuum. Among the most persistent has been the suggestion that the CIA killed Fletcher to ensure British support for future military action against Libya. In 1997, a Channel 4 documentary called 'Murder at St James's' interviewed ballistics experts who suggested that Fletcher's shooting could not have happened from the second floor of the people's bureau, as had widely been agreed. Tam Dalyell raised this issue in the House of Commons:

> With the agreement of Queenie Fletcher, [Yvonne Fletcher's] mother, I raised with the Home Office the three remarkable programmes that were made by Fulcrum, and their producer, Richard Bellfield, called 'Murder at Saint James's'. Television speculation is one thing, but this was rather more than that, because on film was George Stiles, the senior ballistics officer in the British Army, who said that, as a ballistics expert, he believed that the WPC could not have been killed from the second floor of the Libyan embassy, as was suggested.
>
> Also on film was my friend, Hugh Thomas, who talked about the angles at which bullets could enter bodies, and the position of those bodies. Hugh Thomas was, for years, the consultant surgeon of the Royal Victoria Hospital in Belfast, and I suspect he knows more about bullets entering bodies than anybody else in Britain. Above that was Professor Bernard Knight, who, on and off, has been the Home Office pathologist for twenty-five years. When Bernard Knight gives evidence on film that the official explanation could not be, it is time for an investigation.[14]

A proper trial of credible suspects seems the only way to prove or disprove such speculation, and to put an end to the periodic cropping up of alternative theories. I am saddened that the tortuous, slow movement towards justice has meant that Fletcher's family and friends have endured this kind of doubt. Over the years they have suffered through a raking over of the facts of her death which must have increased the pain of her loss immensely. For my part, I have resolved not to let the case rest. I am Libya's most enthusiastic advocate in the House of Commons. I believe that Britain can profit from working closely with its talented business community, and from getting to know a country that will be vital to international security in coming years. This relationship must not, however, be built on a foundation of lies. We need to know who killed Fletcher, and then we can move forward. I continue, therefore, to bring this issue up, mentioning Fletcher in most of my speeches on Libya. On 28 April 2009, I was able to pass the following early day motion: 'That this House marks the 25th anniversary of the murder of WPC Yvonne Fletcher; notes that this brave, courageous policewoman died having been shot in the back; sends its condolences to her family; and urges the Foreign and Commonwealth Office to intensify discussions with Libya to secure and detain her murderer.'

In November 2009 I took Paul McKeever, the chairman of the Police Federation of England and Wales, to meet the Libyan chargé d'affaires, Omar Jelban. We were accompanied by John Murray, a colleague of Fletcher's, who was standing next to her when she was shot. Murray has promised to find Fletcher's killer on a number of occasions. Jelban informed us that negotiations were ongoing and that we should leave it to the Libyan and British governments to resolve. I have very little confidence, however, in the present government's handling of this issue.

After this meeting, McKeever told me of his frustration at successive governments' failure to bring this case to a just conclusion. His feeling is that Fletcher's murder has the most profound significance for police officers and for policing in modern Britain:

> An important part of British culture is based on us having an independent police who are of the people, for the people and who police with the consent of the people. This culture is epitomised in the form of the unarmed constable who always looks to use the least force possible in any conflict they encounter. The unarmed status of the police constable is largely recognised and respected within British society generally and is even tacitly acknowledged by most offenders. Therefore, it is a truly shocking event when an unarmed British police constable is gunned down in the streets of London. An extra dimension is added to that shock when the constable is a female officer who is totally incapable of defending herself. The murder of Yvonne Fletcher created a small but incremental move away from the status of British police constables remaining unarmed.
>
> The shock and anger that was generated within the British police service

cannot be overstated. Many of the police officers who were serving at the time of Yvonne Fletcher's murder are still angry about her killing. I am one of those officers. We were denied justice at the time of the killing and we have now waited twenty-five years for justice to be done. We will not go away. I was a serving Metropolitan Police officer at the time of Yvonne Fletcher's murder and I continue to serve today. I do not want to have to wait another twenty-five years for justice to be done.

It is my fervent hope that the Foreign Office will stay focused on Yvonne Fletcher's case. When I raise it publicly, I am likely to receive telephone calls of protest from the Libyan people's bureau. I tell Jelban that I respect him and I respect his country, but that Britain, an open society and an open democracy, will not let the issue lie. I hope that the coming years will not prove me to have been naïve.

# REAGAN VERSUS GADDAFI

At two o'clock on the morning of 15 April 1986, the roar of US fighter planes was heard over the skies of Tripoli and Benghazi. Foreign correspondents posted in Tripoli dangled telephones from hotel windows, by this rough and ready means transmitting the sounds of the bombardment throughout the world. It was widely assumed that President Reagan had scheduled the attacks to coincide with prime time on US television. He appeared on ABC at nine o'clock in the evening, two hours after the bombing, telling his countrymen and women of indisputable evidence of Libyan involvement in horrific acts of terrorism, and describing the aerial attack on the sleeping cities as a justified act of self-defence. He finished with the declaration that 'today we have done what we had to do. If necessary, we shall do it again.' The majority of Americans reacted with joy, and Reagan's popularity rocketed. As *The Economist* wrote, the United States could no longer be taunted as a Gulliver impotent in the face of the attacks of thousands of lethal Lilliputians.[1]

The bombing of Libya in 1986 was a moment of the greatest significance for Colonel Gaddafi. It demonstrated to him that the conflict with the Americans would not remain a matter of rhetoric and economic sanctions alone, and could not be relied upon forever to shore up his domestic image as Libya's saviour against the American demon. Following the attack, Gaddafi's paranoia escalated, and in the succeeding months, he sought to crush all opposition and to smoke out anyone he suspected might have encouraged the US. It was a moment of truth, and one that was undoubtedly to influence all his major decisions in the succeeding years.

In balance, however, the American attack is likely to have benefited the Colonel more than it harmed him. For one thing, it confirmed his importance and ascribed to his regime a truly astounding level of significance as one of the major enemies of a global superpower. Gaddafi exploited this for years to come, claiming to have fought off American aggression, and also speaking with pathos of the very personal loss of his adopted daughter, Hanna. Importantly, he had also survived. Many experts had thought that his was a regime rotten to the core, which would crumble and fall after an American attack. A power vacuum did indeed seem to gape open invitingly in the days immediately following the bombing, but no-one stepped forward to fill it. Eventually, Gaddafi re-emerged to put an end to a decade of revolutionary madness, paving the way for a more pragmatic approach to international politics that would safeguard his regime for many years to come.

★

The official anthem of the US Marine Corps opens with the line 'From the halls of Montezuma to the shores of Tripoli', aptly enshrining Libya as a key battleground in the American imagination. The song harks back to the opening years of a relationship that was never smooth. In 1804 President Jefferson dispatched the US frigate *Philadelphia* to take decisive action against Tripolitanian pirates, who were demanding ever-increasing amounts of protection money and thus cutting the profits of American traders in the region. The Tripolitanians did not come out of the resulting conflict well and were forced to reduce their demands considerably. The two nations had very little contact again until the mid-twentieth century, but this early conflagration did not augur well.

Twentieth-century relations between Gaddafi's Libya and the US were initially promising. The Americans awarded recognition to the Gaddafi regime just five days after his September 1969 coup, a rapid validation of the Colonel that even prompted some in the Arab world to suspect that he had been backed by the US. It seemed that the Nixon administration held hopes that Gaddafi would turn out to be a pliant, oil-rich dictator of the type America could happily work with. The US quickly and obligingly evacuated their military base at Wheelus Field, just east of Tripoli, even leaving behind some equipment for the Libyans' use. Two major coup attempts against Gaddafi were said to have been thwarted by US intelligence in 1969 and 1970.

Gaddafi, however, was soon to upset the applecart. Although not a communist, the young Gaddafi was a fervent, if confused, Arab nationalist and a devoted Muslim. He had not taken power to rule quietly and competently; he had taken power to shape Libya into an ideological juggernaut. Very quickly, he set about rejecting colonial and imperial influence. Speech after speech issued forth from Libya in the early 1970s, denouncing the US and Britain and proclaiming Gaddafi's support for radical groups working against their governments. In the years to come condemnation of American imperialism would become, in a sense, the populist bread and butter of the regime. Gaddafi had proclaimed himself the defender of Libya against the neo-colonial West, and angry, public exchanges of fiery rhetoric meant that this role could become a reality. Accordingly, Libya extended a helping hand to groups hostile to the US government. This was not confined to groups working outside the US; the Libyans provocatively sent money to the Black Panthers and radical black Muslim organisations.

From 1973, the US cut back its diplomatic representation in Tripoli and launched itself on what was to be a lengthy attempt to rein in Gaddafi's excesses. With evidence piling up of Libyan involvement in terrorist attacks, the Americans in the same year launched the first of many attempts to punish Libya economically, implementing an arms embargo.

President Carter, taking office in 1977, did little better than his predecessors in restraining Libya. The late 1970s brought more of the same, with Gaddafi talking death, destruction and liquidation, while the Americans monitored his actions and pondered their options. In 1979, Gaddafi irked the US by declaring publicly his support for the Iranians, who had stormed the US embassy in Tehran and taken fifty-three Americans hostage. The same year, the American embassy in Tripoli was stormed by an enormous mob and burnt to the ground. The motive seemed to be a desire to protest any action the US planned to take against Iran.

In late 1980 Libya invaded Chad. This was to be a lengthy, expensive conflict, and it contributed to the Americans' growing view that Gaddafi's exploits in Africa were perfectly suited to Soviet interests and were highly likely to destabilise the entire continent. Meanwhile, the murder of dissidents on the streets of Western capital cities that ensued from Gaddafi's 'stray dogs' campaign was becoming deeply embarrassing to the nations involved, which were effectively rendered Libyan battlefields. Six Libyan diplomats were expelled from the US in 1980 as a result of this policy.

This was the height of the Cold War, and conflict between Gaddafi and the Americans was naturally flavoured by the broader political context. Gaddafi flirted with the Soviets, took advantage of their military assistance, and often talked up his links with Moscow purely to agitate the Americans. In their turn, the Americans, especially under Reagan, chose to believe Gaddafi had a much stronger relationship with the Soviets than was actually the case. The Americans did have reason to be wary of Gaddafi and the Russians. In 1975, it was announced that the Soviet Union would assist Libya to build its first nuclear reactor. Nuclear co-operation between the two continued, and in 1978 Gaddafi even raised the somewhat ridiculous prospect of Libya joining the Communist equivalent to NATO, the Warsaw Pact. In 1981, a smiling Gaddafi was photographed with an ailing President Brezhnev on a Libyan state visit to the Soviet Union. The same year, American intelligence operatives suspected that the Soviets had made a delivery of enriched uranium to Tripoli. Libya was known to benefit from the presence of thousands of Soviet military advisors and was one of the Soviet Union's most reliable customers, purchasing billions of dollars' worth of weapons and equipment. To the further chagrin of the Americans, Gaddafi's Eastern Bloc connections also reportedly encompassed Cuban advisors, East German security experts and North Korean pilots and trainers.

The closeness between Libya and the Soviet Union, however, had obvious limits. Gaddafi declared himself a practitioner of 'positive neutrality', and said he was an advocate of Third World emancipation, not of the East or the West. He was a frequent critic of communism, and often broke with the revolutionary movements he supported worldwide if he believed they were getting too Marxist in their approach. An opportunist, he developed the relationship with the Soviets to maximise Libyan gain, building up an impressive arsenal in the process, but Libya was never anything like a client state. The Soviets, like everyone else who dealt with Libya, found Gaddafi frustrating and erratic, and always kept him at arm's length. In a 1986 interview Gaddafi accused the Americans of being obsessed with a fear of Soviet influence, and declared in one of his typically menacing jokes, 'I am not a communist, but I might be obliged – just to nag America – to become a communist out of spite.'[2] It suited the Americans to exaggerate Gaddafi's Soviet friendship, but it is likely that they, as much as anyone, were well aware of its limitations.

Gaddafi welcomed Ronald Reagan's 1981 election victory, as he has tended to do with all US Presidents, apparently because after between four and eight years, his relations with their predecessor have invariably become so dire that any alternative looks like a good prospect. Reagan, however, came to power on a tough-guy platform, promising an America that would face up to its enemies. The high-profile, swaggering and rhetorically incontinent Gaddafi seemed likely to be first among those faced up to. The Reagan administration carefully and strategically portrayed Libya as a dangerous, erratic friend of the Soviets, and quickly decided they would use the awesome military might of America to put as much pressure as possible on the regime. Inside this hawkish administration, Reagan had particularly strong support from CIA chief William Casey and Robert McFarlane, his national security advisor, both of whom were passionately convinced of the need for strong action against Gaddafi.

Nor did Gaddafi disappoint the hawks – he continued to meddle in African politics, he traded arms with the Soviets, he supported terrorists, and even where it was not known whether he had aided them, he hailed their crimes publicly and in the most glowing terms. The year before the bombing of Tripoli saw numerous acts of terrorism: in 1985, 23 Americans were killed and 139 injured in terrorist incidents. Gaddafi's praise of the machine-gunning by terrorists of El Al and TWA passengers and staff at Rome and Vienna airports on 27 December 1985 was particularly contentious. He proclaimed to the world that this attack was justified because Israel had bombed the Tunisian headquarters of the Palestine Liberation Organization that October. Five Americans died in the airport attacks, and Reagan saw the incident as compelling justification for his increasingly determined plan to hold someone accountable for acts of international terror against Americans.

The Americans also suspected that Gaddafi had made plans to assassinate Reagan himself. The renowned investigative journalist Bob Woodward wrote that in 1981 one of the CIA's most reliable Ethiopian sources reported that Gaddafi had held a meeting in Addis Ababa with Lieutenant Colonel Mengistu Haile Mariam, the Ethiopian leader. The two were said to have openly discussed Gaddafi's plan to assassinate Reagan.[3] In early December 1981, American newspapers ran stories claiming a Libyan hit squad had entered the US. Gaddafi was interviewed live on ABC television, vehemently denying that he had any plans to assassinate American politicians. He called Reagan a liar, and said that assassination was the American rather than the Libyan way of doing things.

In fact, it is not thought that Reagan considered assassinating Gaddafi (although there would have been few tears shed had he been hit at Bab el-Aziziyya in 1986). Reagan had reaffirmed the American policy against assassination and was reputed to have rejected approaches from other countries to join plots against the Colonel's life. Tough-guy action against Libya, however, was to become a hallmark of Reagan's presidency, and the policy was launched quickly. In 1981, the President ordered the closure of the Libyan people's bureau in Washington. US oil companies were told to begin scaling back operations in Libya, and were advised to cut down on the number of US citizens they employed. NATO countries were asked to support embargoes on arms and oil exploration, and to refuse to host state visits from Gaddafi. In March 1982, the Americans launched an embargo on Libyan oil and restricted all exports to Libya other than food, medicines and medical supplies. Americans working in Libya were ordered to return home, and 3,000 did so (although many of them quickly returned, as few had felt in any immediate danger). Exxon announced it would withdraw in 1981; Mobil followed suit in January 1983. The 1982 boycott was strengthened in 1985 with a complete ban on the import of all Libyan petroleum products. In 1985 there was a spate of terrorist attacks with alleged Libyan involvement, and Reagan reacted with still harsher economic punishment. In December that year, the Americans terminated all direct economic activities with Libya, putting a freeze on Libyan assets and instructing Americans working in Libya, of whom there were now between 1,000 and 1,500, to return home immediately. The Libyan threat to the US was declared a national emergency.

Libya was already struggling badly under the strain of falling oil prices and an expensive involvement in the war in Chad, so the sanctions were an unwelcome development. At the time of the first set of restrictions on the oil trade in 1981, the US had been an excellent customer, despite the tense diplomatic relationship, and had accounted for 40 per cent of Libyan oil exports. Libya had supplied 10 per cent of American oil needs. The American departure in the early 1980s thus saw the sudden and dramatic loss of more than a third of Libyan oil revenues. The relatively flexible and well-run Libyan oil sector was able to adapt as the US withdrew, turning its attention to the European market. The technological expertise and financial clout of the Americans was nonetheless missed in the immediate aftermath of their departure, as well as in coming years.

Reagan's first year in power saw the two nations come very close to outright war. The Americans' new belligerence was expressed in a display of naval muscle in the Gulf of Sirte, which had long been a bone of contention between the Libya and the US. The Americans said that Libya's extensive maritime claim there was a violation of international law (based on a 1958 international convention which Libya had not signed) and of the principle of the freedom of the seas. The Libyans, on the other hand, felt that the gulf had for centuries been under their possession and control, and that the Americans had no right to dictate its fate. The Americans chose in 1981 to reignite a conflict that had been simmering quietly for years. The US Sixth Fleet embarked on naval exercises involving two aircraft carriers and numerous squadrons of F-14 Tomcat aircraft. The Libyans staunchly resisted the undoubtedly strong temptation to retaliate. On 19 August, two US Tomcats shot down two Libyan planes, Soviet-built Su-22 Fitter ground attack craft, that were monitoring the American presence. Provoked to the extreme by the US, it still seemed as though the Libyans were doing their utmost to back away from direct military confrontation. To many onlookers, it seemed very much as if Reagan had been in search of a rash military response from the Libyans, which could then be used as a pretext for the decisive action he craved. This rash response was not, at this stage, forthcoming.

Meanwhile, the Americans were also pouring money for weapons into Africa, supporting any regime willing to resist Gaddafi and pressuring him by arming his neighbours to the hilt. They carried out joint military exercises with Egypt, they supported Gaddafi's opponents in Chad, and they gave extensive military aid to Sudan, Tunisia, Algeria and Liberia. Rumours circulated that during 1980 and 1981 the Americans and the Israelis were vigorously encouraging Egypt to launch an attack against Libya (although the assassination of President Sadat in October 1981 would have put paid to that possibility). Other efforts were made during the period to get the Egyptians on side, and it is likely that if the US had been able to persuade Egypt to support it, Libya might have suffered an earlier and more extensive attack on its territory.

The US was also said to be carrying out an extensive information campaign, encouraging the world media to speculate on Gaddafi's psychological state, the health of his regime and the strength of his opponents abroad. The CIA was believed to be providing support and training to opposition organisations working outside Libya, an almost unbearable provocation for Gaddafi, who had an unholy dread of such groups.

By the mid-1980s, relations had deteriorated badly. Gaddafi had not been pushed into a military engagement with the Americans, but he was feeling the strain of their hostility. In the wake of an attempted coup against his regime in 1984, he declared to the world that 'we are capable of exporting terrorism to the heart of America'. The threats piled up – Gaddafi repeatedly urged the killing of Americans, spoke of their 'liquidation', encouraged suicide attacks and urged the burning of their property worldwide.

★

By 1986, the US and Libya were thus familiar enemies. It was universally acknowledged, however, that the bombing of Libya was about more than just Libya. It was about an America under siege, which perceived a need to take action in order to prevent death by a thousand terrorist cuts. The US of the early 1980s was a superpower under strain. The profound unpopularity of the Vietnam War had left politicians wary of foreign conflict, but at the same time, the terrorist threat was worsening rapidly: American citizens were dying in bombings and hijackings carried out all over the world with frightening regularity. The US embassy and Marine Corps barracks were bombed in Beirut in April 1983; TWA Flight 847 en route from Athens to Rome was hijacked in June 1985; and, as mentioned earlier, passengers and staff queuing at Rome and Vienna airports were machine-gunned by terrorists on 27 December the same year.

America's image in the world was also suffering as its client states dropped away one by one: the Shah of Iran had been deposed, Nicaragua's Somoza dictatorship had collapsed. The prospect of Gaddafi destabilising some of the remaining reliably pro-American states in Africa was thus most unsavoury. The Iranian hostage crisis, during which fifty-three Americans were held between November 1979 and January 1981, had also enraged the nation and left it feeling under siege in the Middle East. In general, the American public was said to be in a state of chronic anxiety about their weakness in the face of myriad new threats. Jimmy Carter lost the 1980 election as a result of this, and Reagan was determined to be different. Gaddafi would prove useful as a human face against which America's fear and loathing could be directed. Reagan promoted the idea of Gaddafi as a sort of dangerous devil, publicly describing him as 'the mad dog of the Middle East', a 'barbarian' and a 'flake'. The press enthusiastically supported him in this. In July 1981, for example, *Newsweek* ran a story calling Gaddafi 'the most dangerous man in the world'.[4] American journalists circulated rumours about Gaddafi ranging from mental illness to cross-dressing to the allegation that he took a teddy-bear with him on his travels.

Gaddafi's usefulness as a target of American wrath was increased by the fact that, in contrast to other enemies of the US, he had very few loyal, powerful friends. It was unlikely that the Soviets, his Maghrebi neighbours or Arab brother countries would rush to protect him, as by now most had been scarred to some extent by his erratic, interfering presence in the region. Few allies were likely to feel that supporting Libya would be worth the antagonism this would introduce into their own relations with the US.

The bombing of Libya appears to have been a carefully planned action, seen by Reagan as a safe option with which to prove his credentials as the leader of a resurgent US. While Gaddafi had undoubtedly sponsored some horrific violence throughout the world, it is doubtful that he was really among the US's most powerful enemies. The Europeans often urged the Americans to ignore Libya, arguing that Reagan's portrayal of Gaddafi as a powerful merchant of evil was in fact his biggest source of influence at home and abroad. Gaddafi spouted lots of angry rhetoric against the US, but he had largely avoided practical action that might destabilise the relationship. He had been consistently keen to keep American companies working in Libya's oil industry. In the aftermath of the attacks on Libya, he told *US News & World Report* that the American action must have been purely designed to aid the Israelis, as 'there is no Libyan–American problem'.[5]

Tellingly, it was rumoured that Reagan referred to the Libyan leader as 'Gaddafi Duck'. Like Warner Bros' Daffy Duck, it seems as if Gaddafi was viewed as a loud-mouthed, well-known figure who was in reality rather weak, and who would make a soft target for a quick, clean military action that might go some way to soothing wounded American pride.

★

Spring 1986 saw the Americans take action that would dramatically escalate hostilities. They again dispatched their fleet to carry out manoeuvres in the Gulf of Sirte. This time, Libya did respond. They launched an attack on US ships that was judged a complete failure. The Americans, in an operation called Prairie Fire, hit back by sinking several Libyan craft. Gaddafi took to the airwaves, condemning American aggression and describing a 'line of death' across the opening of the Gulf of Sirte, which the Americans would cross again at their peril. Behind the scenes, though, Gaddafi was desperately seeking an escape route. He made repeated overtures to the Americans to open talks, but these were all rejected. He sought help from the Saudis and others to try to open diplomatic channels, but with no success.

The attack on the La Belle disco in West Berlin was to present the Americans with what White House spokesman Larry Speakes described as 'an opportunity for some payback'.[6] On 5 April, a bomb exploded in the crowded venue, killing a US sergeant and a Turkish woman, and injuring more than 200 others, of whom about 60 were Americans. The Americans were closely monitoring Libyan communications and they claimed that at the time of the bombing, the Libyans in East Berlin had told Tripoli by telephone that an operation was 'happening now'. After the bombing, the Americans said that they had intercepted communications between the East Berlin Libyan people's bureau and Tripoli to the effect that there had been a successful operation which it would be impossible to trace to Libya.

The idea that, in the course of the nine days between La Belle and the attack on Libya, the Americans had been able to prove conclusively that Libyans had bombed the disco at Gaddafi's orders was questioned by many. In the weeks, months and years that followed La Belle, some suggested that Reagan's certainty had been unfounded, and that there was good evidence of Syrian involvement. In 2001, however, a Libyan diplomat called Musbah Abdulghasem Eter was convicted of the crime in Berlin, along with two Palestinian accomplices and a German woman. The judge commented in his findings that it had not been proven that Gaddafi or Libyan intelligence agencies had ordered the attack, although evidence had been presented that did suggest this. In 2004, the Libyan government said they would pay $35 million compensation to the non-American victims, and in 2008 it was agreed that money from the joint compensation fund to be set up by the Americans and the Libyans would be used to compensate the American victims of La Belle.

Reagan was able to win little support for his crusade against Libya from most of Europe, even after the Americans had so stridently linked the atrocity at La Belle to Gaddafi. He had been keen to find allies in the imposition of dramatic economic sanctions against Gaddafi in early 1986, and was quoted in the *New York Times* saying that 'we call on our friends in western Europe and elsewhere to join with us in isolating him. Americans will not understand other nations moving into Libya to take commercial advantage of our departure.'[7] Despite such menacing words, the Europeans were not keen to support either trade embargoes or a military attack on Libya. Several European governments got a high proportion of their oil supply from Libya, and had extensive economic ties there. Along with considerable economic interests went large resident expatriate communities who would be placed at risk of being taken hostage should their national governments endorse an American attack. The Europeans also often suggested that the Americans exaggerated Gaddafi's influence and his effectiveness, contributing greatly to his prestige and sense of importance. There was concern in Europe that a military attack against him would in reality only shore up his domestic position as the patriotic defender of Libya against the aggressive neo-colonialism of the US.

There was also a general European feeling, particularly in France, that the Americans were too belligerent with regard to Libya and were determined to proceed with the least possible consultation of their partners in NATO. This was very much resented, particularly as the proximity of southern Europe to Libya meant it would likely be the target of any retaliation (an objection proved prescient when, post-attack, the Libyans did indeed bomb the Italian island of Lampedusa). The Austrians, the Greeks and the Italians insisted that firmer evidence was needed of Gaddafi's involvement in particular raids before Libya could justifiably be attacked.

The question of how to take effective action against state sponsors of terror is, of course, still the subject of vast differences of opinion, and made more complex by uncertain outcomes in Iraq and Afghanistan. Back in 1986, several European governments felt that bombing cities and killing civilians was not the right kind of response to a country charged with sponsoring international terrorism. French, Greek and Italian politicians were much more likely than the Americans to take the view that the root causes of terrorism – mostly, the situation in Palestine – should be taken into account in responding to it. Bombing without talking could be futile or, worse still, a spur to terrorists worldwide and a blow to the West's hopes for peace in the Middle East. This queasiness found expression in the headlines immediately following the attack. *Le Figaro*, for example, led with the statement that 'The French government deplores that the escalation of terrorism has led to an act of reprisal that is an escalation of violence itself'.[8] The consequence of all of this was that no major continental European power granted permission to the Americans to fly over their territory, forcing the attacking planes to take an extremely long and challenging route to Libya, involving several complicated mid-air refuellings.

Britain, however, was a different prospect to mainland Europe. Britain and the US have a long-standing 'special relationship', and much greater pressure could be applied to obtain our support. This support, however, was far from a foregone conclusion. In January 1986, as tensions escalated between the US and Libya, Margaret Thatcher had even spoken out publicly to caution the US against attacking, saying that international law could not justify retaliatory strikes. She reminded the Americans that retaliation was not permitted under the UN Charter.

On 9 April, Thatcher took a telephone call from Reagan. Reagan personally requested her agreement to allow US fighters to launch an attack on Libya from British bases. There was now much to consider for the Prime Minister. Her popularity ratings were low, and it was known that the British public would not support an attack. Like the other Europeans, she felt there was great uncertainty about the likely aftermath of an attack on Libya. Two British hostages were being held in Lebanon by the Abu Nidal Organization, which was known to be very close indeed to the Libyans (as she feared, these hostages were indeed killed in the wake of the bombings). At the same time, there were plenty of arguments in favour of reining Gaddafi in. Britain had suffered directly from his nefarious activities, both when PC Yvonne Fletcher was murdered on British soil and through Libyan funding of the IRA.

By some accounts, Lord Howe had opposed the decision to allow the attack on Libya to be launched from Britain. When I met him, however, he told me a rather different story, in which Thatcher and her Foreign and Defence Secretaries had gradually reached agreement. He described a difficult, painstaking process of negotiation with the Americans that took place over the week before the attack. Testing questions were put to the Reagan administration, including whether an attack would start a cycle of revenge, and the likely fate of Western hostages held in Lebanon at the time. Howe said that ultimately the Americans had a strong rationale and a set of clearly defined targets for the attack, and that they had given consideration to minimising harm to civilians. In retrospect, he thought that the British decision had been justified and formed an instructive contrast to Iraq, when the grounds for attack were far less clear. President Mitterrand, Howe said, had told him on the Thursday of the week of the bombing (which took place on the Monday) that 'we very nearly gave consent, and we respect the fact that you did so'.

Charles Powell gave me a rather more open account of the days leading up to the offering of British support. Now Lord Powell, he has been described by the *New York Times* as 'the Cardinal Richelieu of 10 Downing Street': as Thatcher's private secretary, he was by her side as she took some of the most important foreign policy decisions of our time.[9] Powell is renowned for his deep knowledge of international relations, and is also British political royalty of a kind: his grandfather worked for Winston Churchill when he was Home Secretary and he is a descendant of one of the knights whom Henry II ordered to kill Thomas à Becket.

By Powell's account, the granting of our support to the Americans was a unilateral decision supported by none of the luminaries of Thatcher's cabinet – including Norman Tebbit and indeed Howe. Rather, the Prime Minister alone felt that Britain's obligation to support our American ally was reason enough to agree. Thatcher, of course, famously rose early. Powell's memory of the day on which the decision was made was that 'she came down at 6.30 in the morning and said, "We've got to support the Americans, that's what allies are for."'

I also interviewed Lord Owen, like Howe a former Foreign Secretary, who in 1986 was the leader of the Social Democratic Party (the SDP, which in later years joined with the Liberal Party to form today's Liberal Democratic Party). Owen has been tagged a 'serial resigner', due to a series of principled departures from office. He has a reputation as a politician people either loved or hated, and is seen by some as an arrogant man. My impression was of a man of powerful intelligence and an impressive commitment to avoiding obfuscation. He struck me as one of the most forthright and open politicians I had met.

According to Owen, the SDP was weak at the time, and the rest of his party was firmly set against the attack on Libya. For this reason, he had made a speech opposing the American bombing, arguing instead for a maritime blockade, which would have been unambiguously permissible under the UN Security Charter. According to Owen, if it had been his decision alone, he would have supported Thatcher:

> This is not my finest hour in British politics. If left to my own, I would not have criticised Thatcher. It was perfectly obvious we were going to have to do something about Gaddafi . . . She was very strong, and this is one of the reasons she deserves the accolades history has given her.

Owen toed the party line, as he felt he had to, but chose not to launch what would have been the most damaging line of attack: to accuse Thatcher of participating in an action that was retaliatory (and thus forbidden by the UN Charter) rather than an act of self-defence. It was Owen's feeling that American support to Britain during the Falklands War was the crucial factor in Thatcher's decision. As he said, 'Margaret Thatcher had a big debt of honour to Reagan and six years later she paid it back.'

Reagan had channelled extensive support to the British in the Falklands, despite advice to the contrary from many of his most senior advisors. The US-supplied ammunition and missiles meant the British did not have to turn around and go all the way home to restock. Without this support, some have argued, Britain would have lost to the Argentinians.

Thatcher's decision to allow the Americans to launch their raid from Britain was justified to the British public in terms carefully designed to evoke the Second World War. She declared to the Commons that 'terrorism thrives on appeasement'. She also appealed to the special relationship between Britain and the US, which she described as an alliance that guaranteed the freedom of Europe. Thatcher was also very careful to describe the attack as contributing to America's self-defence. As Owen told me, the Americans were not quite so worried about this: 'Thatcher was very careful to refer to self-defence, while he [Reagan] was talking quite gaily about retaliation.'

★

Operation El Dorado Canyon, as the US named the attack on Libya, took place on the night of 14 April 1986. US fighter planes attacked three targets in Tripoli – the Bab el-Aziziyya barracks, where Gaddafi resides, a government agency implicated in Libyan-sponsored terrorism and an airfield. The Bab el-Aziziyya barracks are inside a heavily guarded, six-mile-long compound, where the army headquarters are also housed. The primary intention in bombing them was, it was claimed, not to assassinate Gaddafi but to cripple the intelligence organisations based there. Lieutenant Colonel Oliver North, the deputy director for political-military affairs who helped to plan the attack, was reported, however, to have said, 'If we get him, that's a bonus.'

Tripoli was bombarded by eighteen F-111 strike aircraft from the US Air Force, which flew all the way from Britain. Because the European powers had refused to allow the US planes across their airspace, they had to take a circuitous thirteen-hour, 6,000-mile round trip around the Iberian peninsula and into the Mediterranean via the Strait of Gibraltar. Numerous mid-air refuellings were required during the arduous journey. The attack on Tripoli was said to have lasted eleven minutes, and it was reported that heavy anti-aircraft fire from the Libyans brought down one of the F-111s, which crashed into the ocean.

In Benghazi, a military base and the al-Jamahiriyya barracks were the two targets. The attack was launched from the aircraft carriers *Coral Sea* and *America*, and carried out by fifteen A-6 naval fighters, accompanied by an EA-6B electronic aircraft that jammed Libyan radar and communications equipment. It was said that the attack in Benghazi destroyed numerous expensive MiG-23 fighter planes, wrecked an airfield and extensively damaged the al-Jamahiriyya barracks, which the Americans claim had been used in terrorist training.

American talk of surgical strikes and precision bombing proved to have been somewhat exaggerated. Libyan government agents escorted foreign journalists around the sites of the bombings, showing them ruined houses and scores of dead bodies and injured civilians, including the body of a middle-aged man in his pyjamas and the tiny corpse of an eighteen-month-old toddler. Attempting to attack Libyan security headquarters, the Americans managed to destroy several homes, and to damage the Austrian, Finnish, French and Romanian embassies and the Swiss ambassador's residence. It was thought that at least 100 Libyan civilians were killed in the attacks. Gaddafi said that his wife and family had been inside the Bab el-Aziziyya barracks at the time of the bombing, and that his adopted baby daughter, Hanna had been killed and two of his sons injured.

Saif al-Islam Gaddafi, Gaddafi's second oldest son, corroborated his father's claim when he told a London court in 2002:

> One of the worst times in my family's life together was the US bombing raid on Tripoli and Benghazi (the two biggest cities in Libya) in 1986. I was only fourteen at the time and my family were all together in our home in Tripoli. One night, without any warning, the bombers came and, for five minutes, rained rockets down on us. I was woken up by loud crashing sounds and explosions, it was absolutely terrifying. Our house had been directly hit. I knew that we had to go to a shelter which had been built within the house. Sadly, some of my brothers and sisters were too young to know what to do, and they became trapped in one part of the house when a corridor collapsed. They were stuck there until the rescue services arrived, and when we dug them out we found that Hanna, my youngest sister, had died. She was just four years old.[10]

Gaddafi had injected unimaginable amounts of money into building up one of the world's most lethal arsenals. He was one of the most reliable customers of the Soviet Union's arms trade, and also bought an impressive range of American military technologies through various back doors. Yet, over the years sceptics had wondered how on earth a tiny, under-skilled desert nation would be able to put all of this to use. The 1986 bombing proved that their cynicism was justified, as the response from the Libyans was bafflingly weak. A few bursts of anti-aircraft fire were said to have been heard, one US fighter was rumoured to have been lost, but by and large there seemed to be almost no response. Was the pernicious rumour that the Libyan air force could not fly at night true? Or was the army letting the Americans wreak devastation, hoping that someone from among their ranks would emerge to wrest power from Gaddafi? This remains unclear even today.

The attack also showed that, at the end of nearly two decades of subversion, terrorism and interference in the affairs of others, Gaddafi had few friends. His Soviet allies were keen to sell him weapons, but had shown no sign of sending any kind of substantive assistance. The weapons they had sold the Libyans seemed to all intents and purposes to have proven completely useless. In the aftermath of the bombing, it became clear that the Soviets had also been at great pains to ensure that their forces were as far from Libya as possible, and that any sort of conflict with the US was carefully avoided. Gaddafi's Arab and African friends sent messages condemning the US, but also failed to produce a scrap of practical help.

The Americans had hoped that their attack would create a power vacuum, allowing opponents of the regime to emerge from their hiding places to take power. After all, reports had emerged from Libya of assassination attempts against Gaddafi in 1984 and 1985, and there were rumours of deep-seated discontent inside the army. It is certain that many Libyans hoped that the American bombing would prove the end of the Gaddafi era. Ahmed, the Libyan businessman I spoke with in June 2009, said of the bombing that 'if it had got rid of Gaddafi, everyone would have been happy. That was the only sorrow. People thought that Gaddafi had been killed. For a number of days there were so many rumours, and everyone thought that would be the end.'

In researching this book, I also interviewed Guma el-Gamaty, a former biochemist now studying for a PhD on Libyan politics. Gamaty has been a

member of London's Libyan dissident community for thirty-five years, and
was present the day PC Yvonne Fletcher was murdered. It has been too
dangerous for him to return to Libya since 1980, but his grasp of Libyan
politics is unrivalled and his knowledge of the resistance unique. Like
Ahmed, Gamaty said of the American bombing of Tripoli:

> Generally, believe it or not, the general population felt it was a shame the
> air raids did not get him, it was a big shame. They say that for about twelve
> hours, from eight o'clock to ten o'clock the next morning, the country
> was in complete chaos, no-one was in control. Anyone who was organised
> could have taken over then . . . The story that he was with his children was
> an absolute fabrication. He was told by the Russians he was going to be hit
> that night, so he ran. He was miles from Tripoli.

In the event, rather than creating space for an opposition to emerge
triumphant, the American attack ensured domestic opposition to Gaddafi
was all but destroyed. Gaddafi was said to have retreated to the desert for
some months in the wake of the attack, by some accounts meditating and
drawing on the inspiration of the desert environment, and by others sinking
into a severe depression. When he returned from this retreat, he launched
a tremendous purge of the army, which could now easily be attacked as a
result of the pathetic show it had put up against the Americans. The military
leadership was dramatically weakened. It was clear to all that Gaddafi's
enemies had missed a big chance, a unique opportunity that would not
come to them again. The Colonel, meanwhile, now had more than enough
excuse to smoke out and punish those who did not support him.

The attacks on Libya were very popular in the US. In the wake of the
bombing, there were nearly 5,000 phone calls made to the White House to
praise the attack, with only about 1,000 against. Americans even called the
British embassy to thank Margaret Thatcher for giving Britain's support.
President Reagan's approval ratings leapt: 77 per cent approved of the strike
and 76 per cent approved of his foreign policy, compared to just 56 per cent
the previous week.

The attacks did not do much, however, for America's image in the world.

Television pictures of bombed homes and wounded Libyans alienated many. This was compounded by a subsequent public scandal that arose from the revelation of an American campaign of global disinformation. In the summer after the April 1986 bombing, the US national security advisor, Admiral John Poindexter, had sent a memo to Reagan recommending that a false story should be circulated to the world media that the US was planning a full-scale invasion of Libya. Poindexter's memo was leaked to Bob Woodward. Woodward was able to prove that the faked information circulated by the administration had made it to page one of the *Wall Street Journal* in August 1986. Reagan bluffed it out, telling the media openly that he was happy for Gaddafi to fall asleep each night fearing what the Americans might be planning. Still, the world was disgusted, and some of Reagan's domestic support melted away, as many began to wonder how far they could actually trust any of the government's pronouncements on Libya.

The British public keenly disapproved of the attack and the part we played in it. Polls taken immediately after the bombing suggested that two thirds disapproved. Labour politicians criticised the government's interpretation of the special relationship – Neil Kinnock, the Leader of the Opposition, accused Thatcher of being a 'compliant accomplice' rather than a 'candid ally' to the US. From the ranks of the Conservatives, Ian Gilmour declared that Reagan could not at once be 'a sheriff in the Middle East and a rustler in Central America'.

What was the long-term effect of the campaign on Gaddafi? This question is difficult to answer. Lord Powell told me that in his opinion, the Tripoli bombing 'made Gaddafi draw in his horns for a while'. As he admitted, though, the argument that the bombing subdued Gaddafi stumbles against the rather large hurdle of Lockerbie, still the most fatal terrorist attack ever carried out on British soil. If, as many have suggested, Lockerbie was not the work of the Libyans, then Powell's argument carries rather more weight. If Lockerbie is set aside, Gaddafi was far less involved in the sponsorship of worldwide terror from this time onward. He did, however, continue enthusiastically attempting to assemble an arsenal of chemical and nuclear weapons for Libya.

It is my opinion that, ironically, the American attack was actually crucial to keeping Gaddafi in power for so long. Being on the receiving end of the awesome military might of a superpower was a deeply sobering experience. It was compounded in 1991 by the spectre of his fellow dictator, Saddam Hussein, watching Iraqi cities burn under American fire. The adaptive Colonel, motivated above all by the desire to hold on to power, went on to prove himself capable of the most astonishing about-turns in his quest for peaceful relations with his former enemies in the West. I doubt he would have been capable of this if it had not been for the frightening and very real picture shown to him that April night of what it might be like to lose power. So, not only did the US attack convincingly prove the weakness of his opposition, it also steeled him to make the difficult choices that accompanied his readmittance to the corridors and meeting rooms of international respectability. The Americans had laid the ground for the renovation of Gaddafi into a dictator who suited their needs.

The strangeness of all this was perhaps embodied by a ceremony held in Tripoli in April 2006. Lionel Richie and José Carreras were among the Western stars to grace 'Hanna Peace Day', the twentieth anniversary commemoration of the US bombing. In front of the demolished buildings preserved as a constant, politically useful reminder of American aggression, the two stars delivered rousing renditions of their classics. Libyan organisers told the media that the festivities were designed to emphasise the strong commitment of the regime to better relations with the West. To underscore this, the concert finished with children dressed as angels waving candles and singing 'We Are the World', the humanitarian anthem co-written by Richie with Michael Jackson. An encouraging picture for the politicians of the West, certainly, but perhaps a little hard to swallow for the Libyans, who still wait and hope for their freedom.

# LIBYA AND LOCKERBIE

The 1988 explosion of Pan Am Flight 103 from Heathrow to New York over the quiet Scottish border town of Lockerbie is notorious as the most fatal terrorist attack on British soil. Two hundred and fifty-nine passengers and crew died that night, along with eleven Lockerbie residents. The consequences of this act of violence have unfolded slowly over the ensuing decades, and today many relatives of those killed at Lockerbie continue what has been a protracted and nightmarish search for the truth. For many, it has seemed that the facts of what happened that December night have grown more rather than less elusive. A Libyan agent, Abdelbaset Ali Mohmed al-Megrahi, spent eight years in a Glasgow prison, convicted of the atrocity, but many doubted his guilt. The veracity and validity of his trials continue to be questioned by a host of victims' families, journalists and legal experts, many of whom wonder if Libya really was the only or indeed the chief sponsor of the Lockerbie murders.

For Colonel Gaddafi, Lockerbie was to be the cruellest lesson yet in the workings of international diplomacy. It was also, however, proof of his unshakeable power. Sanctions choked his oil industry, rendered Libya all but inaccessible to the outside world and ratcheted up the international media's portrayal of Gaddafi as demon dictator. Yet although Gaddafi was rocked, he never looked like falling. In the years following the trial of the two Libyans for the Lockerbie affair, he has managed to come in from the cold, drawing closer to the West than he has ever been. The Colonel has in a sense faced the worst that could be thrown at him, and it seems he has emerged stronger than ever.

★

On 21 December 1988 at 7.03 p.m., Pan Am Flight 103 from Heathrow airport in London to John F. Kennedy airport in New York exploded mid-air over Lockerbie. A bomb concealed in the luggage hold blew a hole through the fuselage, which spread rapidly, and the walls of the plane broke apart. The aeroplane's wings, carrying more than 40 tons of fuel, fell onto a small street called Sherwood Crescent. The plane's four motors, still working at full throttle, also plummeted to the ground, causing unimaginable scenes of destruction. Michael Gordon, a police officer in Lockerbie at the time, later told a journalist:

> I heard this noise above the wind. It sounded like thunder and it was getting louder and louder. It was similar to the noise of a jet fighter . . . As I looked out my window, I could see debris falling from the sky. Then I saw a long, black shape with a firestream heading towards Lockerbie . . . I saw dark objects falling from the sky. When the plane crashed, I could hear the tiles on the roof of my house lifting . . . When the plane hit, it was the most horrendous explosion. The streets, lawns and houses were on fire and it was difficult to move without my shoes and trousers burning. Then I found the cockpit. It was like the jet's nose had just been chopped off.[1]

News of the incident was quickly relayed throughout the world, and families of those on board watched their televisions in disbelief, telephoning the offices of Pan Am and panic-stricken workers at Heathrow to find out the fate of their loved ones. Flora Swire, a 23-year-old medical student, was one of those who died that night. Her father, Worcestershire GP Jim Swire, recounts the experience:

> Jane calls my name. Her voice has a choking sound. There's a plane down, an airliner. She has sensed something, her mother instinct telling her of

horror to come. We stand side by side transfixed in front of the television as the nine o'clock news comes on. A Pan Am jumbo jet with more than 250 people on board has crashed tonight in the Scottish Borders. It hit a petrol station in the centre of the town of Lockerbie. Police say there are many casualties . . . Now we are on a horrible merry-go-round, trying to get confirmation of whether or not Flora is on the flight. We can't get through on the numbers flashing on the screen. We dial and redial until our fingers are sore . . . I take the direct route. I get through to a girl on the Pan Am desk in New York. 'Can you tell me the names of the people on the plane?' She replies in a neutral voice: 'No, sir, I can't.' She puts the phone down.

This is my first contact with the aviation industry. Why, with all those damn computers at their disposal, can't they tell me immediately whether my Flora, my child, is on the plane? But the girl, too, is stunned. The world is stunned, and she is fighting for control, her desk besieged by hysterical relatives.

We all sit holding hands, silent, into the small hours; searching, switching channels until they all close down. Then we tune into the BBC World Service, each bulletin adding just a little more death.

The phone rings. Flora is on the plane. There are no survivors, no point in going to Heathrow, no point in doing anything. Being a doctor is a help and a hindrance. I am too familiar with death.[2]

As shocked relatives like Jim Swire contemplated the end of life as they knew it, politicians and the police in the UK and the US confronted the clear public need to hold someone to account. In the immediate aftermath of Lockerbie, there were many competing theories about who was responsible, but ultimately two main ones emerged. The first was that Lockerbie had been a revenge attack sponsored by Iran. This theory was seen as the most credible for the two years following the attack, and many observers of the case feel it has never satisfactorily been put to bed. At the heart of the Iran theory was a group called the Popular Front for the Liberation of Palestine – General Command (PFLP-GC). The PFLP-GC was known to have become suddenly flush with cash shortly after Lockerbie, and had links with both Syria and Iran. The Iran theory was given credibility by the existence of a very strong motive. In July 1988, the US missile carrier *Vincennes* shot down an Iranian civilian Airbus by mistake. Two hundred and ninety people on board, mainly Iranians, were killed. The US government somewhat provocatively awarded military decorations to the officers involved and welcomed them home as heroes. A CIA agent named Vincent Cannistraro repeatedly claimed that the Iranian government had paid PFLP-GC $10 million to carry out an operation against a US civilian aircraft.

Over the course of 1989, expectations built that an indictment of PFLP-GC members would soon be announced, and public officials in both the UK and the US issued statements to that effect. Tam Dalyell spoke to me of his memory of the day in 1989 when

> Paul Channon [the Transport Secretary] said to six senior journalists at the Garrick Club that the perpetrator of Lockerbie would be found within days. Now I don't believe that Paul Channon was either a liar or a fantasist . . . I knew him well, he was absolutely straight, and if he said this, he really believed it, I was quite sure.

Attention, however, soon moved from the Iran/Syria hypothesis to one focused on Libya. From October 1990, evidence began to emerge for a version of events that challenged the PFLP-GC theory. The main piece of evidence was a piece of circuitboard allegedly found in the wreckage from a timer similar to one that had been sold to Libya by a Swiss electronics company. This tiny piece of glassfibre was to be the foundation of the prosecution's case, and it was the subject of thousands of hours of legal wrangling over subsequent years. An investigation led by Dumfries and Galloway Police gradually drew on this and other evidence to construct a second version of events: two Libyan agents had hidden a bomb with a sophisticated timer mechanism inside a tape recorder and stowed it in a brown Samsonite suitcase filled with children's clothes. This suitcase was loaded onto a flight from Malta to Frankfurt, whence it was transferred to Heathrow and Pan Am Flight 103. The bomb exploded thirty-eight minutes after take-off, over Lockerbie. Clearly, it should have exploded later in the flight, over the Atlantic, when it would have left no evidence. Reasons given for the early explosion have ranged from a mistake with time zones to the flight's alleged late take-off.

Extra credibility was given to the Libya theory by the fact that in 1989 France had issued international arrest warrants for four Libyan officials identified as involved in that year's bombing of a UTA flight (see Chapter 3). This was an attack that had many parallels with Lockerbie.

On 14 November 1991, the Lord Advocate, Lord Fraser of Carmyllie, and William Barr, the US deputy Attorney General, led simultaneous press conferences in Edinburgh and Washington respectively. It was announced that after a long investigation, two Libyans were to be formally charged with the atrocity at Lockerbie. Megrahi and Lamin Khalifah Fhimah stood accused of conspiracy, murder and contravention of the Aviation Security Act. Megrahi had worked in Malta for Libyan Arab Airlines (LAA), regularly travelling through the island's Luqa airport. Fhimah was station manager for LAA at Luqa. The US and the UK demanded that both be immediately extradited for trial in Scotland, although neither country had an extradition treaty with Libya. Barr described previous allegations of Syria's involvement as 'a bum rap' for Damascus, and claimed there was no evidence that any country other than Libya was involved. He and Fraser called on the Gaddafi regime to accept responsibility, disclose all relevant information and compensate victims' families.

Colonel Gaddafi's reaction to this was to dismiss the Lockerbie charges as 'laughable' and immediately to refuse to extradite the Libyan suspects. He was supported in this by the Arab League and by the Organisation of the Islamic Conference, both of which quickly made statements opposing any military or economic action against Libya. Gaddafi maintained from the beginning and throughout the years of tortuous negotiation which followed that he knew nothing about the Lockerbie bombing.

Jim Swire travelled to Libya in 1991 to plead with Gaddafi to agree to the extradition of Megrahi and Fhimah. Swire described to me his visit to

Gaddafi's personal headquarters in a Bedouin tent in Sirte, and the reaction of the Colonel to the suggestion that Libya was involved:

> I was in this canvas space, with ornately designed canvas hangings and stuff, in the Muslim tradition of course of not being representational. And around the edge were quite a lot of people in khaki, they were all women and they all had sub-machine guns. To cut a long story short, Gaddafi held out his hand, and said 'Pleased to meet you, Doctor, and I'm so sorry to hear about the murder of your daughter', and we shook hands, which of course is what the press all take photographs of, photographs are in the archives of that happening. And then we all sat down and he said 'Would you like tea or coffee?' and I said 'Arabic coffee' and 'That's all right, sir', and that sort of thing . . . I don't know how much it showed, but my God, yes, I was nervous. And we discussed Lockerbie, and the gist of his approach was to say, I, Gaddafi, don't know what happened at Lockerbie, maybe a satellite crashed, maybe the plane was in collision with a military aircraft, maybe this, maybe that, maybe it was giant hailstones, all sorts of things, some of them way-out impossible, others of them just about peripherally feasible. All of the time to make me, to try to convince me that he knew nothing about it. In retrospect that was clearly the intent.

Gaddafi's words to Swire are similar to many other statements he has made on Lockerbie over the years. The Colonel's cheap conspiracy theory claims of hailstones and satellites undoubtedly smack of untruth. Many feel that even if Gaddafi did not himself order the attack at Lockerbie, it is likely that he knows who did, given his unique position as an insider in the world of international terror. If, as many believe, Megrahi and Fhimah had no involvement in the Lockerbie attack, it is still possible that Gaddafi, a lifelong supporter of militant Palestinian struggle, could himself have paid the PFLP-GC. Yet the decision to make Libya the only focus of investigation has often been questioned. Whatever Gaddafi's involvement, there is a feeling that, for a satisfying resolution of this case, the strands of evidence leading elsewhere should also have been properly investigated.

It has often been suggested that Gaddafi was used as a soft target – always

King Idris I, Gaddafi's predecessor as Libyan leader. (Getty Images)

The memorial to PC Yvonne Fletcher in St James's Square, location of the Libyan people's bureau, where she was killed in April 1984. (Getty Images)

French authorities seize Libyan-sourced arms from the *Eksund*, intended for the IRA, in November 1987. (AFP/Getty Images)

Damage to Gaddafi's residence
inside the Bab el–Aziziyya barracks,
following the US bombing raid
on Tripoli, April 1986.
(Time & Life Pictures/Getty Images)

After the raid this sculpture of a fist
crushing a US warplane was erected
in front of the ruined building.
(DPA/Press Association Images)

The remains of the Boeing 747 and ruined homes in Lockerbie
in the aftermath of the mid-air explosion on Pan Am Flight 103,
December 1988. (Getty Images)

The two men accused
of the Lockerbie
bombing, Abdelbasset
al-Megrahi *right* and
Lamin Khalifah Fhimah
(Time & Life Pictures/
Getty Images)

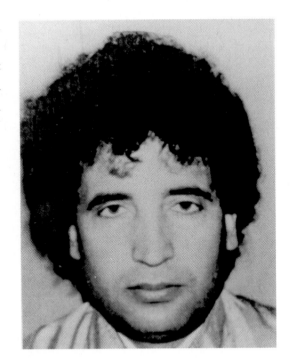

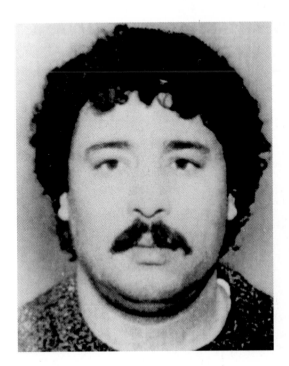

Wreckage following the explosion of UTA Flight 772
from Brazzaville to Paris, September 1989. (Getty Images)

Gaddafi has enjoyed mixed relations with leaders of the Arab world during his rule. *Above* in September 1970 with *from left* King Faisal of Saudi Arabia, President Iryani of North Yemen and President Nasser of Egypt; *below* greeting Yasser Arafat in June 1996 at the Arab Summit in Cairo.
(Getty Images; AFP/Getty Images)

More recently, Gaddafi has sought to build bridges with the West.
*Above* Gaddafi meets Tony Blair in his Bedouin tent at Sirte in May 2007;
*below* he visits President Sarkozy in Paris in December 2007.
(Getty Images)

to be relied on to spout angry rhetoric, ensconced in the public eye as a sort of insane demon, and recently named as the sponsor of a number of other terrorist acts. There was no shortage of potential motivations for Libya, with decades of hostility between it and the US having culminated in 1986 with President Reagan's bombing of Tripoli.

In contrast, teasing out the tortuous threads of Iranian and Syrian involvement was politically extremely difficult – Iran's position on key oil routes between the US and the Middle East made further conflict undesirable, and both Iranian and Syrian support was vital in the 1991 Gulf War against Iraq. Moreover, Syria was soon to become a key player in the highly publicised, US-sponsored, Arab–Israeli peace process. The pursuit of Gaddafi was a safer option, touching few vital interests in the US and the UK, and nicely satisfying public demand for meaningful action on Lockerbie. According to Tam Dalyell, 'Libya was scapegoated, in my opinion, because Iran and Syria were much more powerful and the Americans didn't want the finger of blame to be pointed at them at that stage.'

The force of this argument was also acknowledged in 2001 by Michael Scharf, senior lawyer at the US Department of Justice, and the author of the United Nations resolutions against Libya:

Finally, one of the things that was going on behind the scenes was that Iran and Syria were becoming very inconvenient targets politically, whereas Libya was a very convenient target. This is because, at the same moment in time that the prosecution's case is starting to veer toward Libya a little, something happened in the Persian Gulf, and that was that Saddam Hussein invaded Kuwait. The United States desperately needed to build a coalition and it had to start with Iran. And for the peace process to follow, Syria was crucial.

I'm not saying that the government said let's force the investigation this way, but I'm saying it was a much more convenient turn. People were celebrating when they heard there was evidence indicating that it was Libya, not the Iranians or Syrians. And that may have affected how broad the continuing investigation into Iranian and Syrian responsibility was.[3]

Swire told me that the Conservative government of the day under
Margaret Thatcher had not welcomed his questions, nor had any
subsequent government. Some observers of the case felt that those high
up in power had never really thought that Lockerbie was the work of
Libya. Many commented on the downright peculiar omission of Lockerbie
from Thatcher's memoirs. It surely must have represented a moment of
memorable stress for her. Dalyell commented stridently on this in the
House of Commons in 1997:

> It is an incredible fact which I draw to the attention of my Hon. Friend the
> Minister of State that, in the 800 self-serving pages that Margaret Thatcher
> wrote, she never mentioned Lockerbie once. What she did say was that the
> 'much-vaunted' Libyan retaliation for her unwarranted attack on Benghazi
> and Tripoli in 1986 never came about. If the British Prime Minister, with
> her access to intelligence, really believed that, how on earth could she
> suppose that the Libyans were responsible for the Lockerbie crime?[4]

It is something of an irony that in the tense years of negotiation that were to
follow, Libya the rogue state and Gaddafi the demon dictator held fast to the
tenets of international law, while the US and the UK resorted to hardcore
superpower politicking. As the US and the UK ratcheted up pressure in
the UN Security Council, Libya cited the 1971 Montreal Convention on
aviation security, which provided that a person suspected of attacking an
aircraft should be tried in their country of origin. Libya demanded the right
to try the two men in Libya and for the British and US governments to
hand over to them all evidence in the case. Gaddafi clung tenaciously to
his rights under the Montreal Convention, and it is widely acknowledged
that he had every right to do so.

The UK and the US were clearly bound by this convention, but it is
equally clear that they never considered the possibility of a Libyan trial.
Such a trial would be utterly suspect, the verdict essentially risible in a
country where justice was questionable to say the least. This was reinforced
powerfully in 1992, when the world media arrived in Tripoli to witness the
Libyan court's indictment of Megrahi and Fhimah: instead of witnessing a

full cross-examination of the suspects as was expected, journalists saw the men led into the courtroom for just two minutes, appearing bewildered and saying little. There was much speculation as to what was going on behind the scenes in the Libyan legal system. Yet for Gaddafi, the refusal of the US and the UK to abide by their obligations under international law would certainly have reinforced his violent cynicism of the West and its liberal institutions. He was continually harangued on the grounds of not being a responsible international citizen, yet was himself barred from reliance on the rules of this US-dominated system.

Swire, presented by Gaddafi with this argument, offered to take a letter from him to the Foreign Office restating Libya's position and its request for evidence. When Swire contacted the Foreign Office, he claims to have been told to 'put it in the post if you like', a strange reflection on the attitude of civil servants to Libya and Gaddafi, and to this case, which, after all, centred on the worst terrorist atrocity committed in Britain to date. During Swire's first visit to Libya in 1991, the country's chief justice confirmed to him that they wanted to put the two on trial there, as they were fully entitled to do. He claimed that the reason they could not was that the West would not hand over the evidence which it claimed to have against the two accused.

As Gaddafi righteously proclaimed his fondness for international law, the US and the UK began their campaign to mobilise the full force of the Security Council. Their first success was in 1992. On 21 January, Resolution 731 was passed, calling on Libya to co-operate in the investigations of the attacks on Pan Am 103 and on UTA Flight 772. The Security Council declared that it was 'deeply concerned over the results of investigations, which implicate officials of the Libyan government' and that it strongly deplored the Libyans' failure to co-operate with requests to provide full information.[5] Libya refused to meet the conditions of this resolution, and so followed Resolution 748, adopted on 31 March. Resolution 748 was an unusually forceful instrument and was highly unusual in the history of the UN. It represented only the second time that the Security Council had imposed sanctions on a state for failing to comply with its demands (the first time had been the previous year, when Iraq invaded Kuwait). The resolution stated that Libya's failure 'to demonstrate by concrete actions its renunciation of terrorism' represented a 'threat to international peace and security'. It imposed sanctions that asked member states to suspend any arms trade with Libya, to reduce the scale of Libyan diplomatic representation and to suspend all flights to and from Libya.[6] Meanwhile, the US was also putting into place additional sanctions of its own. The Bush administration had announced shortly before Resolution 748 that it would freeze the US assets of forty-six Libyan businesses. UN Resolution 883, of November 1993, went on to further strengthen sanctions, freezing Libyan assets overseas (apart from its petroleum-related assets), banning the sale of oil-related equipment to Libya, and strengthening the restrictions on commercial aviation.

Where, one might ask, as Libya's dramatic isolation and economic punishment were hammered home, were Gaddafi's friends? Much to the Colonel's disillusionment, international action against Libya was not much opposed by either Arab or African states, with most of which he shared a colourful history of mutual betrayal and unpredictable, erratic friendships. As the UN turned on Gaddafi, it was clear that support from the Arab world was generally lukewarm. While the Saudis had made some initial attempts to assist Libya, raising the issue in Washington and London, they were strongly rebuffed by the West and soon backed away (although towards the end of the 1990s their behind-the-scenes diplomatic contribution was to be crucial). Although the Arab League expressed its regret over the sanctions, it also included in its principal statement on the UN resolutions a denunciation of international terrorism in all its forms and a declaration of its own willingness to co-operate in addressing it. This incensed Gaddafi, who in 1995 declared that his former Arab allies were no longer to be trusted. The imposition of UN sanctions from 1992 marked the point of several years of unprecedented diplomatic isolation for the Libyan regime, with few willing to deny the sanctions regime very convincingly. Disillusionment with his Arab brother states during these years was to be long-lasting: the lifting of sanctions saw a deliberate shift in Libyan foreign policy away from the Arab world to focus instead on Africa and African unity.

★

These days, the public is familiar with the often extreme suffering economic sanctions can bring, having watched horrific images of Iraqi children dying in under-equipped hospitals as sanctions were imposed on Iraq in the lead-up to the second Gulf War. Libyan sanctions were not, however, of this order. Their effect on Colonel Gaddafi certainly played a role in his decision to hand over Megrahi and Fhimah, but it cannot be said that they brought Libya to its knees. A report published by the US Department of Commerce recorded:

> UN sanctions imposed in April 1992 have not yet had a major impact on the economy because Libya's oil revenues generate sufficient foreign exchange that, along with Libya's large currency reserves, sustain food and consumer goods imports as well as equipment for the oil industry and ongoing development projects. In 1994, Libya's imports totaled $6.9 billion, compared to exports of $7.2 billion . . . The sanctions have, however, had an effect in painting Libya as a rogue state.[7]

Adel Darwish, a seasoned journalist who has spent his career covering Middle Eastern politics, felt that the sanctions were nonetheless effective:

> The well-aimed sanctions can take much of the credit; Tripoli-based Western diplomats agree, saying that sanctions are a blunt instrument, and often hurt anybody but their intended target – Iraq is a case in point. The UN sanctions imposed on Libya were the exception to the rule: they had a precise aim, they severely inconvenienced Libya's ruling elite – by placing an embargo on air transport, arms and some oil parts and financial transactions – without harming ordinary citizens.[8]

Gaddafi and many Libyans may not agree with this analysis. Sanctions were certainly the subject of violent resentment there, irrespective of social class. A Libyan report to the UN claimed that there had been deaths due to the inability to import medicines and medical supplies by air. Sanctions undoubtedly held Libya back in the development of its oil industry, during a decade when the world was more than ever crying out for stable oil sources. In a 'distributive state', where everyone depends on a government that exists mainly to share out oil revenue, this had dramatic effects on everyone. Yet it is broadly accurate to say that these sanctions mainly worked because they managed to hit those at the top hard. In particular, the ridiculous contortions needed to get in and out of Libya under the period of sanctions on commercial air travel would have been difficult to stomach. For the elites needing regular access to the West and for Gaddafi himself, the lengthy, rough journey from Tripoli through the desert into Tunisia would have been a nasty inconvenience. Worse, it formed a potent symbol and a constant reminder of the Gaddafi regime's pariah status in the international community.

Sanctions never completely isolated the regime. This is a remarkable testament to Libya's significance in the world economy. Even when all the power of the United States was deployed to push for Libya's complete isolation as a 'rogue state', this proved unachievable. Even the harshest UN sanctions were not allowed to include a complete ban on oil exports from Libya, nor did they prevent foreign oil companies continuing with profitable gas and oil drilling and exploration projects there. The US pushed for a complete embargo, but Germany and Italy were too dependent on Libyan oil to entertain this. The Italians even suggested that their oil refineries could not process non-Libyan crude oil. From 1995, the Bank of England retracted its rule forbidding British oil companies to send cash to Libyan subsidiaries, and began to allow them where the 'merits of individual cases' for doing so could be proven. In April 1995, the UN allowed Libyans to fly to Mecca to join the annual worldwide Muslim pilgrimage there. In 1996, US legislation designed to discourage new foreign investment in Libya was criticised vigorously by the European Union, which felt the US did not have the right to pass legislation impacting on other nations' trade interests. Even American companies sought and found ways around sanctions. Halliburton, for example, while under the chairmanship of the future Vice-President Dick Cheney, built public works in Libya using a British subsidiary, obeying the letter if not the spirit of the harsher US sanctions regime.

Support for sanctions against Libya gradually weakened as the 1990s wore on, with a growing sense that they were extreme and that the US was employing this blunt instrument of diplomacy too freely against Arab and African states in general. In March 1997 the Vatican led the way by re-establishing a diplomatic relationship with Libya. In September of the same year, the Arab League resolved to allow its member states to suspend sanctions until a better solution to the Lockerbie situation could be decided. In May 1998 the Clinton administration agreed with EU nations to relax the rules restricting multinational companies dealing with Iran, Cuba and Libya. The UN sanctions committee allowed the President of Egypt, Hosni Mubarak, to fly into Tripoli on a visit to Libya two months later. Even before Gaddafi handed over Megrahi and Fhimah, the pressure on the Libyan regime was easing. It is often said that the visibly lessening power of sanctions as a policy instrument at this time was a factor in persuading the US to agree to the public trial of Megrahi and Fhimah, a trial which many thought could be the source of considerable embarrassment to the superpower.

Sanctions were likely, however, to have increased Gaddafi's deep-seated fear of opposition forces working against his regime. Sanctions closed Libya off from the rest of the world and put limits on its prosperity. It was easy for Gaddafi to believe that in this context, discontent with his regime and efforts to overthrow him might increase. There were a number of coup attempts in the mid-1990s, and murky reports of mass rioting sponsored by Islamic fundamentalists emerged from Libya. Despite these periodic eruptions of discontent, in the long run sanctions did not significantly destabilise the regime. It is thought by many that the centralised control exerted by Gaddafi was actually strengthened by the late 1990s, with poor economic circumstances forcing an even stronger dependency by citizens on the state. Yet Gaddafi is likely to have felt an increased fear of dissidence during this period of isolation, making readmission to the international community much more attractive.

For many relatives of those murdered at Lockerbie, the pressure to reduce sanctions and the lack of support for a stronger approach were seen as a betrayal. For Gaddafi, the incomplete nature of the sanctions must have shown him that his Libyan regime was so thoroughly integrated

into the world system that the worst the US could throw at it in terms
of economic punishment could not bring him to his knees. His re-entry
into the international scene, therefore, was not conducted from a position
of complete weakness. Making the overtures needed for reintegration
could easily be framed as the canny business decision of a leader still
doing relatively well, in contrast to Robert Mugabe, for example, who
had brought Zimbabwe to what seemed like the point of no return. Oil
had again provided a cushion – Gaddafi could fall, indeed he has done so
repeatedly, but never so hard that he did not recover.

*

By the second half of the 1990s, sanctions against Libya were becoming
an increasingly thorny problem for all the countries involved. The non-
Western world was becoming restive and defiant, reluctant to continue to
punish Libya, threatening to undermine the very instrument of economic
sanctions. In this context, an unusual situation promoted by unusual players
on the international scene became more and more attractive. This was the
idea of a trial for the accused in a neutral third country. This compromise
solution was the brainchild of a Lockerbie-born professor of law at
Edinburgh University, Robert Black, who later worked closely with Jim
Swire to devise a solution that all parties might accept, and the two lobbied
extensively to promote the third-country option, enlisting the support of
the Arab League and Saudi Arabia. In 1998 they travelled to Libya to discuss
the plan with Gaddafi. They met with a warm reception, to the extent that
jokes were exchanged about President Clinton's disastrous affair with his
White House intern, Monica Lewinsky. Black's plan to try Megrahi and
Fhimah in a third country rapidly gathered steam, and was promoted with
particular enthusiasm by South African and Saudi Arabian diplomats.

One of the strangest sights of the Lockerbie negotiations was Nelson
Mandela, revered worldwide for his principled struggle against apartheid
in South Africa, hand in hand in Tripoli with Gaddafi, notorious for
sponsoring most known terrorist organisations over the last thirty years.
Libyan bagpipes droned and crowds shouted 'Long live Mandela' in English

as the two leaders combined in 1997 to present Libya with its best publicity in years. Yet this meeting had its roots in a potent history: the odd friendship between the two leaders had been cemented by Gaddafi's generous funding of the African National Congress during the time when it was itself seen by the West as a terrorist organisation. Mandela's visit was not just to discuss Lockerbie, but also to confer on Gaddafi the Good Hope Medal, the highest South African honour that can be awarded to a non-national. Mandela's statements in support of Gaddafi and against US criticism of the visit were quoted in newspapers all over the world. In answer to those who said his visit was wrong, Mandela said, 'Those who say I should not be here are without morals . . . This man helped us at a time when we were all alone, when those who say we should not come here were helping the enemy.'[9] The Mandela visit was undoubtedly powerful: here was perhaps the one world leader deeply respected by all countries involved, speaking out in favour of a judicial solution. Following the meeting, diplomats swung into action, commencing years of the delicate discussions needed to persuade both sides to agree.

The Mandela visit may also have been important in providing the Colonel with a piece of theatre of the kind that he thoroughly enjoys. With the flashing cameras of the world's media on him again and Mandela's congratulations in all the papers, Gaddafi had a welcome taste of the international limelight he had undoubtedly missed. Indeed, it seems likely that for the quixotic, flamboyant Colonel, pure boredom played a role in the decision to bow to the international community over Lockerbie – the end of sanctions would mean the chance to take to the stage again and renew his unique brand of international diplomacy.

In 1998, Gaddafi was finally persuaded to agree to the third-country trial option, and the UN Security Council passed Resolution 1192, calling for a special court to be set up at Camp Zeist in the Netherlands. Megrahi and Fhimah would be tried under Scottish law, using Scottish judges. Robin Cook, the then Foreign Secretary, hailed the solution as 'an historic innovation in international legal practice' and held out the hope of 'ending the long wait for justice of the relatives of those who were murdered'.[10]

In public, Cook and the other politicians involved made euphoric pronouncements hailing the likely advent of justice. Behind the scenes, however, the great powers were nervous. The trial was an odd solution that had gained a momentum nobody expected, thanks to Black, Swire, Mandela and a host of unseen diplomats. Many feel that neither the UK nor the US ever expected that a legal trial of this type would take place, or that Gaddafi would actually hand the two men over. By the time the British and American politicians gave the green light to the third-country trial they had altered its parameters from those proposed by Black, substituting his panel of judges from several countries with one of exclusively Scottish judges. This change may have been what prompted Mandela to warn publicly, at a Commonwealth heads of government conference in Edinburgh, that 'no one country should be complainant, prosecutor and judge'.

Michael Scharf has publicly stated that the US always saw sanctions against Libya as an instrument of punishment, not a means to find justice:

> So, my argument was, let's use something else, let's use the rule of law. I wasn't the only one. I was part of a chorus of voices saying this. What they did though was not use the rule of law with the idea that we would get a conviction and have truth come out and have justice come out, that wasn't the idea. The idea was let's use the rule of law so we can set the stage for the money bomb, UN sanctions.[11]

The Camp Zeist trial was not the kind of interaction that the West usually had with the countries it labelled rogue states. Events on the world stage had propelled Blair, Clinton and Gaddafi to accept a third-country trial of this type, but none knew quite what to expect from an unprecedented judicial experiment. Many observers felt that a deep-seated political fear of fallout from the trial led all the states involved to take actions that compromised justice.

The case against the two Libyans had not changed a great deal since it was first presented to the UN in the early 1990s: Megrahi and Fhimah had smuggled a bomb concealed in a tape recorder onto Pan Am 103 via two connecting flights. Hidden in a suitcase full of children's clothes, the bomb was triggered by a sophisticated timer. A shopkeeper named

Tony Gauci provided a crucial identification of Megrahi as the purchaser of the children's clothes wrapped around the bomb. A CIA double agent, Abdul Majid Giaka, linked Megrahi to the suitcase. Edwin Bollier, a Swiss businessman selling sophisticated and rare electronic timing devices, testified that the Libyans had had exclusive access to devices of the kind found in the ruins of Pan Am 103, and connected Megrahi directly to its purchase (though later confirming that he had also supplied some to the Stasi in East Germany).

Weaknesses in the case, however, were plentiful. Most analyses and indeed the trial proceedings themselves record that none of the witnesses for the prosecution were reliable. Giaka claimed to have evidence linking Megrahi and Fhimah to the brown Samsonite suitcase. Cross-examination revealed that he was financially dependent on the CIA and that prior to producing his damning testimony, the CIA had threatened to stop paying him unless he produced some leads. His testimony was described by the trial judges as contradictory and confusing. Bollier was found to have been an unreliable witness and to have contradicted himself numerous times in his testimony. Despite admitting that Bollier and Giaka lacked credibility, the judges relied heavily on parts of their statements. They also relied on Gauci's identification, despite describing it as 'not absolute'. Perhaps most seriously, however, some observers felt the court had failed to thoroughly explore the alternative scenarios the defence had suggested might explain the Lockerbie attack.

Megrahi's ultimate conviction was immediately appealed, in part based on inconsistencies in Gauci's identification. The appeal took place between 23 January and 14 February 2002, again at Camp Zeist. Public interest in the case was such that the appeal became the first Scottish trial to be broadcast live on television and on the internet. On 14 February the appeal was rejected unanimously by the three judges, in a verdict that took just three minutes to read. Megrahi's wife wept openly, and Megrahi himself told the Arabic newspaper Asharq al-Awsat, 'God is my witness that I am innocent, I have never committed any crime and I have no connection to this issue.' The court, however, had found that none of the grounds for appeal was well founded, and Megrahi returned to prison to resume his twenty-year sentence. Many of the American families who lost relatives at Lockerbie supported his conviction. Jack Flynn, whose son John Patrick Flynn was killed, told *The Scotsman*:

> I went to the trial every day either at Camp Zeist or to the closed circuit
> television link in New York. I saw all the evidence. I noted it and discussed
> it with attorneys and everybody agreed he was guilty. Yes, he was the right
> man. Yes, he did it.

In contrast, several of the British relatives, including Jim Swire, were unconvinced by the evidence against Megrahi. Swire even went on to found the 'Justice for Megrahi' campaign, which has lobbied for the Libyan's release.

One of the most intriguing developments of the appeal was new evidence that security at Heathrow airport was breached the night before the bombing. Ray Manly, a security worker at Heathrow, was interviewed by Scotland Yard's Anti-Terrorist Branch in the investigation carried out in the months following the attack. He told the Yard that in the early hours of the day of the attack on Pan Am 103, a padlock securing the baggage transfer area at Terminal 3 had been 'cut like butter', in 'a very deliberate act, leaving easy access to airside'. Thirteen years later, Manly followed the course of the Lockerbie trial at Camp Zeist with interest, and was shocked to find that there was no mention in court of the Heathrow break-in. Manly's evidence at the appeal now raised the possibility that the bomb had been introduced onto Pan Am 103 not at Luqa or Frankfurt, but in London. Manly was not a strong witness: he had been obviously ill, he had warned the court that he might have to leave the stand to be sick, and he became confused during his testimony. Some even felt that he had weakened the case for Megrahi. Many observers were outraged, however, that the breach of Heathrow's security had not been raised at the original trial, and the reason for this omission has never become clear.

For the Lockerbie relatives, news of the Heathrow break-in was a bitter pill, as many had spent years following the case, mounting their own investigations based on the information made available to them. Moreover, the fatal accident inquiry held in Britain in 1990–91 had proceeded without any knowledge of the break-in. This threw into question the decision at the time that the inquiry should focus mainly on what might have gone wrong at Luqa or Frankfurt airports, not on events at Heathrow. Swire came to see me in my constituency and told me:

> But the real putting into perspective of this is that the guy who discovered the break-in reported it immediately to the Heathrow authorities that same early morning. It was recorded in the Heathrow log. He was interviewed by the police, who came and did a sweep of Heathrow after Lockerbie happened, of course; he was interviewed by the Special Branch, by the Metropolitan anti-terror squad; and yet the fact that there had been a break-in at Heathrow was concealed from the court at Zeist, from us, the relatives, and from the defence at Zeist until after the verdict at Zeist had been reached. That was twelve years. Now, since the anti-terror branch were involved, it's very difficult to see how someone of the magnitude of Number 10 wouldn't have known that something had happened at Heathrow. Why would they hush it up for twelve years? Or is it the fault of the Crown Prosecution Service in Scotland, the Crown Office? Because they were in charge of the investigation and the defence were dependent on the prosecution to hand it to them . . . And I can't believe that the Scottish police, when they went to Heathrow, didn't find out about the break-in, and somebody in Westminster must have known about the anti-terror interview that this guy had . . . Heathrow had been penetrated, there was a break-in, the court agreed there had been a break-in, from landside to airside in the small hours of the morning of the disaster. Nobody knew who'd broken in, nobody knew why he'd broken in; why was that concealed till after the verdict had been reached? Somebody must have had a reason for doing that. Was it the prosecution in Scotland? Was it Number 10? As I say, I don't know a way of penetrating these layers of government . . .

I was one of only two relatives who represented themselves in that court, and I spent most of my time delving into why Heathrow's baggage security system wasn't secure, because it was presumed that the device had come

in from Frankfurt and had gone through [Heathrow's] baggage security
system to get onto the fatal aircraft. I wouldn't have done that if I'd known
about the break-in at Heathrow. I'd have majored on perimeter security
at Heathrow, and on why on earth did the airport not suspend all flights
until they found out who'd broken in and why he'd done it? I believe that
if Heathrow had acted responsibly, my daughter might well still be alive.
And that's a source of – to put it mildly – considerable vexation, to think
about that.

Few felt that Megrahi's trial had met their expectations. While some
relatives, particularly the American contingent, gratefully welcomed the
conviction and the comfort it brought, others felt it evident that even if
he were guilty, Megrahi was still merely an agent, and wondered how
the whole weight of the murderous terrorist attack could rest on one
man. The president of one of several American victims' groups told the
BBC, 'We only have part of the truth and a small measure of justice. We
have a footsoldier – we don't have Gaddafi.' Bruce Smith, a Lockerbie
widower, said, 'I don't know anyone in the world who thinks those
guys acted alone.' Tam Dalyell commented, 'It stretches the imagination
that Megrahi alone devised a scheme which led to the biggest murder
of Western civilians since 1945.' Strangely, neither the defence nor the
prosecution had pursued questions about who had given Megrahi his
orders. Gaddafi had claimed in May 2000 that an 'agreement' had been
made with the US and the UK, hinting that his decision to hand over the
suspects had been made conditional on limits to the questions that would
be asked about Libyan government involvement. This was vigorously
denied by the US and the UK, but some feel the Colonel may have told
the truth.

There was also serious criticism of the judicial process at Camp Zeist.
One of the key public figures to emerge during the trial was an Austrian
professor of philosophy, Dr Hans Koechler. The UN had appointed five
independent observers to attend the trial, one of whom was Koechler, in his
capacity as president of the International Progress Organization. Koechler
is also a specialist in legal philosophy. His report on what he viewed as the

shocking flaws of the trial process took the media by storm, producing headlines such as:

Unfair, incomprehensible, irrational and arbitrary (*Scotland on Sunday*, 8 April 2001)

Lockerbie verdict 'politically influenced' (BBC News, 7 April 2001)

UN claims Lockerbie trial rigged. EXCLUSIVE: Court was politically influenced by US (*Sunday Herald*, 8 April 2001)

Koechler's most serious charge was that of political interference. As already noted, Nelson Mandela had warned at a 1997 meeting of Commonwealth heads of state that the trial would not be effective if Britain acted as 'complainant, prosecutor and judge'. According to Koechler's report, Mandela's fear that politicians would yield to the temptation to interfere with the workings of justice was well founded. Koechler wrote that two state prosecutors from the US Department of Justice had sat with the prosecutors throughout, passing notes and documents. The American lawyers had no official role, and were not even recorded as present at the court. Yet, according to Koechler, the impression given was that they were supervising the prosecution's case and deciding what evidence should be released in the open court. On the effects of this, Koechler wrote:

It has become obvious that the presence of representatives of foreign governments in a Scottish courtroom (or any courtroom for that matter) on the side of the prosecution team jeopardises the independence and integrity of legal procedures and is not in conformity with the general standards of due process and fairness of the trial. As has become obvious . . . this presence has negatively impacted on the court's ability to find the truth; it has introduced a political element into the proceedings in the courtroom. This presence should never have been granted from the outset.[12]

On the Libyan side, political interests had also clearly affected proceedings, possibly in a way that weakened the defence. A high-ranking legal advisor to the Libyan government, Mr Maghour, acted as the official defence lawyer, but he was not seen to interact in any way with the Scottish defence team and seemed to have been the choice of his government rather than of the defendants. In both the trial and the appeal, Koechler felt that the efforts of Megrahi and Fhimah's defence team were so weak as to lack credibility. The defence did not appear to pursue vigorously the numerous pieces of evidence that were withheld and which might have furthered their case; nor did they push the court to consider any of the alternative theories about what happened at Lockerbie. Koechler wrote that virtually all of the prosecution's witnesses were unreliable. Many logical flaws were pointed out, but perhaps most damning was the fact that the prosecution's entire case had rested on the story that both suspects had acted closely together in devising and carrying out the attack. When Fhimah was found not guilty (a strong exoneration under Scottish law, which offers three verdicts – guilty, not guilty or not proven), the sudden reconstituting of a different story in which Megrahi had acted alone was described as 'totally incomprehensible for any rational observer'. The report on the first trial suggested that 'there is not one single piece of material evidence linking the two accused to the crime' and finished:

> Regrettably, through the conduct of the court, disservice has been done to the important cause of international criminal justice. The goals of criminal justice on an international level cannot be advanced in a context of power politics and in the absence of an elaborate division of powers. What is true on the national level, applies to the transnational level as well. No national court can function if it has to act under pressure from the executive power and if vital evidence is being withheld from it because of political interests. The realities faced by the Scottish court in the Netherlands have demonstrated this truth in a very clear and dramatic fashion – the political impact stemming, in this particular case, from a highly complex web of national and transnational interests related to the interaction among several major actors on the international scene.[13]

There were relatively few staunch defenders of the proceedings at Camp

Zeist. It is notable that Michael Scharf said publicly in the aftermath of the trial that the Americans had viewed a trial at Lockerbie as an effective means of putting a difficult situation to bed, more than an as an exercise in justice. He wrote of the trial in the *Boston Globe*:

> Despite its inadequacies, the judicial response has apparently succeeded in severing the cycle of violence between the United States and Libya. Libya has made a show of terminating its support for terrorist groups, and its actions are now more closely scrutinised by the international community. Libya will soon pay billions of dollars to the families of the victims to settle the pending lawsuits. And the renewed flow of Libyan oil to the West may help stave off worldwide inflation and recession. From the standpoint of US security interests, the Lockerbie trial was an unmitigated success.[14]

Robert Black, the legal expert who had spent years lobbying for the Camp Zeist trial, wrote of Megrahi in 2007:

> Since the date of the trial court's verdict against him, my position has been a clear one: on the evidence led at the trial his conviction was simply an outrageous miscarriage of justice, about which the Scottish criminal justice system should feel nothing but shame. As a result of today's meeting I am satisfied that not only was there a wrongful conviction, but the victim of it was an innocent man. Lawyers, and I hope others, will appreciate this distinction.[15]

The Italian newspaper *La Stampa* had claimed in the lead-up to the verdict at Camp Zeist that, 'whatever the outcome of the trial, there's already an assured winner, and it's not the victims' relatives . . . The winner is Colonel Gaddafi, who on agreeing to the extradition of the two defendants saw the lifting of the sanctions imposed by the United Nations for the past seven years.' This was proved prescient. Megrahi went quietly off to his Glasgow cell, Fhimah returned to Libya to be hailed as a conquering hero, and Gaddafi came forward to reclaim his place in the international system. The trial had not furnished foreign media with embarrassing insights into

Libyan state security, nor had it chosen to dive into the shadowy details of who had issued Megrahi's orders. Ultimately, it seemed that it had been a relatively small price to pay for the restoration of Libya's economy and the end of its pariah status. If Megrahi had not been guilty, his fate was grim indeed. Tam Dalyell felt strongly that this was the case, telling me, at his home in Scotland:

> Megrahi was a sanctions buster for Libyan Arab Airlines and the Libyan oil industry. You asked me about this meeting with Gaddafi. Gaddafi sat there . . . and he was thinking, 'Well, this man Dalyell is probably right. I know that Megrahi is not guilty, but my problem is I've got to get into the international trading circuit, and for the sake of the Libyan oil industry and Libyan Arab Airlines and the spare parts, this is far more important to my country than the liberty or otherwise of one individual.'

Gaddafi had clearly decided to play the West's game when it came to Lockerbie, but this is not to say that negotiations post-Zeist were easy. As ever, angry rhetoric, conflicting statements and bluster were the order of the day. Gaddafi baulked at the US and UK's demands that he take written responsibility for the Lockerbie attack and pay billions of dollars in compensation to relatives. Nelson Mandela supported Gaddafi in seeing this demand as a betrayal, saying that the West had shifted the goalposts on sanctions and that 'the condition that Gaddafi must accept responsibility for Lockerbie is totally unacceptable'. The trial had not touched on ultimate responsibility within the Libyan hierarchy, and thus, Mandela said, 'unless it's clear that Gaddafi was involved in giving orders it's unfair to act on that basis'.[16] The Libyans were horrified by what they saw as a new set of demands, and the local media immediately asked why the Americans should not, in their turn, pay compensation for the 1986 bombing of Tripoli. The Libyan position was articulated by Gaddafi's son Saif al-Islam, who told the media in 2003 that 'we regard ourselves as innocent and we had nothing to do with that tragedy', and that Libya's only commitment had been 'to accept the outcome of the trial'. All of this, however, was somewhat disingenuous, as it was reasonably likely that compensation and the issue of responsibility would be on the negotiating table once a satisfactory verdict was reached. It was perhaps incumbent on Gaddafi to produce a lot of noise on the issue for the benefit of domestic audiences, but ultimately the two issues were resolved. On 11 March 2003, Libya agreed to pay up to $10 million per victim, amounting to around $2.7 billion in total. On 15 August of the same year, a letter accepting responsibility was sent to the UN. The letter carefully distanced Gaddafi and his government from any involvement in the bombing and made no reference to Megrahi's guilt or innocence. It merely stated that Libya 'accepts responsibility for the actions of its officials'.

This was enough, however, to clear the way for the end of the punitive sanctions regime. On 12 September 2003, the UN Security Council formally voted to lift sanctions against Libya, with thirteen votes in favour and none against. Two countries, France and the US, abstained, the latter keeping its unilateral sanctions in place.

★

Many relatives, some MPs and a number of veterans of the first trials had been left feeling that the case against Megrahi was terribly weak. Megrahi and his supporters clung to the prospect of another appeal, and in 2003, the Scottish Criminal Cases Review Commission (SCCRC) agreed to consider whether there would be grounds for this. On 28 June 2007, the SCCRC, following four years' scrutiny of the evidence, found six grounds on which a miscarriage of justice might have occurred, and allowed a second appeal. Tony Kelly, the lawyer heading Megrahi's defence team, claimed that all findings of the original trials would be questioned, saying, 'There's not one aspect of the case that's been left untouched.' The SCCRC's report was 800 pages long, with 13 volumes of appendices, and was said to be the longest, most complicated and costliest in the commission's history.

The claims that emerged over the brief period for which the new trial was convened in 2009 prompted observers to comment that 'you couldn't make it up'. Since Zeist, Lord Fraser of Carmyllie, who as Lord Advocate of Scotland had initiated the trial, has publicly described Tony Gauci, on whom the prosecution had hinged, as 'not quite the full shilling' and 'an apple short of a picnic'.[17] Several witnesses had also been paid. Edwin Bollier's repeated claims over the years since the trial that the crucial timer evidence had been tampered with between his first and second sighting of it was confirmed in 2007 when a former employee came forward to corroborate what he had said.[18]

The appeal, unfortunately, was a short-lived affair. In August 2009, Megrahi was released from his Glasgow jail cell and allowed to return home to Libya, with the condition that he surrender his appeal. The decision was taken by the Scottish Justice Secretary, Kenny MacAskill, on compassionate grounds, given that medical reports suggested he was very close to death. Megrahi's release prompted a deluge of outrage. I myself wrote to MacAskill asking him not to release Megrahi, feeling that this was an unwise diplomatic step. The Libyans had given too little ground in many aspects of the relationship, including their continuing lack of co-operation with the Fletcher investigation, to justify such an enormous, dubious concession. Upon Megrahi's release, journalists expressed not only doubt at the morality of releasing a convicted terrorist, but also disbelief at a government line that even the most naïve and credulous member of the public would struggle to accept. The position of the UK Justice Secretary, Jack Straw, was that the Westminster government had nothing to do with this decision, which he said had been entirely a matter for Scotland. Megrahi had been let go not under the aegis of the Prisoner Transfer Agreement negotiated in 2007 by Tony Blair, but through the unilateral decision of the Scottish Government to grant him release on compassionate grounds.

Conveniently, this allowed Straw and Gordon Brown to claim total non-involvement. Few observers, however, bought this stance as anything other than an ill-conceived attempt to dodge the inevitable flak that would follow Megrahi's release. As Gareth Peirce (a highly regarded lawyer with expertise in miscarriage of justice cases) argued in a 6,500-word article in the *London Review of Books*, 'Only a simpleton could believe that Abdelbaset Ali al-Megrahi, convicted of responsibility for the Lockerbie bombing, was not recently returned to his home in Libya because it suited Britain.'[19] The idea that the British government had no involvement in so crucial a political decision seemed laughable, and the declaration of its own non-involvement, if anyone were to believe it, would anyway have served only to make it appear grossly negligent.

With a government saying so little, everyone was free to think the worst. Often, they were likely to be right. It is hard to escape the conclusion that Megrahi's release was the result of years of very secret negotiations, likely to have included some loaded conversations about British oil and business interests in Libya. Megrahi's freedom had been sought by Gaddafi since the day the verdict was passed, and it had undoubtedly come up again and again in the long-standing British–Libyan efforts to invigorate mutual trade.

The only aspect of the release that Brown was willing to comment on for several weeks was Megrahi's welcome home to Libya. Megrahi was greeted at Tripoli airport by a 'spontaneous demonstration'. This scene attracted a storm of opprobrium from the Prime Minister and most of the Western world, the public shocked by pictures of a convicted terrorist being cheered and welcomed by supporters brandishing Scottish flags. I warned Glenn Campbell of BBC Scotland, two weeks before Megrahi's return, that this would happen. Why did none of the leadership at either Westminster or Holyrood seek a written assurance that there would be no reception for Megrahi on his return to Tripoli?

To those who knew the case and knew Libya, the reaction to Megrahi's return home was not surprising. The scene, in fact, enshrined a number of key truths about the whole situation. Libya and Gaddafi had held consistently that Megrahi was innocent and viewed his return home as a diplomatic triumph, after years of protesting the Camp Zeist verdict. Secondly, in Gaddafi's eyes, this was a most under-stated and modest affair – he had not attended personally, and the 'spontaneous' demonstrators, undoubtedly organised by the regime, numbered in the low hundreds. For Libya this was subtlety, for Western observers it was shocking insensitivity, but for Brown it was a gift, as he had now found an unambivalent aspect of the Lockerbie case on which he could speak out publicly without getting himself into trouble.

The furore did not stop at Lockerbie. The press had smelt blood on the issue and laid open to scrutiny every aspect of the British relationship with

Libya. The ensuing revelations were interesting, to say the least. Perhaps the most shocking and saddening was the news that the Northern Ireland police had participated in police training in Libya, not only strengthening the muscle of a dictatorial state, but providing assistance to the country that had delivered shiploads of explosives used in some of the IRA's deadliest attacks. Somebody here certainly made the wrong decision. It also emerged that back in 2006, the Foreign Office had given the Libyans a secret guarantee that Britain would not be asking for PC Yvonne Fletcher's killer to be tried in Britain.

At the same time, the blanket media outrage manufactured over every aspect of the relationship in the wake of Megrahi's release seemed excessive. The tabloids even shouted against the NHS helping to train Libyan doctors, but were unsurprisingly unable to explain very convincingly why this should be a problem. The oil trade between our countries was hysterically and repeatedly denounced as morally bankrupt, but few commentators gave thought to the tricky problem of where, if anywhere, we might find a nicer country from which to purchase this rather important commodity. I fully concur that handing Megrahi over to further our oil interests would be repugnant, if that was what was done, but I do not support the vague position, difficult to defend, that any oil trade with Libya is evil. Those who wish to criticise oil deals must also engage with the reality that safe oil sources are a pillar of national security, and with the unpleasant fact that ensuring stable supplies is one of the greatest challenges that governments face.

Perhaps the most repellent aspect of the whole situation, however, was the convenient disappearance of the potential political disaster that was Megrahi's appeal. Megrahi's release on compassionate grounds caused the British and US governments the direst political embarrassment, so one can only imagine the outrage that would have followed an acquittal. It was clear that this was something both the Scottish and the British governments wished to avoid at all costs. For the many victims' families who saw this appeal as a rare chance to get more information into the public domain, it was a tragedy that the prospect of an appeal was fading away. Robert Black, Jim Swire, Archbishop Desmond Tutu, Father Pat Keegans (Lockerbie parish priest at the time of the bombing), *Private Eye* editor Ian Hislop, former MP Teddy Taylor and a number of other luminaries all signed an open letter to the UN urging them to conduct a public inquiry so that the families could at least see the evidence painstakingly compiled for the appeal. Megrahi himself clearly felt the pain of this sacrifice, as he and Tony Kelly took the step of publishing a 298-page dossier of documents on the internet, doing what they could to clear his name before his imminent death.

★

Delving into the events of Lockerbie has left me feeling angry. Angry that so many close and intelligent observers of what went on have concluded that the trial of Megrahi and Fhimah has stained our judicial system, perhaps indelibly. Angry when I heard Jim Swire say that his country's justice system is incapable of achieving independence from international politics in order to produce the truth. And above all, angry because I believe that our own integrity must be the foundation of our dealings with foreign regimes. How much more difficult will it be for me and my colleagues to ask Libya to co-operate in the case of Yvonne Fletcher when this cynical episode lies behind us? Gaddafi has offered up two of his agents, paid a whacking great sum of cash and bought his way back into the international system, meanwhile suspecting strongly, as many of us do, that the real perpetrators are still out there. This record is not honourable, and I hope that the next government will provide for the relatives of the Lockerbie victims what they have requested from every British Prime Minister since 1988: a full, public, impartial inquiry into the events at Lockerbie and the handling of the investigation, and, as far as can be achieved, a putting to bed of the many competing theories about who was responsible. Such an inquiry could acknowledge the difficulties involved in teasing out twenty-year-old links between shady terrorist organisations and their sponsors, and could admit that a final identification of the bomber may be out of its reach. What an inquiry could do, however, is finally to put all the evidence on the table for families to see, and to make it clear where, when and to what extent our institutions – be it the police, the law, Westminster or Holyrood – failed British citizens desperate to find out why their relatives died. I asked Gordon Brown for a public inquiry at Prime Minister's Questions, but, avoiding responsibility, he said it was for the Scottish Parliament to decide.

For Colonel Gaddafi, the events surrounding Lockerbie were transformational. He experienced a new degree of ostracism, even for a regime that had been vigorously sanctioned and bombed throughout the entire decade of the 1980s. Times were changing, however – the new threat of Islamic fundamentalism had struck fear into his heart, the economic prospects of full engagement with the West were growing more attractive, and disillusionment with his Arab brother states had festered. All of this fed into his decision to allow the trial of Megrahi and Fhimah to go ahead, and to do what was necessary to put Lockerbie behind him. Anger clearly remains – Gaddafi and, it seems, many Libyans see the Lockerbie trials as a grave injustice – but a sea change had begun, and a smoother era for Libya, Britain and the West had commenced. Despite his awesome range of lunatic peccadilloes and his bizarre diplomatic history, Gaddafi had this time acted with startling rationality, taking the steps that would best protect his own power.

# 9

# A GADDAFI FOR OUR TIMES

The world has changed radically and drastically. The methods and ideas should change, and, being a revolutionary and progressive man, I have followed this movement.

Colonel Gaddafi, 1999

It was 2004, and Tony Blair's government was struggling in the wake of an unpopular and bloody invasion of Iraq, justified to the British people by an increasingly elusive set of weapons of mass destruction (WMD). Good news stories were few and far between, but one of them, surprisingly, was Libya, which had recently announced with great fanfare that it would surrender its own WMD. Libya was now an Arab state in which Blair could claim a real triumph, a rare regional victory. So, that March, he took the enormous symbolic step of making an official visit to the country, where no British Prime Minister had set foot since Gaddafi's 1969 coup. The prime ministerial team of advisors were beset by dreadful anxiety in the lead-up to the meeting: would the Colonel keep the Prime Minister waiting for hours, humiliating the British delegation? Would he turn up at all? If he did, would he bestow the traditional Bedouin greeting of a kiss to both cheeks? Any such kiss would be dynamite in the ruthless hands of the British tabloids. Would Gaddafi keep to the agreed script, or would he venture into one of his tirades on neo-colonialism or the evils of Israel?

In the event, the meeting went off without a hitch. Blair was delivered safely to a prompt and disciplined meeting with Gaddafi. The two sat on plastic chairs in a dusty canvas tent, surrounded by grazing camels, and conversed for an hour on topics of mutual interest. No dangerous kisses were exchanged. Blair's four-hour stopover in Libya had been a success, and in its wake Britain's relations with Libya were dramatically invigorated.

This was an historically unprecedented diplomatic makeover, and Blair was not alone in accepting a penitent Gaddafi back into the fold. He was, however, ahead of the pack. In October 2009, I met with Mike O'Brien, now a minister in the Department of Health but back in 2002 the Foreign Office minister responsible for responding to the initial overtures from Gaddafi. O'Brien's pride in reopening relations with Libya was very clear. It was his view that this was a coup for British diplomacy and for the Foreign Office. O'Brien told me of the British–Libyan negotiations over rapprochement:

> The Americans thought it was an entirely pointless exercise. We took the view that it could produce beneficial effects . . . It was a calculated risk . . . We had the support of the Foreign Office, and there were a lot of benefits for us. Remember, at this stage, we did believe Saddam Hussein had WMD – we were also being briefed that Gaddafi was doing the same, to a lesser extent, though arguably it turned out to be to a greater extent. We secured a lot of information . . . Our MI6 people did a tremendous job and the Foreign Office deserves a lot of credit . . . The Americans were absolutely stunned by this. This was a stunning achievement for the UK, which produced a very unexpected political change in Libya.

O'Brien and the Foreign Office had set in motion the process by which the demonic dictator of the 1980s morphed into a kind of a new model for rogue states seeking renovation. This was a result of mutual need. The West had much to gain from better access to Libyan oil, and also from the rebuilding of a successful, peaceful relationship with an Arab nation. Gaddafi, in turn, needed to secure his grip on Libya in changing times. Engagement with the United States, Britain and Europe meant more oil money and the chance to satisfy the demands of a new generation in Libya that was crying out for jobs and education. It also meant some very powerful help with one of his most pressing problems: the rise of Islamic fundamentalism.

In 2006, the pop group Asian Dub Foundation staged a rock opera about Gaddafi, called *Gaddafi: A Living Myth*. In it, Blair was shown receiving an enormous cheque from the Colonel. This is just one, albeit rather unusual, example of the flak Blair received for his reinvigoration of the Libyan relationship. Many observers declared it immoral to meet with Gaddafi, citing the sufferings of the Lockerbie victims, the murder of Yvonne Fletcher and the domestic excesses of the Libyan regime. Libyans, too, expressed discomfort. Sir Oliver Miles quotes a Libyan journalist who wrote of Blair's 'savage, vicious, bloodthirsty smiles in front of the cameras as he clings his claw in the Arab flesh' on the occasion of his second Libyan visit in 2007.[1] For my part, I generally find relatively little to commend Blair on, but here I think he took a courageous and creative diplomatic step. We cannot realistically ignore the potential of Libya as a friendly, oil-rich state that is but a three-hour flight from Heathrow, and it is to be hoped that we will continue to develop a profitable, mutually beneficial and honest relationship.

★

Gaddafi's search for respectability began much earlier than is commonly realised, starting from the end of the 1980s. The US bombing of Tripoli in 1986 had been a sobering moment, showing him that his enemies would no longer be content to play a role in keeping his oil industry alive while he covertly sponsored horrific acts of terror and caused endless trouble in Africa. British relations were in tatters as well, after Yvonne Fletcher's murder in 1984 and as a result of ongoing sponsorship of the IRA throughout the 1980s. Libya had been enmeshed in war with Chad between 1978 and 1987, in which both France and the US supported the other side. The conflict in Chad had humiliated the Libyans deeply, exposing their army as a massively expensive and massively incompetent force, defeated time and again by one of the world's poorest nations. Neighbouring rulers in Africa and the Arab world no longer had much time for Gaddafi, who had repeatedly proved himself to be duplicitous, untrustworthy and dangerously unpredictable. The export of the Libyan revolution and the search for Arab or African unity had proved fruitless, and there was little appetite at home for the continuation of revolutionary experiments with foreign policy.

The year 1991 brought the first US invasion of Iraq, an event which many claim frightened Gaddafi. The parallels between him and Saddam Hussein were uncomfortably close: both dictators unpopular with the West, both ruling over territory exceptionally well endowed with oil, and both with few friends in the world. Gaddafi felt exposed, an easy target should George Bush seek to replicate the relatively quick and successful first Iraq War in Libya – in fact Libya was a much more long-standing enemy of the Americans than Iraq, which the US had supported in its war against Iran during the 1980s.

Like all dictators, Gaddafi's one overarching imperative is the need to maintain his grip on power. At the end of the 1980s and into the 1990s, it became clear that friendship with the powerful nations of the West would be essential in achieving this. In the context of the economic sanctions imposed after Libya was accused of sponsoring the attack on Pan Am Flight 103, life became more difficult for Libyans, creating the ideal conditions for shadowy opposition forces to prosper, and ratcheting up the Colonel's not insignificant or unjustified fear of revolt or assassination. The mid-1990s saw increasing unrest in Libya, with a major coup attempt in 1993 and reports of serious riots in 1995. Robert Fisk wrote in *The Independent*, 'Certainly, Colonel Gaddafi – once one of the most honoured nationalist revolutionaries – is worried about a real revolution, that of the growing Islamist movement which opposes his deeply corrupt regime.'[2]

Enemies from the ranks of Islamic fundamentalists were something of a novelty to many of us in the West as they emerged during the 1990s. Gaddafi, however, had been grappling with them for years. His crusade against a range of Islamic organisations was unambiguously successful: leaders were harassed and imprisoned, even publicly hanged, so that most groups were fragile, disparate and forced abroad. They kept cropping up, though, particularly as al-Qaeda gained in power and influence and jihadist groups mushroomed worldwide. The Libyan Islamic Fighting Group and other similar factions caused considerable unrest throughout the 1990s, including at least one assassination attempt against Gaddafi. In the years following 9/11, closer relations with the West could offer the Colonel powerful allies in his continuing mission to eradicate fundamentalism in Libya, and more money with which to pursue it.

The prospect of more money was tantalising. While the Lockerbie furore had sidelined Libya in the international oil industry during the 1990s, oil prices had shot up. The Libyans, barred from buying and selling essential new technology, were increasingly left with rusty, superseded infrastructure that meant they were very far indeed from achieving the full financial potential of their oil reserves. There was a drastic need for international expertise and technology to raise and expand oil production.

Money would also be important in finding ways to look after the younger generation in Libya, who are, of course, the segment of the population most likely to foment political challenges. Here in Britain we struggle to think of ways to plan for the ageing of our population, but in Libya the opposite is true. It is thought that half of the population there is aged under twenty. With a stagnant and declining economy and high unemployment, Libya's young men and women were profoundly under-occupied. In the late 1990s and early 2000s, unemployment was unofficially said to hover at around 30 per cent, and the situation for youth was likely to be even worse. A closed and isolated Libya offered little prospect of bettering this situation, whereas an open Libya would mean potential jobs with foreign companies, better access to foreign universities and more opportunities to lift employability through learning English.

Of course, rapprochement was not just about Libya. It made little sense to anyone for one of the world's richest and least exploited sources of oil to be locked permanently out of the world economy. In the early 2000s, three quarters of Libyan oil territory remained unexplored. As well as bountiful oil, the Libyan interior was known to offer enormous reserves of natural gas, which had barely begun to be exploited. Oil company executives clamoured for action on Libya, so that American, British and European companies could buy into the enormous potential profits on offer. While the relatives' groups formed around the Lockerbie and the UTA bombings and other atrocities linked to Libya were powerful, the business community in most countries pushed politicians hard to respond positively to Libyan overtures.

The post–Cold War landscape was also an entirely different geo-political terrain. Gaddafi, Blair and Bush now shared a common enemy: Islamic fundamentalism. The chance to secure an ally in north Africa, whence many of al-Qaeda's most powerful lieutenants were emerging, was not to be scoffed at. Gaddafi would benefit from Western support in his battle against the forces of fundamentalism, but so too would his new friends in Britain, the US and Europe.

★

Libya certainly had some powerful motives to reconnect with the West. What is notable about the period from the mid-1990s is just how all-encompassing its efforts to restore relations were. On every significant issue, the Libyans stepped forward to take solid action to repair relations and pave the way for future co-operation. This was a policy to which the Libyans were committed, and it was obvious to all involved that it had the strong support of Gaddafi. This is not to say that the new Gaddafi was an angel – his rhetoric was still aggressive and unpredictable, and the Libyans continued to be linked to some shady incidents (of which more below). But when it came to the substance of its Western relationships, it seemed that Libya could now be trusted to stick to its word, and that its desire for peaceful and productive interactions was genuine.

The most painful and pressing issue, of course, was Lockerbie. As Chapter 8 discussed, sanctions over its involvement in the bombing of Pan Am Flight 103 had isolated Libya between 1992 and 1999. Encouraged by Saudi, South African and Egyptian diplomacy, Gaddafi handed over the two Libyan suspects in the bombing for an international trial to be held in the Netherlands. When they were convicted, he signed a statement broadly indicating that Libya accepted the court's verdict, and agreed to the payment of sizeable sums in compensation to the victims' families. Libya paid $10 million for each victim, $4 million when United Nations sanctions were lifted, $4 million when US sanctions were lifted, and $2 million when Libya was removed from the American list of states sponsoring terrorism. Many victims' families chose to accept this as an appropriate resolution to the Lockerbie tragedy, and the compensation paved the way for the full restoration of diplomatic relations with the US. The final payment was made in 2009, and as a result the Libyans welcomed the first US ambassador to Tripoli for thirty-six years. For the Libyans, this was seen as a price well worth paying. Indeed, it was suggested that just a few months of economic boom following re-engagement with the US would cover the cost of the compensation payments.

In 2008, Gaddafi declared to the world that 'there will be no more wars, raids or acts of terrorism'.[3] This represented the culmination of a decade of effort (admittedly interspersed with the occasional apparent relapse) to distance Libya from its notorious past. Back in December 1991, Gaddafi had announced that Libya would sever all relations with terrorist organisations. Aid to the IRA ceased early in the 1990s, and in 1993 Libya provided the British government with vital intelligence on its connection to the IRA. In the same year, Gaddafi expelled the notoriously violent and cruel Palestinian terrorist Abu Nidal from Libya, where he had made a comfortable home since 1985.

To smooth things over with Britain, Gaddafi agreed in July 1999 that Libya would take 'general responsibility' for the murder of PC Yvonne Fletcher and paid £250,000 compensation to her family. This paved the way for the resumption of diplomatic relations with Britain, suspended since the murder fifteen years before. Sir Richard Dalton was dispatched to Tripoli as the first British ambassador since Sir Oliver Miles left back in 1984. Dalton told me of arriving in a Libya that did not quite know what to do with a British embassy. In the early months of his residence, a small travel agency was opened outside the embassy, which no-one was ever seen to use. By this rather unsubtle means, the Libyans ensured that they kept an eye on the unknown quantity that was the new ambassador and his staff.

From the early 2000s, the British Foreign Office had begun to believe that Gaddafi might be amenable to further rapprochement. His fear of Islamic fundamentalism was growing, and economic circumstances were increasingly trying. According to Mike O'Brien, it was a difficult decision to make:

> A key question was, what were the UK's national interests? Did we want someone who would engage with the West or did we want to push him back? Our view was that, although there were many deep concerns about Libya, we were better to see if we could work with the regime in a way that would enmesh them productively. An additional factor was that Gaddafi had changed his foreign policy objectives. He was looking to Africa. The US thought this was pretty much a front, but we thought he was serious. Another key reason we thought he'd move on this was his desire to be the 'philosopher-king of Africa'. Particularly post-9/11 it became clear to him that the price of involvement with terrorist groups was high. We were clear that it was Africa where his interests lay.

O'Brien met Gaddafi in 2002, preparing the ground for the Blair visit in 2004. By 2007, when Tony Blair conducted his whirlwind farewell tour of Africa, things were on such a courteous footing that he and Cherie paid a second visit to Gaddafi, with whom he told the media he was now on first-name terms.

Since this time, Gaddafi has not only moved away from sponsoring terrorism against Israel, he has also toned down his rhetoric considerably. In 2009, he shocked those familiar with his long history of anti-Israeli fervour by writing an editorial in the *New York Times* calling for 'a just and lasting peace between Israel and the Palestinians' and the formation of a shared state called 'Isratine', as well as declaring that 'the Jewish people want and deserve their homeland'.[4] He also promised that Libya would embrace the return of any Libyan Jews who might wish to bring business skills and investment with them. It was doubtful that any of the world's Jewish population would be rushing to take up residence in Tripoli, but the statement was certainly light years from the rabid pronouncements of the past.

This new Gaddafi's statements on Palestine, while still idiosyncratic, are often positively placatory. This is partly, of course, because times have moved on, and most players in the conflict are now focused on finding a peaceful long-term solution. The extremist Gaddafi of earlier times would be hopelessly anachronistic. Yet Gaddafi has made strong and public efforts to move to a more internationally acceptable position, declaring in 1999 that Libya would in future deal exclusively with Yasser Arafat's Palestinian Authority, eschewing the more radical and violent groups with which it had dealt in the past. In 2001, Libya signed up to the Saudi-sponsored Arab League proposal for peace in the Middle East, agreed at the Beirut Conference that year. Gaddafi remains committed to the Palestinians he has supported for so long – in 2009 he was reported to be sending humanitarian aid to the citizens of the Gaza Strip via unapproved, non-official channels – but the fact remains that he has seemed broadly willing to toe the line on this issue.

Gaddafi also extended the olive branch to many fellow leaders in Europe. In contrast to the Americans, who were still held back by an extensive regime of bilateral sanctions, Europe had maintained a very strong economic presence in Libya throughout the years of its diplomatic isolation. For every year between 1991 and 2004, Libya was the biggest source of oil for both Germany and Italy. Eighty-five percent of Libyan exports went to Europe during the 1990s. The economic relationship of mutual dependence had easily survived Libya's isolation over Lockerbie, but it was clear that the potential was there really to invigorate economic partnerships, should some troubling political hurdles be overcome.

For France, the bombing of UTA Flight 772 was the major stumbling block to better relations (see Chapter 3). As with Lockerbie, the case of PC Fletcher and the Berlin disco bombing, the UTA affair needed to be settled before Gaddafi could comfortably deal with the French. In 2003, therefore, Libya issued a carefully worded statement that 'accepted responsibility for the actions of its officials', without explicitly agreeing to their guilt. In 2004, the Gaddafi International Foundation for Charity Associations paid compensation of $1 million for each of the 170 victims.

This was sufficient to put French relations back on track. After decades of intense political hostility, including on-again, off-again war against the French in Chad, Gaddafi made a historic visit to Paris in December 2007. The new French President, Nicolas Sarkozy, signed a deal to sell Libya twenty-one Airbus planes, and the two countries agreed on areas of peaceful nuclear co-operation. The French would work with the Libyans to develop nuclear reactors for energy, as well as a desalination plant to address Libya's water security.

Sarkozy was virulently criticised in France for hosting Gaddafi. His own human rights minister made a dramatic statement to the press, declaring, 'Our country is not a doormat on which a leader can wipe off the blood of his crimes.'[5] The French press was also abuzz with rumours as to the true nature of the nuclear deal struck between the two nations, and questioned the responsibility of sharing cutting-edge nuclear technology with Libya. Journalists were cruel: the satirical weekly Le Canard Enchaîné wrote that Gaddafi had

> remade himself as a virgin. He's no longer a terrorist at all. Pardoned: the attack on the Boeing over Lockerbie and on a DC-10 blown up over the desert of Ténéré. Forgotten: the attempts to make weapons of mass destruction, notably nuclear ones. Ended: the status as a refuge for criminals and terrorists that gave Tripoli its charm. Even from the psychiatric point of view, things are going better: the dangerous paranoid, the angry wild man has become a delectable companion who's perfectly urbane. To take tea with him is pure happiness.[6]

Notwithstanding such taunts from his critics, Sarkozy had made the pragmatic decision that working with rather than against a reformed, wealthy Libya was the only realistic option. Many of his colleagues across Europe were to follow. It is my hope, and I imagine Sarkozy's as well, that principled engagement with Libya will have more of an effect than criticism from a somewhat barren moral high ground.

Italy was the first of the Western nations to announce a full restoration of diplomatic relations with Libya, in July 1998. Economic collaboration with Italy, always one of Libya's chief import and export markets, has since grown considerably, while the political relationship has also been closer than ever before. In August 2008, the Italian Prime Minister, Silvio Berlusconi, flew to Benghazi to publicly apologise for Libyan suffering under Italian colonisation and to commit to the payment of £3 billion compensation for the wrongs of the colonial era. In return, Italy was guaranteed a reliable source of gas and a set of lucrative infrastructure contracts. Italian–Libyan ties only grow closer: the Libya Energy Fund in 2009 announced plans to buy a 10 per cent stake in the Italian national oil company, Eni.

The closeness of the Italians and the Libyans is likely to benefit both, but problems have also arisen. In July 2009, I objected in Parliament to the aid package agreed as part of this rapprochement. The Italians are now building new roads and a railway from Tripoli to Benghazi, aid that was given on the condition that it would be Italian companies which delivered the work. This flies in the face of all the progress made in recent years against so-called 'tied aid', in which donor countries cynically ensure that they benefit as much as the recipients of their largesse, and in which the recipient is unable freely to choose the cheapest and best service provider. It is also blatantly against the EU's own rules. Libya is wealthy, but its development needs are great. Just like any other developing economy, it should not be subject to exploitation by more powerful nations.

Italy and Libya are also linked in that they are respectively the destination and the embarkation point of thousands of doomed, desperate journeys undertaken each year by sub-Saharan African migrants. In 2008 the UN High Commission for Refugees (UNHCR) estimated there were 30,000 refugees in Libya. The waiting time for an appointment at UNHCR in Tripoli was eight months. The Italians and the EU need desperately to gain control over this flow of migration. This has given Gaddafi a great deal of leverage with Italy, which he has used very effectively. Cynics have even suggested that the dramatic relaxation in 2002 of migration regulations for African workers looking to enter Libya was enacted with an eye to increasing this leverage. Whereas in the past Libya mainly turned a blind eye to the migration flows out of Tripoli into Italy, the reformed Gaddafi has agreed to take on a much more active role. Libya now allows joint Italian–Libyan patrols in the waters between Tripoli and the Italian island of Lampedusa, and accepts the return of the migrants intercepted by the patrols.

The process by which this co-operation over migration has been achieved has not been pretty. Many observers were horrified: the UN's high commissioner for refugees rightly protested the dumping in Libyan prisons of genuine refugees from political persecution, Berlusconi unashamedly described returned migrants as lucky, because Italian conditions for refugees were like concentration camps, and Gaddafi declared to the world that it is impossible for an African to be a political refugee by dint of his or her racial characteristics: 'The Africans do not have problems of political asylum. People who live in the bush [or] the desert don't have political problems . . . [They] don't have a political identity; they don't even have a personal identity.'[7]

It is important, however, to look past the populist, racist overtones of these negotiations. The point remains that Libya is a vital stage in the struggle to regulate migration from Africa into Europe. Hundreds die each year in ramshackle boats, after paying exorbitant sums to exploitative traffickers, and only a few find what they want and need in Europe. Taking meaningful action to improve the situation for host and source nations caught up in the often tragic flow of international migration requires that Libya be part of discussions. We might not like what Gaddafi says, but I see it as positive that he is now part of the conversation. It is my opinion that a revitalised, reintegrated Libya offers us a really important opportunity to do something positive about the chaotic, destructive human traffic between Europe and Africa. I sponsored a debate to this effect in Parliament in June 2009, in which I drew the attention of our Foreign Office and its ministers to Libya's new role in controlling European migration. At present, the UK gives no aid to Libya whatsoever, and it is my feeling that we need to do better. We must work with the Libyans to give them encouragement and assistance to treat African migrants fairly and humanely, and to help Libya find a way to do something positive for the desperate economic migrants landing on its doorstep in increasing numbers.

For the Italians, increasing co-operation with Gaddafi on issues of really vital national interest has brought a certain set of diplomatic obligations.

We can only wonder how Berlusconi feels about the need to continue the exchange of visits with Gaddafi. Gaddafi made a visit to Rome in June 2009, which as usual grabbed the front pages of the world's newspapers. Journalists delighted in the usual colourful entourage of female bodyguards, the Bedouin tent he pitched in hotel grounds and his determination to make his hosts uncomfortable: pinned to his Bedouin robe was a large picture of Omar Mukhtar, the hero of the Libyan resistance who was publicly hanged by the Italians in 1931. The press also relished the delicious irony of Gaddafi's request to address Italian women on women's rights, at a time when Berlusconi was facing down numerous sex scandals: notably, one cartoonist depicted an uncomfortable Berlusconi shrinking in the face of a berobed Gaddafi declaring, 'I come to liberate your women!'

In April 2004, Gaddafi launched another of his well-publicised visits. This one was to Brussels, on an official trip to the EU. He was welcomed personally to Brussels airport by the then president of the European Commission, Romano Prodi. Two hundred demonstrators from an obscure NGO called the Arab African Immigrant Child Support Committee sang, danced and waved his portrait in welcome, while fifty dissidents shouted that Gaddafi was a wolf in sheep's clothing and a terrorist. The press mainly reported on his outfit – a red fez, grey-green robes – and on the ruckus at the airport, but this meeting signalled that Gaddafi was now to be taken seriously by the EU. Announcements were made heralding increased co-operation in culture, migration and economic reform. Although the EU had suspended economic sanctions back in 1999, these were fully lifted in 2004, removing all impediments to co-operation. In 2009, negotiations were proceeding on setting up a Libya–EU framework to improve mutual relations further.

Underlying this dry Euro-bureaucratic terminology is a genuine desire to bring the oil-rich Libyans as fully as possible into the European fold. As with the Italians, Gaddafi has great leverage with the EU, stemming from his important role in controlling migration into Europe, and this, together with his important economic role in the region, has guaranteed him a sympathetic reception in the corridors of Brussels. Gaddafi has taken a strong interest in the emergence of the EU as a power bloc, seems to enjoy dealing with it and has often referred to his desire to model the African Union on it.

European relations, however, had to surmount the considerable hurdle of Libya's detention, imprisonment and alleged torture of five Bulgarian nurses and a Palestinian doctor. Bulgarian health workers have a long history in Libya, where they were historically able to earn much higher salaries than at home, and generally led peaceful and productive lives tending to their Libyan patients. In 1999, this mutually beneficial exchange was abruptly terminated. Libya arrested the six medics and accused them of deliberately infecting more than 400 children at the El Fatih Children's Hospital in Benghazi with HIV. The five nurses and the doctor were seized from the hospital and blindfolded, gagged, beaten and imprisoned. In 2006 they were condemned to death by firing squad. All six reported being tortured in Libyan prisons while held in custody for eight years. It was reported in *The Guardian* that confessions were obtained from three of the accused 'after an interrogation process in which they were stripped, beaten, attacked by dogs, electrocuted and, in at least one case, sexually assaulted with a police baton'.[8]

The detention of the doctor and nurses was a disturbing incident, stirring up memories of Libya's darker days and drawing international attention to the fact that while Libya's outward face had become more acceptable, internally it was still a closed and oppressive society. The international medical community concurred that the mass epidemic of HIV/AIDS in the children's hospital was a result not of crazed, child-killing health professionals, but of appalling hygiene practices in the Libyan health system. The Libyan leadership, however, was unwilling to publicise the poor condition of the nation's health service, and instead pinned the blame on vulnerable foreigners, always an easy target in Libyan politics. Gaddafi even informed an outraged Libyan public that the CIA or Mossad of Israel had specially prepared a strain of killer virus and sent it to the medical staff to use in an experiment on Libyan children.

Yet the issue was less of a hurdle for Libya than might have been expected. Indeed, it showed how profound Gaddafi's rehabilitation had been since the late 1990s. Bulgaria joined the EU in 2007, and immediately the diplomatic pressure on Libya to release its nationals escalated. Europe, however, was highly reluctant to see years of rapprochement unravel and invested serious diplomatic effort into resolving the crisis. In July 2007, a deal was reached with the EU under which the six medics were extradited to Bulgaria (where, to protests from Libya, they were pardoned on their arrival at Sofia airport). Rumours abounded as to what Libya received in return, including the suggestion that the French nuclear co-operation deal signed in 2007 was a reward for releasing the doctor and nurses. It also was reported in the world media that the sale of French anti-tank missiles to Libya had been part of the deal. In a *Newsweek* interview, Saif al-Islam Gaddafi referred to 'secret accords' that he 'couldn't really talk about'.[9] At the very least, Libya was given hundreds of millions of dollars to use for compensation payments to the infected children's families, and similar sums to pay for improvements to the nation's hospitals.

Rather than being excoriated for the blatant victimisation of the nurses and doctor, Gaddafi was hailed for his keenness to engage with Europe. Praise was showered on him from on high: the European commissioner for external relations, Benita Ferrero-Waldner, declared that after the medics were released, 'we open a new page in relations with Libya'.[10] Much of the publicity around the release focused on the role of Cécilia Sarkozy, the then wife of the newly elected French President, Nicolas Sarkozy. It was said that Gaddafi had found Mrs Sarkozy irresistible. Whatever the truth, Gaddafi had negotiated hard and well, and Libya emerged from this unsavoury episode with a strengthened rather than a weakened relationship with Europe.

★

Compared to Europe, where most countries were engaged with the Libyans in some way even during the mid-1990s, the US has had a tougher time rebuilding bridges with Libya. Its leadership had spent decades presenting Libya to its populace as Public Enemy No. 1, it had imposed an extensive bilateral sanctions regime, and the families of the Lockerbie victims had become a vocal and effective group of political lobbyists.

Gaddafi's efforts to remedy the poor state of Libya's American relationship began as far back as the first Gulf War in 1991, when, to the world's surprise, he condemned the Iraqis for invading Kuwait. The Libya expert George Joffé suggests that Gaddafi even contemplated sending Libyan soldiers to join the American–led coalition force, but was advised against this by those close to him.[11] Gaddafi was still far from being an acceptable partner for alliance with the US, even in the eyes of his own advisors.

In 2000, the Secretary of State, Madeleine Albright, announced that the US would no longer refer to 'rogue states' but to 'countries of concern', suggesting the winds of change were gathering in regard to Libya. In September 2001, Gaddafi offered a ringing condemnation of the 9/11 attacks on the World Trade Center in New York and even volunteered to send donated Libyan blood for the survivors. He described the subsequent US invasion of Afghanistan as completely justified. This was a crucial moment in US history, and it also marked the point at which it became obvious to Gaddafi that he and the Americans now shared an enemy: the Islamic fundamentalists he had been working to suppress throughout most of his rule in Libya.

By 2003, the Libyans had made the decision to renounce their WMD, after years of negotiating with the British and the Americans (of which more below). Giving up their WMD ambitions brought instant reward. The first ever US Congressional delegation made an official visit to Libya in March 2004. Senator Joe Biden (today Barack Obama's Vice-President) attended a meeting of the General People's Congress and congratulated Libya for its determined efforts to re-enter the international community. The US and Libya re-established diplomatic relations, which had been suspended since 1980. In February 2004, the US lifted its ban on its citizens travelling to Libya. Travel restrictions had been a significant brake on the activities of US businesses in Libya, so this was a key step in normalising relations. In 2006, the US State Department removed Libya from its list of state sponsors of terrorism.

Compensation was a thorny issue, but this was a game the Libyans now knew how to play. Lockerbie was resolved by the staged payment of the final cheques due to victims' families. In a position of much greater influence than in the late 1990s, however, the Libyans would no longer allow compensation to be a one-way process. Taking heed of the success of relatives' groups in the West, Libyan victims formed an organisation called the Families of the American Aggression Victims' Society. This group called for compensation for those whose relatives had died in the 1986 bombing of Tripoli. It was finally agreed that they would be paid from a joint fund established in 2008 to settle all compensation claims between the two countries once and for all (the US–Libya Comprehensive Claims Settlement Agreement). The joint fund would also cover the victims of the 1986 bombing of the Berlin disco La Belle. This was a politically difficult step for the Americans to take, given the popularity of President Reagan's attack on Libya and of his generally militaristic presidency. It indicated the Americans' determination to wrap up painful decades of wrangling with the Libyans over a mutually difficult past.

By 2008, all outstanding compensation claims had apparently been resolved (although there was some ambiguity about how and when payments were to be made into the joint fund) and ambassadors had taken up postings in Tripoli and in Washington. The restoration of full relations was commemorated by the visit to Libya on 5 September 2008 of the US Secretary of State, Condoleezza Rice. Rice was the most senior American politician to visit Libya since Vice-President Richard Nixon in 1957. As a prominent black woman leader, she had long attracted Gaddafi's interest. In 2007 he had proclaimed:

> I support my darling black African woman. I admire and am very proud
> of the way she leans back and gives orders to the Arab leaders . . . Leezza,
> Leezza, Leezza . . . I love her very much. I admire her and I'm proud of
> her because she's a black woman of African origin.[12]

The significance of Rice's presence in Libya was matched by the caution of her own statements to the media at the time: 'It is a historic moment and it is one that has come after a lot of difficulty and the suffering of many people that will never be forgotten or assuaged, Americans in particular, for whom I am very concerned.'

Rice's successor, Hillary Clinton, and those who follow her in office will likely need to become accustomed to paying these unpredictable visits to Gaddafi's desert tent.

As relations improved, the US–Libya partnership quickly became extremely prosperous. In 2004, when the majority of US economic sanctions were lifted, foreign direct investment in Libya stood at $4 billion, six times as much as in 2003. US companies including Amerada Hess, ChevronTexaco and Occidental Petroleum rushed to take advantage of new opportunities in Libya, and the financial benefits for both sides will be immense.

★

Through the 1970s, 1980s and 1990s, Gaddafi alternately denied any nuclear ambitions or was belligerent about them: sometimes he said Libya merely wanted cleaner power and opposed nuclear war; at other times he terrified his various audiences by asserting the need for an 'Arab bomb' to match the Israeli nuclear capacity. The nations of the West were well aware, however, that Gaddafi had long pursued the development of nuclear and chemical weapons for Libya. Regular controversies had erupted: in the 1980s and 1990s, the Americans accused Libya of using an underground facility at Rabta and an industrial complex in Tarhuna to move towards a chemical weapons capability. It was widely reported that the Libyans had sought out sources of nuclear technology wherever they could find them ever since Gaddafi took power. France, China, India, Argentina, Pakistan, Bulgaria, Yugoslavia, Japan and the Soviet Union were among the states reported to have been approached to sell technology and materials to the Libyans.

The Soviet Union did provide considerable assistance to Libya in its development of WMD, mainly under the guise of setting up a civil nuclear power programme. This stopped from the mid-1980s, however, as the Soviets under Mikhail Gorbachev began to express strong concern about proliferation. Evidence suggests that they were cautious about just what they sold to the Libyans, always keeping a keen eye on their own security and making sure that their erratic ally did not proceed too far down the road to a longed-for nuclear arsenal.

Indeed, most states with which Libya dealt tried to limit the extent of their nuclear trade, as evidence of Gaddafi's temperamental and erratic nature mounted. By the mid-1980s, there were in general far fewer states left in the world willing to co-operate with Gaddafi, as his experimentation with subversion and terror became more widely known. India, for example, is said to have agreed in 1977 to exchange peaceful nuclear expertise for oil at cut-price rates. New Delhi backed off quickly, however, letting the agreement lapse as it became increasingly clear that Gaddafi was also dealing with Pakistan.

Later in its nuclear career, Libya became a major customer of the Pakistani nuclear scientist Abdul Qadir Khan. A. Q. Khan was a unique character in twentieth-century history. He was termed the 'merchant of menace' by *Time* magazine but revered at home as father of a holy Islamic bomb. He was said to keep a jasmine bush outside his house in Islamabad trimmed into the shape of a mushroom cloud. As head of Pakistan's nuclear programme, he helped the nation to build the atom bomb – in 1998 five nuclear bombs were exploded underground, escalating a dangerous sub-continental arms race with neighbouring India.

From the early 1990s, Khan is alleged to have set up an illegal proliferation network selling nuclear technology all over the world. He was motivated both by financial gain and by the desire to see Muslim nations develop a nuclear capability. In 2004, he made a spectacular appearance on Pakistani television to admit to his nuclear smuggling network, but was quickly pardoned by President Musharraf.

Khan's connections with the Libyans were discovered to have been extensive. Libya bought gas centrifuge technology from the renegade scientist, and also paid for sets of instructions and for Pakistani nuclear expertise. Khan's network allowed an intensive reinvigoration of the Libyan nuclear programme from 1995, after years of relatively low-level activity. It was reported in the *Washington Times* that Libya admitted in 2003 to having spent $500 million on its nuclear weapons programme during the late 1990s.[13]

News of Libya's WMD capabilities was a surprise to many. The journalist Robert Fisk, for example, expressed his disbelief that Libya had been able to run any such programme. He wrote, 'The problem I have with the whole Gaddafi saga is that the Libya I know can scarcely repair a drain or install a working lavatory in a hotel.'[14] This touches on an important aspect of the decision to give up on Libya's nuclear ambitions. Put simply, it just wasn't working. Although there was always money to pay for nuclear equipment, the infrastructure and the scientists needed to build the weapons were absent. Even those willing to sell Gaddafi bits and pieces were not keen to sell him the whole package: relatively few parties in the international nuclear trade wanted to see Libya make fast progress in nuclear armament. Gaddafi tried hard to attract nuclear experts to Libya – offering huge salaries, free accommodation and numerous other perks to scientists from Arab nations – but it was difficult for him to attract the quantity and calibre of scientists needed to run a successful weapons programme. In 2003, when the historic announcement was made, the Libyans had spent millions of dollars over four decades, but still had not produced any weapons-grade uranium. Although Khan had given them the best chance yet to develop a fully functioning programme, nuclear warheads probably remained a distant dream. The kudos that resulted from surrendering the programme may have been an easy way out, an escape from the money-drain the nuclear programme had become.

Events in 2003 confirmed the wisdom of surrendering Libya's nuclear programme. Malaysia was caught early that year shipping nuclear technology to Gaddafi (a considerable scandal erupted there as it was discovered that a company headed by the son of the new Malaysian Prime Minister, Abdullah Badawi, had sold the parts to Libya). After Iraq was invaded on the grounds of its alleged production of WMD, the US was clearly unlikely to mend fences with Gaddafi until he took some major action in this area. The Libyans carefully avoided any suggestion, however, that George W. Bush's invasion of Iraq had had any influence on their decision, citing years of negotiations in the years leading up to the announcement.

Opinion remains violently divided as to whether the invasion of Iraq in 2003 had any impact on Gaddafi's decision to renounce Libya's WMD.

It is certainly clear that Gaddafi had been seeking respectability for many years before the Iraq War, that there were many lucrative rewards on offer, and that Libya was gaining little from its formidable arsenal. Yet those who dismiss Iraq entirely as a factor in Gaddafi's thinking are perhaps under-estimating a fundamental psychological truth of dictatorship: the dictator always lives in fear of losing power and ending up in the hands of the enemies lurking around his throne, of whom he is constantly, anxiously aware. According to my dissident friend Guma el-Gamaty, the fall of Saddam Hussein and his capture by the Americans was likely to have had a powerful impact on Gaddafi: 'When he saw those pictures of Saddam Hussein in a hole in the ground, this was the biggest influence on Gaddafi in the modern era. It persuaded him to change course, to realise if he didn't change course, he would have the same fate.'

In the end, it was Gaddafi's son Saif al-Islam who took much of the responsibility for the publicity surrounding the decision. He presented things in relatively bland terms: according to Saif, the decision was taken because Libya would be safer without nuclear weapons, and because the enormous expense of funding the programme could more rewardingly be channelled into Libyan development.

Years of backroom negotiations between Britain, Libya and the US had led to Libya's 2003 announcement, and this was perhaps the definitive moment at which Libya could be considered reintegrated into the world. The handing over of 11 tons of nuclear materials and folder after folder of detailed weapons designs was an enormous PR coup for all involved. The dire state of Arab relations with the West in the wake of the Iraqi invasion meant that an international success story in regard to an Arab nation was seized upon enthusiastically. This was an almost unprecedented event in world history: an entirely positive resolution of a thorny issue with an Arab state the West had long struggled with. It was regularly suggested that Libya's commitment to suspend all of its WMD production provided a model of peaceful resolution of a difficult issue that Iran, Syria and North Korea could profit from at some stage in the future. Libya's declaration was publicised with the greatest energy, with journalists happy to weigh in because, of course, Gaddafi sells newspapers. Ultimately, the surrender of nuclear weapons represented an important truth about Gaddafi: erratic and experimental though his rule has been, he is highly adaptable to the *esprit du temps*, clever in his ability to read the writing on the wall, always willing to take the action most likely to increase the security of his own position.

★

Tying up all the loose ends left over from Gaddafi's years of involvement with terrorism and handing over Libya's nuclear capability was an expensive and time-consuming business. In all, it took more than two decades for him to reach the position he occupies today, in part due to the maelstrom that hit Libya over the Lockerbie bombing. The rewards, however, have been considerable for both sides. US, European and British oil companies, travel agencies, service businesses and consultancies have rapidly moved in to capitalise on what is widely known to be one of the most lucrative and least exploited markets on the international scene. British oil companies have been among those agreeing potentially highly lucrative exploration deals. During Tony Blair's second Libyan visit in 2007, BP signed a natural gas contract worth $900 million. The return of BP to Libya after the nationalisation of its assets in 1971 was a truly historic moment, signalling the degree to which Gaddafi's regime is now regarded as a trustworthy, reliable partner.

I feel the greatest excitement about this revival of the Libyan economy, and am pushing hard for British businesses to be even more involved. This is a grand opportunity to help model Libya into a functioning, effective economy that will contribute enormously to the wellbeing of the wider region. British businesses, particularly consultancies, can contribute a great deal on the skills front, helping the Libyans to plan really effective, sustainable development. It is my hope and belief that the more modern infrastructure goes up, the more health and education are developed and the more the communications industry prospers, the more likely it is that Libya will begin to demand more open and accountable politics. The men and women of business can build links that are beyond what can be achieved by politicians and diplomats, because to do business means to share risk and to share reward in a really meaningful way.

I am not naïve, however. While I think past experience shows that Gaddafi is unlikely to jeopardise the safety and security of the business environment (in particular when it comes to oil), a future of rosy partnership between Libya and the West is certainly not guaranteed. Although he no longer seeks to be involved in war and terror abroad, it is clear that Gaddafi is still a wily strategist, unlikely to be a compliant friend to the West. Already, in the lead-up to his 2008 meeting with Condoleezza Rice, Saif Gaddafi told the press that Libya had chosen Russia as its strategic partner and gave interviews claiming that the Arab world was standing behind Russia in its conflict with Georgia that year. As always, Libya is wary of putting all of its eggs into one basket.

Libya is a weak state, with radically under-developed political structures. History shows it has been subject to rapid and arbitrary changes of direction ordered from on high. While Gaddafi has been consistent in his desire to re-engage with the West, it is still the case that foreign leaders must trust in his personal commitment to change, unsupported by any other social structures – there are no political parties, no transparent or powerful political processes, no independent judiciary or economic regulators. There will always be a certain element of risk involved.

Gaddafi is now generally a well-behaved dictator, at least in international relations. It is unlikely, however, that he will ever be easy to deal with. As usual, in the years following the restoration of relations, he has run hot and cold. In the lead-up to his historic meeting with Rice in 2008, he told journalists that 'it is not necessary for us to be friends with America. What is necessary is that relations are free of aggression, terrorism, wars and explosions' and described the Libyan relationship with the US as neither friendship nor enmity.[15] Alarmingly, in 2004 the Libyan Prime Minister, Shukri Ghanem, told BBC Radio 4 that the Libyans were not responsible for Lockerbie, profoundly destabilising the expensive truce over the issue that had taken years to negotiate. The statement was rescinded quickly, but it showed the ongoing unpredictability of Libyan behaviour.

Shadows of the Libya of old are still regularly to be seen. Dissidents

abroad report frequent harassment. Ashur Shamis, a founder member of
the National Front for the Salvation of Libya, reported in 2005 that his and
five others' names had been put on a website advertising a million-dollar
reward for their capture. He also said that in March 2001, a Libyan diplomat
in London had attempted to hit him with a metal object during a seminar
at the School of Oriental and African Studies.[16]

Gaddafi continues to find it particularly difficult to restrain himself when
it comes to the Saudi royal family. Without the generous assistance of
Saudi diplomats, it is doubtful that he would have been able to resolve the
Lockerbie situation. Yet Gaddafi has still continued regularly to hurl abuse
at the Saudis in major international forums. At an Arab League meeting in
2003 to discuss a response to the invasion of Iraq, he told Crown Prince
Abdullah of Saudi Arabia that the latter had made 'a deal with the devil' by
accommodating American troops in the first Gulf War. Abdullah angrily
rebuffed Gaddafi's comments.[17] The next year it was reported throughout
world media that Gaddafi, while going full throttle to convince the West
he had changed, had sponsored an attempt to assassinate the Saudi Crown
Prince. In March 2009, Gaddafi enlivened another Arab League summit
by calling Abdullah, now King, a 'British product'. *The Economist* reported
that the Libyan leader had 'mumbled insults at King Abdullah of Saudi
Arabia from behind his wraparound sunglasses'.[18] He was said by some
newspapers to have then stormed out and spent the afternoon of the Arab
League session taking a tour of an Islamic cultural museum. While the
rehabilitated Gaddafi of the 2000s is certainly a wholly different prospect
from the Gaddafi of old, he is still a lover of chaos, and will never be easy
to deal with.

# AFRICAN KING OF KINGS

Colonel Gaddafi famously has little time for ambassadors. Diplomats posted in Tripoli are unable to contact him, except via a formal note requesting an audience. Sir Richard Dalton told me that during his stint as British ambassador in Tripoli between 1999 and 2003 he came face to face with the Leader only rarely. On one of these unusual occasions, all of Tripoli's European ambassadors had received an urgent summons. As was customary, they were then kept waiting in an ante-room for several hours. Finally, Gaddafi entered. The urgent business for which they had been summoned, it turned out, was a lengthy lecture on the politics of European colonial possessions in Africa and elsewhere. The Spanish were castigated for Ceuta and Melilla, their Moroccan enclaves, the British for their remote South Atlantic island territory of St Helena. Gaddafi demanded of the diplomatic luminaries how on earth he could hold his head up in Africa while their governments insisted on retaining these vestiges of empire. I asked Dalton what he thought the purpose of such a meeting had been, and he replied, 'It's about his vanity, his view of himself as a great statesman in Africa playing to the gallery of the world.' In Gaddafi's eyes, Africa is his last-chance saloon, the one remaining forum in which he still sees an opportunity to become an internationally powerful statesman with a place in the history books. Few nations now want Libya involved in negotiating Palestine's future, and Gaddafi's Arab brothers have largely had enough of him. Therefore, the world now watches as he bestrides the stages of international forums as the champion of the peoples of Africa.

Many African states, struggling with poverty, war and environmental devastation, are only too happy to work with wealthy Libya, and many provide accommodating partners for cosy chats about the evils of the West. In August 2008, a group of 200 African kings and traditional rulers met to bestow the title of 'African King of Kings' on Gaddafi. Wearing a flowing, gold-embossed robe, Gaddafi accepted the title with a most regal air. The occasion emphasised the vast distance that has grown up between the Gaddafi of old – virulent hater of monarchs and monarchies, principled Arab revolutionary, ardent Nasserite – and 21st-century Gaddafi – master of compromise, 'king of kings', African leader.

Gaddafi's enthusiasm for Africa was evident even in the pre-Lockerbie era. At the end of the 1980s, he proposed a new unity agreement for north Africa. Unlike his previous history of wildly ambitious bilateral unions, this was to be a multilateral forum designed along the lines of the EU, an institution Gaddafi has always seemed to regard with a degree of awe and admiration. In Marrakesh in February 1989, Libya, Tunisia, Algeria, Morocco and Mauritania formed the Arab Maghreb Union (AMU). Its goals were to promote economic integration by reducing market barriers between the member states. A chief benefit was said to have been expanded shopping opportunities for Libyans in Tunisia, where they could now buy a bigger and cheaper range of the many consumer goods that had still not reached Libya. This was, unfortunately, about where it ended. The larger story of the AMU has been one of failure. The organisation now seems moribund, its successes have been few, and it has been profoundly destabilised by Libya's quixotic, belligerent and unpredictable behaviour, as well as by the intractable conflict over Western Sahara. It was not a particularly promising beginning to Gaddafi's career as regional institution builder.

Excluded from African organisations during the 1990s by Lockerbie sanctions, Gaddafi nonetheless made his presence felt as a player in the politics and economics of the continent, with characteristic verve. In 1994, for example, he declared his intention to revive Cecil Rhodes's dream of a railway across Africa, starting with a line connecting the nations of north Africa with Egypt. He said he was looking forward ultimately to being able to travel by train from Marrakesh to the South African Cape. This envisaged transcontinental railway would be a symbolic representation of the prosperous and powerful unity he dreamed of bringing to Africa.

Another achievement in Gaddafi's new quest to build regional institutions was the creation of the Community of Saharan and Sahelian States (CEN-SAD): rather unfortunately named given the frequent criticism of many of its members for their restriction of press freedom. CEN-SAD was established in Tripoli in February 1998, with the aim of freeing up regional trade. Sudan, Chad, Niger, Mali, Burkina Faso, Egypt, Tunisia, Algeria and Morocco were among its members, of which there are now twenty-eight. One of CEN-SAD's more adventurous steps was to eliminate the requirement for visas between members, resulting in a massive influx of sub-Saharan immigrants into Libya, which in the space of about a year played host to an influx of up to two million new migrants. In a small country with only six million people and very high unemployment, it was no surprise that this led to rioting and violence. In September 2000, riots in Tripoli and al-Zawiyya, 25 miles west of the capital, were said to have led to the deaths of hundreds of immigrants. Though reformed and reinvented, this was still Gaddafi, and he was not averse to conducting large-scale experiments on the Libyan people in the name of his current grand vision.

By 1998, having handed over the two Libyan suspects for trial in the Lockerbie case, Gaddafi was no longer *persona non grata* and could now really forge ahead with his African ambitions. That year, he attended an important summit of African and EU leaders. He arrived in Cairo complete with camels, glamorous bodyguards, Bedouin tents, dark sunglasses and an assortment of colourful traditional robes. Those present, many of whom were lobbying hard on his behalf for Libya's full restoration to international acceptability, were somewhat shocked by the belligerent approach he took, lecturing Europe on its capitalist decadence: 'We do not love conflicts. You love conflicts. You have bullfights. Capitalists have changed eggs and honey into shampoo. You use cocoa fat as cream for your hair. This is misuse of God's blessings.'[1]

Nevertheless, his reintegration into regional forums by now seemed inevitable. In July 2000, he was welcomed back into the Organisation of African Unity (OAU). The Algerian president, Abdulaziz Bouteflika, received him at the first summit he had attended in twenty years. The OAU was to become Gaddafi's new pet project, into which he injected characteristically large doses of money and energy. His lobbying contributed to the 1999 replacement of the OAU with an invigorated, strengthened organisation called the African Union (AU). The AU had its inaugural meeting in 2002 under the leadership of the then South African President, Thabo Mbeki. All African states were members except for Morocco (excluded due to its continuing occupation of Western Sahara).

The launch of the AU was not without its problems: in the lead-up, *The Independent* reported that Gaddafi and Mbeki were at odds over the location of the inaugural ceremony, and that Gaddafi had paid the subscriptions of a number of lapsed members in order to guarantee his influence. An unnamed diplomat from one of the poorer member states was quoted saying, 'We made a deal with Libya whereby we would support and vote for all resolutions proposed by Mr Gaddafi at OAU summits in exchange for his help.'[2] This, of course, is not light years away from the practices of Western states over the years, but it was a characteristically blunt Gaddafi approach.

In 2009, Gaddafi was elected to the position of chairman of the AU, a result which, to put it politely, was not universally welcomed. Previous leaders had been democrats, and many considered it odd to see Gaddafi leading an organisation that claimed the promotion of human rights and democracy among its aims. The *New York Times* pointed out, however, that contemporary Africa is devoid of some of the big personalities of the past. In the absence of a strong democratic leader, Libya's money at least offered the prospect that proposed schemes might get funded while Gaddafi was in charge. The paper quoted J. Stephen Morrison, an Africa expert, wondering whether regional leaders had thought, 'It may be goofy, but maybe something good will come out of this.'[3]

The most controversial aspect of Gaddafi's work in the AU has been his vigorously promoted plan for a 'United States of Africa' to rival the United States of America, starting with a merger of all the armies of Africa into one grand military force. He has also called for a euro-style single currency called the 'afro' and an African Union passport. His 2009 chairmanship has allowed him even more space to promote these aims. At the July AU meeting, there was unrest among members on a number of fronts: Gaddafi personally delivered an astonishing 25 per cent of all the speeches made at the meeting; Mbeki's successor, Jacob Zuma, observed that Gaddafi 'forgets that there is lunchtime and he forgets that people have to sleep'; and, tellingly, many members said they felt that the chair was pushing the United States of Africa too hard.[4]

It seems relatively unlikely that the United States of Africa will be forming any time soon. Nevertheless, Gaddafi has made some progress as chair. Despite his fondness for lengthy, wandering speechifying, the July meeting produced a draft document planning to simplify the AU's structure and to give it more power in defence, diplomacy and international trade. A stronger Africa is something that many want, and it may yet be that Gaddafi does manage to achieve some good.

★

Gaddafi is not just a regionalist, he is now also a peacemaker, pouring oil, so to speak, on the troubled waters of African conflicts. Robert Fisk, drawing attention to this remarkable transformation, wrote, 'And so international pariah Gaddafi has become international negotiator Gaddafi.'[5] In this new role as broker of African conflicts, Gaddafi has had some success. The cynic might suggest that this is partly because he has a unique perspective on such conflicts, as Libya has at some stage or other played a part in equipping most of them. The channelling of guns and money to virtually every non-state African actor of the 1980s allowed Gaddafi to amass a formidable first-hand knowledge of the history of war in the region, which must surely have stood him in good stead.

In April 1999, conflict between Uganda and Congo was resolved through negotiations led by Gaddafi, who then sent Libyan troops to police the peace agreement. Gaddafi was also congratulated by the AU in 2000 for his (albeit unsuccessful) efforts to resolve the Ethiopia–Eritrea border war, a conflict he had fuelled vigorously over the years. Gaddafi has also been involved in efforts to resolve the civil war in Sudan, a conflict that has claimed the lives of 200,000 people and which has led some to describe the Sudanese leader, Omar al-Bashir, as guilty of genocide against the people of the Darfur region. Gaddafi has had reasonably good relations with Bashir's regime (which has ruled Sudan since 1989) in the past. Peace talks in 2007 between the government and Sudanese rebels were held in Tripoli, a convenient venue because a number of the rebel groups were said to have offices there.

Gaddafi has stood firmly by Bashir's side, perhaps feeling a natural sympathy for the international bogeyman of the day. He has backed Bashir strongly against international pressure to bring him to trial for war crimes in the International Criminal Court (ICC). In the usual fiery fashion, he has labelled the ICC an instrument of Western imperialism, and has urged the West to back off and leave Africans alone to sort out their own problems. Sudan, it seems, has offered a convenient cause for Gaddafi to use in his campaign to present himself as the natural diplomatic leader of Africa and a champion of independence from the interfering machinations of the West.

For myself, I can understand some of Gaddafi's reservations about the ICC. He is right that there is an uncomfortable power differential involved: as he has said, Western leaders are unlikely ever to be brought before it. All of the investigations since the court opened in 2002 have focused on African leaders. It is a stark fact of international power politics that the ICC is only for the weakest of the weak. Of course, it is also the case that the ICC represents a forum in which the victims of some of the world's cruellest and most violent leaders can hold their tormentors to account: these victims are unlikely to quibble with the court's significance in world politics.

As has so often been the case, Gaddafi has seemed to place his beliefs and his desire to cultivate influence before plain good sense. He is right to have reservations about the ICC, perhaps, and many Africans would probably think him spot on in his criticism of it. Yet is Bashir the right man to defend, the right cause to shout so loudly about? In 2007, I met him in his gilded palace in Khartoum, together with Michael Howard MP and Lord Steel. We challenged him over the atrocities in Darfur, which we had visited. We witnessed the suffering of thousands of people who have fled murder and rape in their home towns to take sanctuary in these camps. Even in the camps themselves, reports of abuse and child-trafficking are common, and the struggle to provide enough food, shelter and medicine is horribly obvious.

Other attempts by Gaddafi to win influence in Africa have been equally questionable. He has been a strong supporter, for example, of Robert Mugabe, who has overseen the virtual destruction of the state of Zimbabwe since he began to allow the seizure of white-owned land back in 2000, a campaign that brought economic chaos to the former 'bread basket of Africa' and which was followed by a brutal crackdown on political opposition. Gaddafi sent $1 million to support Mugabe's campaign for re-election in 2002. The previous year Libya gave Zimbabwe $100 million and also signed a $300 million oil deal. Also in 2001, Gaddafi undertook a ceremonial drive from Zambia to the Zimbabwean capital, Harare, in order to draw attention to the crippling fuel shortages Zimbabwe was confronting. Along the way he exhorted the country's small population of Asian Muslims to launch a jihad against white Zimbabweans, and declared to the world media that all whites should be forced out of the country. The same year, Libya sent troops to help their ally, Mugabe, beat opposition forces into submission. Deals with the Libyans were said to have included the provision of 10,000 Zimbabwean passports for Libyan nationals, who would be able to travel internationally more easily on a Zimbabwean than on a Libyan passport.

Mugabe, in return, has stood firmly at Gaddafi's side on many issues, offering strong support for the Colonel's United States of Africa plan. In 2008 Gaddafi repaid his loyalty by announcing to the Ugandan Afro-Arab festival that Mugabe should stay in power for life, and that calls for democracy in Zimbabwe represented an attempt to impose a foreign system of government on Africa. Mugabe's opposition reacted with alarm to the prospect of Libyan involvement in domestic affairs. In 2001 a senior Movement for Democratic Change (MDC) official told the *Daily Telegraph*, 'Mugabe is prepared to turn us into a satellite state of Libya.'[6]

I felt the greatest sympathy for Morgan Tsvangirai, the leader of the MDC, when he visited London in June 2009. The visit was to ask Britain and other European nations to provide more aid to help to restore the Zimbabwean economy which Mugabe has laid waste. Tsvangirai appeared exhausted and somewhat dispirited, put off by the rebuffs he was receiving on the grounds that more work towards democracy was needed. Tsvangirai has courageously and riskily committed himself to working in a unity government with the man who plundered and bankrupted his country and who has several times had him clapped in jail and beaten. It is sad to see Gaddafi supporting Mugabe so vigorously, but perhaps not unexpected. It would be difficult for Gaddafi credibly to support Tsvangirai, as he is a proud and principled advocate of multi-party democracy, while Gaddafi has devoted a lifetime to fighting this, ideologically and practically. I have encouraged the chairman of the International Development Select Committee, Malcolm Bruce MP, to arrange a visit to Zimbabwe. I sit on this committee and feel we need to be doing more to help Tsvangirai rebuild his country.

★

Africa will probably continue to serve as Gaddafi's stage of choice in the years to come. Fashioning himself into a wise elder statesman, an arbiter of conflict and a builder of institutions is likely to absorb much of his attention. We are lucky that the Gaddafi of old is no longer with us, and that his desire to exert influence over the continent no longer finds its expression in arms-trading and the sponsorship of non-state violence. But how much has really changed? The Colonel's unerring instinct for supporting distasteful causes still seems very much with him. He has stood up proudly for Robert Mugabe and for Omar al-Bashir, as both merrily ravage their countries and store up reserves of poverty and hatred for generations to come. Where he does support laudable aims, such as strengthening Africa's collective position, he still does it with the simplistic reasoning and the blunt language of a fiery undergraduate student politician from Cairo in 1960. His money and his ability to bring publicity to any cause may be of use, but hopes are not high that this leopard will ever really change its spots and make a useful, solid and lasting contribution to the region.

# LIVING IN LIBYA

To the traveller, life in Libya can look relatively pleasant. While the newer parts of town are marred by brutal concrete edifices, a great deal of rubbish and constant noisy traffic, Tripoli's medina is a crumbling, elegant, Italianate maze of white-walled streets. The craftsmen typical of north Africa sit peacefully in tiny workshops. Steam hisses from hammams and men rest in courtyards with glasses of mint tea or coffee and play leisurely games of draughts or dominoes. It is easy to while away hours drinking the astonishingly sweet tea or relaxing with a hookah pipe. Along the waterfront, avenues of palms rustle in the pleasant sea breeze. Mosques, minarets and Ottoman arches dot the landscape, and in the evening the city comes alive in the usual way of a very hot country after the heat of the day has passed.

The apparently peaceful Mediterranean existence that we visitors witness, however, conceals tumultuous stories, for life in Libya is unlike life elsewhere. Dining on typical dishes such as lamb shank and couscous in your average Libyan restaurant, you would be unlikely to suspect this. It is only if you are invited into the home of a friend who trusts you that you will hear frank accounts of the bewilderment and suffering that have accompanied Gaddafi's unpredictable rule. For the local people, talking to strangers is a dangerous game. There is a constant and queasy awareness, much as there was in communist Europe, that walls have ears, that informers are widespread and that one must be careful indeed whom one trusts.

Many argue, and not without justification, that Libya has impressive advantages when compared to its neighbours. It is a virtually classless society, in which every girl and boy has the right to a free education. Homelessness is not a problem and everyone has enough to eat. On the other hand, Gaddafi's bizarre political experiments have narrowed and impoverished the lives of his citizens, whose main relationship with the government is one of fear. The Libyans may be wealthier than the Tunisians or the Sudanese, but in every respect, they could have expected the bountiful natural resources of their country to bring them happier and more prosperous lives.

One of my main reasons for writing this book is to draw attention to some of our own nation's most valuable possessions: a robust media, a vigorous representative democracy, a fair and transparent legal system. I worry very much that political disasters of recent times – the exposure of an MPs' expenses system unfit for purpose, the emergence of corruption, the lies and deceit that surrounded the decision to take this nation to war in Iraq – will mean that the younger generation will forget how important the components of a democracy are, and will not be equipped to defend them. If they delved into Libyan society, if they looked closely at its very different relationship with government, I would think that many of them would be moved to value what we have more. As Libyan society has become more open to the world in recent times, there has undoubtedly been a very welcome relaxation in the degree of censorship and political repression. Nonetheless, the people of Libya have been stunted and oppressed by Gaddafi's police state for many years. The media is still not allowed to criticise the government. Political opposition is weak, clandestine and persecuted. Public hangings and 'disappearances' ensure that dissent is limited. Mostly, people's lives take place behind closed doors, they work around the corruption of their government, and they hope for better days to come.

★

Libya has a unique relationship with the car. Back in 1999, Gaddafi even designed his own car – the Saroukh el-Jamahiriyya, or 'Rocket of the

Republic' – a missile-shaped, dark green saloon with safety features designed by the Leader himself. A Libyan spokesman claimed that 'the invention of the safest car in the world is proof that the Libyan revolution is built on the happiness of man'.[1] The design was updated for fortieth anniversary celebrations in 2009, but was said to be still awaiting mass production.

Whatever the fate of the Rocket of the Republic, cars are certainly perceived as a fundamental dimension of existence in the *jamahiriyya*. Gaddafi's *Green Book* stipulates that a private vehicle is one of a person's basic needs, along with an income and a house. Renting transport from another individual, according to the Colonel's economic philosophy, represents enslavement. Therefore, just about everyone in Libya has a car, and Tripoli is one of the most congested cities I have ever visited. According to the World Health Organization (WHO), a startling 11 per cent of deaths in Libya are from traffic accidents, and five or six people are killed every day on the roads – a similar figure to the UK, with ten times Libya's population. Clearly, the car is king in Libya, but roads and regulation are woefully inadequate. This situation provides an apt metaphor for the way in which Libyan social development in general has proceeded. Lots of money has been spent, the basics are there, the society is in many ways egalitarian, but good planning has been missing and, in many areas, things are starting to crumble.

When Gaddafi came to power, he focused very quickly on distributing oil revenues better, rapidly building his own legitimacy by ensuring that the man on the street felt the benefits of Libya's skyrocketing wealth. As a revolutionary who claimed to incorporate socialism into his ideology, Gaddafi needed to invest demonstrable effort into social welfare. He had to lay the basics early on, and he did so. The result is that Libyans have universal access to health and education, and generally do better on most development indices than neighbouring countries. Unfortunately, the later years of Gaddafi's regime saw expectations rise and standards fall. In general, the tumult and poor planning that have characterised the Colonel's rule have meant either stagnation or decline in the quality of social services in Libya. Whereas Libyans were lucky in comparison to others, in a country selling enormously profitable quantities of oil, people might have hoped for better. The government became less and less inclined to invest in health and education, particularly during the expensive, lengthy war in Chad between 1978 and 1987.

The education system promoted by Gaddafi has undoubtedly achieved great things. In 1973, the literacy rate was just 40 per cent, whereas by 2003 it had more than doubled to 82.6 per cent overall: 92.4 per cent of men and 72 per cent of women. Libyans all have access to a universal, free system of primary, secondary and tertiary education. University students pay no fees and receive a generous stipend to sustain them through their studies. Libyans are much more likely to be literate than their counterparts in Tunisia, Egypt or Morocco.

On the other hand, Libya has not had the critical mass of teachers and academics needed to provide an educational system of really high quality, of the type that could produce a talented, capable workforce able to participate fully in the flowering of commerce currently taking place in Libya. Despite his generosity towards them, Gaddafi has always distrusted students and kept a tight rein on the universities. The demonstration during which PC Yvonne Fletcher was shot was held by dissidents condemning public hangings of university undergraduates who had protested against Gaddafi's rule. At regular intervals through the 1980s and 1990s, similar violent crackdowns rocked Libya's universities.

As well as this terrifying political action against students, teachers at all levels confronted a constant flow of confusing, threatening edicts that interfered dramatically with their ability to teach. During the 1980s and 1990s, they were forbidden to teach foreign languages – in 1986, for example, Gaddafi threatened to destroy the libraries of the French and English faculties at al-Fateh University in Tripoli, and later closed down both faculties. At one stage, the ever-ingenious Colonel proposed eliminating primary schools altogether, in favour of making mothers teach their children at home. Luckily, popular objection to this idea was so strenuous that it was dropped fairly quickly. In such uncertain conditions, it is unsurprising that the education system was relatively weak.

Libya's tertiary sector is judged particularly problematic, and is acknowledged to be utterly inadequate for the task of preparing work-ready graduates. As it becomes increasingly important that Libyans find employment with the multinationals flooding into the country to run the oil industry, the educational sector desperately needs to change. If Libya is to diversify its economy and become a global competitor in industries outside oil and gas, it needs a population educated to the highest world standards. Quantity, as well as quality, is an issue. A March 2009 article published in *Oea*, an Arabic-language newspaper run by Saif Gaddafi, reported that only 10 per cent of boys and 13 per cent of girls entered tertiary education. If Libya does want its population to find a more prominent role in the oil and other industries, many more graduates will be needed.

Part of the answer to this has been the provision of more opportunities for students to travel abroad. Up until the early 1980s, it was very common for Libyans to travel to Britain or the US for higher education. As Gaddafi's high-profile support for terrorism rendered the nation an international pariah, this became much more difficult. It is only during this decade that Western universities have again begun to open their doors to Libyan students. Nowadays, Britain's universities are again educating thousands of Libyan students, and this is certainly a positive contribution to the future of the country. I hope that these students will find themselves able to return home and pass on the rich educational experiences they have benefited from in our universities.

Sending everyone abroad, however, is ultimately unsustainable. Libyans need a robust and high-quality university system of their own. The challenge here is immense. It has been partly addressed by the regime's recent plans to build twenty-eight new universities. More campuses, however, may not on their own be enough. Will the really capable academics wish to return home to work in Libyan universities, or will they prefer the freer atmosphere of academia elsewhere? Can the atmosphere of rigorous debate and intellectual stimulation that characterises a good university really develop in a micro-managed police state? It is known that the government restricts opportunities for foreigners to visit Libya's universities, thus eradicating one of the most important and fruitful aspects of academic work, international collaboration. Few high-calibre academics are likely to want to work with government security agencies scrutinising their teaching and research, and without the intellectual sustenance of international exchange. It may not be for some years that Libyans are able to access a really good education at home.

The situation in hospitals is similar to that in schools and universities: the basics are there, but standards are low. Libyans who experience ill health have good access to free medical attention. One of the earliest planning documents of the regime was the 1973 National Transformation Plan, which set out a commitment to ensure that every citizen had free access to health services. Gaddafi's regime has since put considerable effort into building up its hospitals and primary healthcare centres, and attracting foreign doctors and nurses to work in Libya. In 2003, there were 129 doctors for every 100,000 people, a relatively high ratio (the ratio in the UK is not that much higher, at 166 per 100,000). Libya has slowly built up the capacity to train doctors from among the local population, so that nowadays the WHO reports that there are actually too many medical students enrolled in the nation's universities. Medics have also come from Egypt, Sudan, Lebanon and eastern Europe to staff Libya's hospitals, attracted by higher salaries than they could hope to receive at home. As a consequence, the health achievements of post-independence Libya have been remarkable: life expectancy rose from 46.7 years in 1960 to 76.9 in 2005. Diseases of poverty that were still common in the 1970s – including typhoid, rabies, meningitis and cholera – were brought under control by the 1980s, a major achievement for a public health system that was judged by many to be well planned and effective. More than 98 per cent of the population now has access to safe drinking water, and 99 per cent of mothers are attended by trained birth attendants when they deliver their children. The vast majority of Libya's children have received the recommended childhood vaccinations. These days, Libya's health problems are those of a wealthy nation – major causes of death include cardiovascular disease, cancer and diabetes.

The quality of medical attention, however, is seen as poor for a relatively wealthy state. Libya has done well, but might have done a lot better. When the regime imprisoned five Bulgarian nurses and a Palestinian doctor in 1999 on charges of deliberately infecting children in a Benghazi hospital with HIV (see Chapter 9), the world's attention swung briefly to the state of Libyan hospitals. Expert after foreign expert (including Luc Montagnier, the French virologist who was a co-discoverer of HIV) declared that the circumstances of the case suggested the prevalence of poor hygiene and little knowledge of injection safety practices. This was just one hospital, but it pointed to a pressing need for modernisation in healthcare. Gaddafi talked wildly of foreign conspiracies, and perhaps it was easier for many in the population to believe this than to believe that going to their local hospital to have their appendix out could leave them infected with HIV/ AIDS. Shocking reports of an outbreak of bubonic plague in the eastern coastal town of Tobruk in 2009 suggested that it is not just urban hospitals, but the entire public health system that needs urgent modernisation and careful scrutiny.

Libya has struggled for decades to build up the skills of the local workforce, and it still lags behind in medical terms. Reliance on foreign doctors and nurses brings many problems, and the lack of local medical skills has held back the development of healthcare in Libya. Part of the problem is the lack of specialisation – Libya tried to develop its capacity by sending its doctors abroad for training in medical specialities, but unfortunately a large proportion chose not to return, and Libya has been forced to continue importing expensive foreign consultants. As in other conservative Muslim nations, nursing has been a profoundly unpopular career for Libyan women, and the quality of the nursing education available is very poor. The country continues to rely on employing nurses and midwives from abroad.

As a result of all this, many of the more complex medical procedures have not been available in Libya. Thousands of Libyans thus travel abroad each year to access care of a type or a quality unavailable at home. The private health sectors in Tunisia, Jordan and Egypt have profited from this, and the WHO reports that the Libyan government spends around £29 million each year to fund overseas medical care for its citizens. Wealthier Libyans travel even further afield, seeking care in other Arab countries and in Europe.

The opening up of Libya to foreign investment will mean that some of Britain's excellent private healthcare businesses and talented NHS staff will be able to help Libya meet the challenges of building a better health system.

The long-term impact of their contribution, however, will depend on the regime making a really solid, well-planned commitment to improving the nation's healthcare. At the moment, Libya's nascent private health industry is struggling with unpredictability and uncertainty in the health policy climate. Whether this will be addressed remains to be seen.

★

Libyans' working lives are unusual, to say the least. Nearly three quarters of the population are employed in a soggy, unproductive state sector, which has chiefly functioned as a way to get oil money to the populace and to sustain the impression that there is mass employment. Many Libyans thus turn up day after day to do dull, meaningless and largely redundant jobs. Reliable figures on Libya's workforce are somewhat difficult to obtain, given that the government is highly sensitive both about the true extent of unemployment and about the presence of expatriate workers, but a Libya scholar, Mary-Jane Deeb, quotes a 2004 figure that 30 per cent of the Libyan workforce was unemployed.[2] One thing is for certain: with a youthful population, the question of productive employment grows ever more troubling.

High unemployment is a particularly sensitive issue, owing to the large presence of foreign workers and migrants. In 2004, one estimate suggested that Libya was hosting 1.6 million foreign workers. As in other oil-rich economies, many of these foreign migrants are vulnerable and unskilled, doing low-status work such as cleaning, waiting and construction, which Libyans are not willing to do. Cleaners, labourers, construction workers and shop assistants are all generally sourced from Libya's neighbours, including Chad, Sudan, Tunisia and Egypt. Nonetheless, Gaddafi is astutely aware of the danger of his countrymen and women feeling that they are sidelined by better-trained foreigners.

Channelling this resentment, Gaddafi has regularly indulged in sudden mass expulsions of expatriates, unleashing havoc on Libyan society. In 1985, one such expulsion was said to have suspended virtually all activity in agriculture and the service sectors. In 1995 Gaddafi provocatively called on the United Nations to immediately repatriate one million people living in Libya. Alarmed UN officials warned that this would be a humanitarian catastrophe, to which Gaddafi responded that he would drive them out across Libya's desert borders if the UN would not deport them by air. These threats clearly caused a considerable headache for surrounding countries and for the UN. He did not carry out the threat to expel the million people, but 30,000 Palestinian refugees were ordered to leave, and expatriates from Chad, Sudan, Nigeria, Mali and elsewhere were also removed.

The large presence of foreign labour makes a discussion of working conditions in Libya problematic. In theory, Libyans have quite good working conditions. The country's labour laws outline pension rights, rest periods, shift regulations, a minimum wage, fair dismissal procedures and working hours. The working week was reduced from forty-eight to forty hours in 2006. While these laws look good, much of the workforce is not covered by them. Most of the foreign workers in Libya are not covered under the law. They experience frequent arbitrary changes in rules and pay and are regularly rounded up without notice and threatened with deportation. Libyan workers have not, however, had a completely smooth run. In particular, wages have been frozen for many years. Although the set public sector wages were raised in 2006, they have not kept pace with the swiftly rising prices resulting from the opening of the economy.

Fruitfully employing and paying an educated population, fussy about the type of work it will do, remains one of the key challenges for Libya. Working it out will be an onerous task for both Gaddafi and for his successors, and the outcome will shape the nation's social and economic future.

★

During his 2009 state visit to Italy, Gaddafi requested a meeting with 700 Italian women. Curious women from Italian politics, culture, industry, law and even reality television welcomed this unusual invitation. Gaddafi gave them a long lecture touching on such topics as working women in Libya and the emancipated attitudes of Libyan men. Exhibiting a characteristically idiosyncratic take on the issues, he decried the fact that in some Arab countries women must apply to the government for permission to drive cars: really, he said, this was not a matter for state involvement when women's husbands and brothers could as easily grant the permission. The reaction of the Italian women granted such insights into the purportedly feminist *jamahiriyya* seemed in general to be confusion, mixed with mild annoyance.

One member of the audience felt there was a conflict between Gaddafi's position as a champion of women's rights and his treatment of his famous all-women legion of bodyguards, who surrounded him on the stage as he delivered his speech. She commented mildly to a *Guardian* journalist, 'I am curious to see, to understand his point of view, but with all these women working for him as semi-slaves it seems a bit of a contradiction to call himself a liberator of women.'[3]

This interviewee hit the nail on the head. Gaddafi wishes to view himself as a liberator of women, but he struggles to comprehend what liberation actually is. As always, for Gaddafi, image is everything. He seems to feel that the visual impact of women in combat fatigues is enough, that it alone proves Libya is different, emancipated. What he will not do, however, is work alongside women as equals, or appoint them to any kind of high- or even middle-ranking position. He has no comprehension that liberation means sharing access to power, influence and wealth. According to Guma el-Gamaty, the Libyan dissident with whom I spoke in June 2009, 'Where Gaddafi failed is in empowering women to important positions in politics, the economy and social institutions . . . to him, women are a commodity, to be used.'

Gaddafi's regime has, however, overseen a big change in the position of women. The society inherited in 1951 when Libya gained its independence under the leadership of King Idris was radically unequal. Many Libyan women, especially in rural areas or smaller towns, married early, were kept in seclusion and only went out fully veiled and accompanied by male relatives. Education for girls was highly limited, and very few were employed. Under Idris, some initial attempts at reform were made – schools were opened for girls, education was made compulsory for all, women were given the vote and legislation designed to improve women's status was passed.

Gaddafi, however, was not content with this rather orthodox, run-of-the-mill approach to raising the status of women. He wanted something much more flamboyant, and hence came up with the idea that Libya needed women soldiers. Maria Graeff-Wassink's essay on women in the Libyan army suggests that Gaddafi wanted to use visibly liberated women soldiers as a symbol of just how progressive and egalitarian his revolution was going to be.[4] In effect, women with guns would be the face of the revolution.

In 1977, therefore, Gaddafi proposed the policy of compulsory military service for girls. In Libya's conservative, religious society, this upset virtually everyone. The idea of women soldiers was enough to imbue many mullahs and imams with the courage to speak truth to absolute power – they stood up and publicly condemned the very idea as shamefully un-Islamic. The General People's Congress was also troublesome, rejecting this aspect of Gaddafi's reform three years in a row. Gaddafi, meanwhile, brought a range of arguments to bear against his opponents. If the Prophet Mohammed's wife Aisha had led an army, why should not Libya's women be soldiers? If Libya were to match Israel, where women served alongside men in the army, then her women would surely need to equal the courage of the Israelis.

By 1980, the Colonel had won the battle (if not the war), and the policy of compulsory military service for girls passed into law. The year before, the Women's Academy was set up to begin training women soldiers. Gaddafi declared that applicants should be among the nation's elite – well educated, healthy and with 'outstanding personalities'. It was to present to Libyans and to the world the image of powerful, talented, strong Libyan women. In 1983, 7,000 women soldiers graduated. Ultimately, however, the policy proved so unpopular that Gaddafi let it lapse, and the school closed.

In the end, it was not so much Libya's women soldiers that embodied Libyan womanhood to the world, but the Colonel's all-female personal bodyguard. In February 1981, Gaddafi enacted one of his more eccentric policies, the founding of the 'Revolutionary Nuns', or *al-Rahibat al-Thawriyat*. These women were to devote themselves wholly to nation and

revolution, forgoing marriage (although it is said that these days, some of
the bodyguards are married with children). Conveniently, they could also
serve as the source of a trusted, faithful and visually pleasing phalanx of
personal security guards for Gaddafi. While many Libyans deeply resented
the new institution, decrying it as un-Islamic, the bodyguards served their
Leader well. Dressed in blue camouflage, all with long hair, enormous guns
and high leather boots, they act both to protect Gaddafi and to ensure he
makes the front pages of the newspapers on all his foreign visits. Journalists
compete to invent outlandish names for them – 'Libyan Lara Crofts', 'Green
Nuns', 'Blue Nuns', 'Gaddafi's Angels'. Few dispatches are filed without
commentary on outfits, make-up, nail polish and the wearing of high heels.
These women have also proved themselves highly capable: in 1998, one of
the bodyguards was reported to have taken a bullet for Gaddafi on a visit to
Athens, and the guard has allegedly also taken on Nigerian police.

What the bodyguards tell us about women's status in Libya is a hotly
contested topic. Some hail it as evidence of a uniquely progressive Islamic
society. Others say that trailing in the wake of a dictator, enacting a kind
of cheap fantasy based on women with guns and high heels, is neither
progressive nor reflective of Libyan attitudes to women. To my mind,
this whole conversation is something of a distraction – it is fair enough to
argue these women are degraded by being positioned as a slice of the kitsch
inevitably associated with dictatorship – but Gaddafi should really be judged
elsewhere, on ordinary women's experience of his rule.

In his favour, Gaddafi built on Idris's early efforts to improve women's
status. He vigorously promoted women's education and established many
more schools for girls. Undoubtedly, the encouragement of women's
education had a highly positive effect. Libya claims that the proportion
of women in the workforce has grown from 6 per cent forty years ago
to more than 20 percent in 2009. Women came forward in increasing
numbers from the 1970s to join the workforce, although they universally
took jobs that were considered suitable 'women's work': predominantly
teaching, secretarial and clerical work. Under Gaddafi's rule, women have
also become increasingly independent. Many choose not to wear the veil,
and Gaddafi has spoken out against it frequently. It is common for Libyan

women to move about freely in the community. A law was passed in 1984 forbidding men to take second wives without the permission of the first, or without a special legal permit.

As is the case with health and education, though, one is forced to ask whether much more could and should have been done in a nation with so much more money to spend compared to other, poorer nations. Large obstacles to true equality of the sexes clearly remain. Only 72 per cent of women are literate, compared to 92 per cent of men. While 71 per cent of boys are sent to secondary school, just 53 per cent of girls are given this chance. The remaining 47 per cent, kept at home and restricted to a primary-level education, are a major concern.

Gaddafi likes to boast of statistics proving the progressive nature of Libyan society, but he does not wish actually to put women in positions of power and to work with them. While a revolutionary, he is still a product of a conservative, Arab society, and it shows. Women are notable for their absence from the ranks of the governing elite. They are rarely appointed to high-ranking posts such as committee secretaries. Between 1977 and 1999, only four women were elected to the secretariat of the General People's Congress. In 2008, there were no cabinet-level women politicians.

It has often been said that in Libya there is a large gulf between a theoretical, politically expedient wish to emancipate women and a set of cultural values that keep women out of the domains of real power. Gaddafi, as much as any other Libyan man, has demonstrated the truth of this. While presenting himself to the world as an emancipator of women, he has also shown a desire to play the traditionalist. *The Green Book* is radical in most ways, but it is socially quite conservative. In it, Gaddafi declares that 'an individual without a family has no value or no social life'. He says that the sexes are equal, but that 'any mother who forsakes her duties towards her children goes against her natural role in life'. Women cannot escape their biological destinies, and must fulfil their duty to look after children: 'Placing a child in a day nursery is coercive and tyrannical and a violation of the child's free and natural disposition.' Women are also to avoid jobs that 'disgrace and taint their femininity' and must not 'study a discipline that would lead them to jobs incompatible with their nature'.

In practice, Gaddafi has often proved reluctant to intervene to protect women victimised in a highly conservative Islamic society. Human Rights Watch reported in 2006 that Libyan women accused of tainting their families' honour were routinely kept in 'social rehabilitation facilities' – effectively prisons. They were locked up, subjected to forced virginity tests, and given no schooling or means of occupying themselves. It is hard to judge Libya the model of liberation and progressive Islam touted by Gaddafi when such institutions exist.

★

Life in Libya, of course, is all about Gaddafi. This foundational truth is reflected in the landscape. Everywhere you travel in Libya, the face of the Colonel looms. Clad in a range of military uniforms, staring enigmatically and benevolently, he is on nearly every wall and lamp-post. Even out in the desert, Gaddafi billboards line the roads. The ever-watching Leader signifies an ever-watching regime. Libya is defined by a frighteningly vigilant state security apparatus, which intrudes on most aspects of life in the *jamahiriyya*. The US State Department reported in 2008 that Libyans live under an extensive and all-pervasive security system, that they have no legal options if they want to complain about the actions of security agencies, that they can be detained and held indefinitely without charge, and that security forces have 'committed serious human rights abuses with impunity'.[5] Ordinary residents regularly have phone calls, emails and internet use monitored, particularly if they are communicating with people abroad.

Criticising the government in Libya remains exceptionally dangerous, not only for oneself, but also for one's relatives. The families of political activists have been targeted for harassment by the regime, and have reported being denied access to water, electricity, telephone services, fuel, food and essential official documents such as passports and driving licences. An extreme instance of this kind of harassment was noted by the UN's Human Rights Committee in November 2007. It was reported that security services descended on the small north-western town of Bani Walid and burned to the ground all the property owned by the relatives of a political activist who had been arrested for demanding a multi-party system.

One of the issues journalists are prevented from discussing is the treatment of Libya's ethnic minorities, who have suffered under Gaddafi's rule. The main minority groups in the country are Berbers, the indigenous inhabitants of north Africa. Berbers do not see themselves as Arabs and have different linguistic and cultural backgrounds from the Arab majority. Discrimination against Berber minorities has included laws forbidding the use of typically Berber names and the banning of Berber languages.

Nomadic tribes also live deep in the desert regions of Libya, clustered along the southern borders. These nomads have also felt the strong arm of Gaddafi's Libya. The Tebu tribe, especially, has been in the news in recent times. Riots erupted in 2007 in the southern town of Kufra, where many Tebu live. The cause of the rioting was difficult to discern, but it was reported that between eleven and thirty Tebu civilians were killed, while others had their Libyan citizenship and rights to state services such as health and schooling withdrawn.

The other significant and seemingly permanent minority in Libya is refugees. Tripoli remains the transit point for hundreds of thousands of refugees quitting sub-Saharan Africa to seek better lives in Europe. The UN's High Commission for Refugees estimates there are between 1½ and 2 million illegal migrants living in Libya, an enormous presence for a country of just six million people in all. Of these, about one million were said to come from Sahelian or sub-Saharan Africa. NGOs have lined up to criticise the inhumane treatment of refugees in Libya, where they are often imprisoned for long periods in filthy conditions, without access to any kind of assistance. Amnesty International has also raised concerns about the forcible return of genuine refugees. In its 2008 report on Libya, Amnesty drew attention to the plight of 500 Eritreans threatened with repatriation. Many of these men were said to have been conscripts and victims of enforced military service.[6] I have seen footage of the boats which desperate migrants hand over their life savings to board in Tripoli, and it is shocking indeed. Ancient, crumbling fishing vessels packed with many more passengers than they can safely carry chug out of Tripoli, low down

in the water due to the immense weight of their desperate passengers. It is a
harrowing sight, and we Europeans have a responsibility to work alongside
Libya to make sure that refugees are given the fairest, fastest and most
humane treatment possible.

Recent years have seen some effort by Gaddafi to address Libya's woeful
record on political freedom. Gaddafi's son Saif, touted as a likely successor,
has shown himself willing to join in discussions on issues such as the use of
torture in prisons. Western NGOs have been given visas to come to the
country and produce reports on life in Libya. In 2007, some of the anti-
Berber legislation was revoked, and Amazigh television programmes were
even screened on state television.

While the NGOs given improved access to Libya welcomed Gaddafi's
greater openness, they also criticised what they saw on their visits to Libya
in the strongest terms, suggesting that there is a long way to go in freeing
up Libyan society. Human Rights Watch was invited in 2005 to make
three visits to Libya. Their findings confirmed most people's suspicion that
Libyans continue to be intensely restricted in all areas of their lives. Scores
of prisoners are incarcerated for peaceful political activities and some have
apparently disappeared, their fate unknown. Many political prisoners will have
experienced torture: Human Rights Watch reported that fifteen of the thirty-
two prisoners it interviewed had been tortured. The US State Department said
in its 2008 country report on human rights practices in Libya:

> The reported methods of torture and abuse included chaining prisoners
> to a wall for hours; clubbing; applying electric shock; applying corkscrews
> to the back; pouring lemon juice in open wounds; breaking fingers and
> allowing the joints to heal without medical care; suffocating with plastic
> bags; depriving detainees of sleep, food, and water; hanging by the wrists;
> suspending from a pole inserted between the knees and elbows; burning
> with cigarettes; threatening with dog attacks; and beatings on the soles of
> the feet.[7]

On 28 June 1996, a particularly shocking incident in the history of
repression in Libya took place at the Abu Salim prison in Tripoli. The

gaol held mainly political prisoners, among whom were a number of alleged Islamic fundamentalists. The prisoners had complained that they were suffering under terrible conditions, with up to twenty-four men in each cell, no healthcare, inadequate food and little provision for communication with their families. Becoming desperate, they took a prison guard hostage and demanded that the prison authorities negotiate better conditions.

According to controversial reports received from dissidents abroad, Gaddafi then sent his brother-in-law, Abdullah Senussi (head of military intelligence and personally responsible for the security of Gaddafi's sons), to manage the situation. This has been denied vigorously by the regime, which ascribes what happened next to rogue guards acting without official sanction. According to dissidents, several eyewitnesses identified Senussi as the man who took charge at Abu Salim that day.

By their reports, Senussi was extremely cunning in his approach to the hostage situation. He agreed to all of the prisoners' demands and had the guard released. The next morning, however, at seven o'clock, he ordered more than a thousand prisoners to gather in the prison's central courtyard. For four hours, guards posted on the rooftops around the courtyard shot at the assembled prisoners. It is said that 1,200 men were killed. One can only imagine the bloodshed and terror of that day.

This was the bloodiest and most terrifying crackdown Libya had seen in years, and the regime was to regret it. In a small country like Libya, murdering this many men is impossible to hush up. There was no way of silencing or punishing the relatives and friends of this many people and inevitably eyewitness accounts leaked out and were published on the internet. Tremendous pressure grew on the regime, which had provided no official explanation to the public or to relatives of events that day, to account for what happened. In 2001, families began to be told of their relatives' fate. In 2004, Gaddafi admitted publicly that there had been an 'incident' at Abu Salim, although his version of events was that prisoners had become aggressive and had been brought under control by an exchange of fire. By 2005, 112 families of the 1,200 involved had been informed of their relatives' deaths. In 2008, each family was offered compensation of

130,000 Libyan dinars, or just under $100,000. By then, 800 families had been told the grim news.

The bereaved families, however, had formed a committee, which refused Gaddafi's offer. This committee put forward its own demands, saying it would not negotiate with anyone other than Saif Gaddafi, that the bodies of the victims must be returned, that all of those responsible should be brought to justice and that compensation should amount to ten million dinars per victim. Out of this tragedy, positive results may come. The courage of the families concerned is impressive. Gaddafi's attempts to hush the incident up, then to let time pass and adopt a 'drip-drip' approach to acknowledging responsibility, and then to buy his way out of accountability, have all failed utterly. Confronted by hordes of relatives with nothing to lose, the Libyan dictatorship has struggled to find a convincing response. At the very least, there will be a reluctance to repeat any such incident in the coming years.

The frequent imprisonment of protestors and the Abu Salim incident shows how dangerous it remains to promote any sort of political cause in Libya. This is also true of most other forms of social organisation. Gaddafi has sought to eliminate most groups from Libyan society, fearful that any sort of organisation, no matter how innocuous, could prove to be a front for organising against him. There are no independent trade unions, no professional organisations, no business groups and few voluntary societies. *The Green Book* waxed lyrical on the evils of sporting clubs in particular. In a somewhat strange exercise of logic, Gaddafi felt professional sportsmen stole the benefits of physical exercise from their fans. *The Green Book* labelled sporting clubs 'rapacious social instruments, not unlike the dictatorial political instruments which monopolise power to the exclusion of the people'. Spectators were 'a multitude of fools . . . practising lethargy'. For many years, Libyans were denied the pleasure of spectator sport of any kind. Football clubs were only allowed after Gaddafi's third son, al-Saadi, a football fanatic and professional player, personally requested that his father relax these restrictions. Gaddafi seems to have been right to have feared the footballers: football has since proved a constant lightning rod for political unrest, and has caused the Colonel numerous headaches.

The regime has justified its dramatic suppression of civil society with the explanation that Libya can only afford to host groups that are in line with the political ideology of the 1969 revolution. The result is a society deeply damaged, in which few people have any experience of working together to achieve anything. Inevitably, the few principles of social organisation left open have become more and more meaningful. For the Libyans, denied unions, clubs or political parties, religious and tribal identities have become very important in society. Libya's Bedouin Arab culture is defined by tribal allegiances, and under Gaddafi these have become more, not less, relevant to people's lives and politics. Similarly, many have turned to religion, probably for a number of reasons – solace, identity, self-expression, participation in a realm of life relatively untouched by dictatorship.

★

Gaddafi himself says that Libyans are among the most empowered people in the world, because they live in the world's purest democracy. According to Gaddafi, in Libya people have a say in every single decision, from street-cleaning through to going to war. He claims his model is superior to that of the West, where elite elected representatives rob citizens of true democratic involvement by making decisions on their behalf. In theory, Libya does indeed have a carefully built structure of popular committees that represents a pioneering achievement in participative democracy. In practice, of course, Gaddafi is the supreme authority, and he is free to push through whatever policy he prefers. Attendance at popular committee meetings is unsurprisingly very low, estimated at around 6 or 7 per cent, and only a very small number of those who do go along to meetings take part in debate. The Economist Intelligence Unit puts Libya 159th out of 167 countries on its democracy index, placing it squarely among those countries considered authoritarian.[8]

I would wager that most Britons would not rate our robust media all that highly if asked to make a list of what was important to them in life. Travelling to Libya is an excellent corrective in this respect, for Libyan society has been deeply impoverished by the intellectual closure of life in a police state, where the leadership must not be criticised and where the papers report only news approved by the government. Libya's press is among the most vigorously suppressed in the world. In 2005, Reporters without Borders was allowed to make an investigative visit to Libya, a welcome development that followed twenty years of rejected visa applications. This was a surprisingly open step, particularly as the NGO then proceeded, as was presumably expected, to publish an extremely critical report. It quoted an anonymous journalist's statement that 'in Libya you can criticise Allah but not Gaddafi', it drew attention to the imprisonment of several reporters, and it pointed out the long list of subjects ruled off limits to the media: criticism of Gaddafi, criticism of the regime, treatment of the Berber minority and corruption, among others.[9]

Individual reporters with the courage to criticise Gaddafi's regime have suffered dire consequences. On 21 May 2005 Daif al-Ghazal, a Libyan journalist and Green Book expert who had risen to the highest ranks of the revolutionary committees, was kidnapped while driving home. He was tortured and shot dead; his body was found in Benghazi on 31 May. Most of his fingers had been cut off, he had stab wounds and there was bruising to his body. Ghazal had embarked on a campaign, partly through international websites, of criticising corruption and oppression under Gaddafi. As the veteran of ten years working for the revolutionary committees, his critique was made from a well-informed perspective that posed what the regime clearly viewed as a grave threat. In 2007, Saif Gaddafi admitted publicly that state officials had killed Ghazal, but claimed they were renegades who had not been acting under official orders. In 2008, three Revolutionary Guard men alleged to have undertaken this 'renegade' action, supposedly with no sanction from above, were sentenced to death.

Two years prior to Ghazal's case, another journalist, Abdel Nasser Younis Meftah al-Rabassi, was given a fifteen-year prison sentence for posting an article on an Arabic-language internet site. His article had drawn attention to high-level corruption in the Gaddafi regime. Reports from Amnesty International indicated that he was tortured, denied legal representation and held incommunicado. Rabassi was fortunate compared to Abdullah Ali al-Senussi al-Darrat, who has been referred to as 'Libya's forgotten man'. Darrat was a journalist who disappeared in 1973, and nothing has been heard of him since. If he is still languishing in a Libyan prison, this makes his sentence the longest ever dealt to a journalist for a political offence. Nobody knows why he was arrested, no-one has asked about his fate, and no visiting leader has raised the case. Most assume he is dead.

Gaddafi has sought to muzzle his critics even when they have spoken against him from beyond Libya's borders. Recent years have seen a number of damaging and expensive libel suits against foreign journalists. In 2007, Ali Fodil and Naïla Berrahal, respectively an editor and a journalist from the popular Algerian daily *Ech-Chourouk*, were jailed for six months and subjected to heavy fines after Gaddafi won a libel case against them. Publication of their newspaper was suspended for two months. In July 2009, Gaddafi successfully sued three Moroccan newspapers for insulting him. The newspapers were ordered to pay a fine of $370,000. It was uncertain as to whether or not the financial blow this represented would close the papers concerned for good. The National Union of the Moroccan Press spoke out against the trial, which they called 'a blow for press freedom in Morocco'.

The unsurprising result of such vigorous restriction of press freedom is that Libya's newspapers, TV channels and radio stations toe the government line with studied and boring obedience. A 1972 media law stipulates indefinite prison sentences for offences such as 'doubting the aims of the revolution', an offence relatively few journalists nowadays dare to contemplate. No criticism of Gaddafi or his leaders is allowed, and much of Libya's news content is drab, depressing political propaganda. The four leading newspapers (*al-Jamahiriyya, al-Shams, al-Fajr al-Jadid* and *al-Zahf al-Akhdar*) sometimes publish identical articles, and all international news comes from the government's news agency, Jana, described by the veteran BBC journalist Kate Adie as 'the nonsense organ of the regime'.[10] *Al-Zahf* is particularly close to the government and carries a story about Gaddafi's activities on the front page every day. The other titles print cautious criticism of minor problems with life in Libya, such as the poor state of roads or low-level corruption, but carefully avoid anything more serious.

Government television is perhaps even less exciting. It is renowned for subjecting Libyans to a lengthy nightly reading from *The Green Book* and is regularly used to broadcast political propaganda. For example, in one recent programme, Gaddafi debated his plan to dismantle the state bureaucracy with his senior ministers, who argued against it. According to *The Economist*, 'There is no doubt that the broadcast was carefully choreographed, and it is expected to presage a substantial toning-down of the original programme.'[11] With such studiously manipulated viewing fare, it is unsurprising to learn that these days state television has largely been deserted for the meatier content provided by al-Jazeera and the Saudi, Lebanese and Iranian stations available via satellite television.

Libyans are also increasingly able to surf the internet, seeing at first hand the contrast between a colourful free press and their own drab, state-sanctioned media. They are taking to the net in ever-increasing numbers: in 2007 it was reported by the International Telecommunications Union that there were 260,000 internet users in Libya. The government is said to block websites run by opposition organisations and other sites considered subversive. Its attempts at censoring the net, however, are reportedly quite unsophisticated, and many of Libya's flourishing internet cafés use satellite connections to Europe, so that attempts at censorship are largely irrelevant.

There is little doubt that the voracious consumption of foreign television and internet content will influence people's opinions on life in Libya. Anticipating the problems this may cause, the regime recently took some tentative steps towards a more open media. From early 2008, Gaddafi allowed his second son, Saif al-Islam, to carry out an experiment in media freedom. Saif declared in April that year, 'Society must have several media establishments that expose corruption, rigging and violations. These establishments have to be independent and not reporting to the information minister, the parliament, the cabinet, or even to Saif al-Islam.'[12]

For the first time in Libya's post-revolution history, privately owned media outlets were allowed to open, including the al-Libiya satellite TV channel, the al-Libiya and Eman radio stations, and the newspapers *Quryna* and *Oea*. This experiment in greater openness, however, was not a huge success. In June 2009 it was announced that these new channels would be nationalised, returning to the protective, censoring clutches of the National Media Services Centre. The experiment had not exactly been revolutionary

– all the new media were owned by Saif, most of the journalists involved also worked for the government outlets, and the new papers were printed on government presses – but it had still been judged a step too far in the direction of a more open society. Similarly, in February 2007, news outlets were permitted to stock foreign Arabic-language publications, but this new freedom was retracted just a month later. Libya's moves towards greater openness in its domestic media have been tentative and piecemeal. The effect of the retraction of reforms such as this may actually be to make things worse. When experiments in openness and freedom are terminated so quickly and so arbitrarily, one wonders how Libyans will ever be able to trust any reform plan proposed by Gaddafi's regime.

★

Libya thus continues to face many problems when it comes to basic freedom and human rights. Memories of events like the gruesome, violent Abu Salim massacre loom large. Many citizens know someone whose relative has disappeared into the shadowy world of the nation's prison system. Despite all this, it must be acknowledged that the 'relaxation' of recent years has been enthusiastically welcomed. It might not have translated into a free and honest press, but it has meant more openness and more accountability. The internet has made news from the outside accessible to everyone; satellite television has formed a window onto the world. Life has become more fun – people are allowed to watch football matches, listen to pop music, watch popular soaps beamed in from Arab neighbours. It will now be difficult, if not impossible, for Gaddafi's regime to turn back, to close Libya down again.

The message here is that connections work. The thicker the web of links between ordinary Libyans and the rest of the world, the more likely things are to get better, and the less likely people will be to accept a return to the bad old days. I hope that the businesses, teachers, doctors and politicians of Britain will join in the task of reaching out to Libya, so that its people do not have to face up alone to what can be a terrifying regime.

# 12

# PAYING FOR THE REVOLUTION

One of the many Gaddafi billboards lining Libya's highways shows the Colonel driving his VW Beetle, a benevolent smile on his face, throwing dollar bills out of the window to admiring crowds. An unfortunate metaphor, perhaps, for the way that he has chosen to spend Libya's money. For nearly four decades, oil receipts granted Gaddafi the freedom to conduct an enormous experiment in his quasi-socialist ideology, using Libyan people as his guinea pigs. Billions have been squandered on Gaddafi's economic whims, and there has been next to no consistency, at least outside the oil industry. Economic dictates have often been terrifying and irrational. The economy today reflects this; it is the economy of what many would term a rich but broken society. Oil receipts mean that there is healthcare and schooling for everyone, but productive, rewarding employment is hard to find. An enormous, lethargic, corrupt public sector, for decades used as a way of giving people jobs, is now an obstacle to reform. Few men in government have the confidence to make decisions, the majority of projects approved for development never make it to completion. Back in 1975, Libya had similar GDP and living standards to Portugal, and was far more advanced than the United Arab Emirates. Now, thirty-five years on, it lags way behind both. In 2009 I visited Qatar for the first time and I was taken aback by the high-rise buildings and splendour on display. Everything was so modern, gleaming and clean. Libya could have been like this if its wealth had been spent wisely.

There are thus many problems for Libya, but it is also the case that in 2010 things look better than they have since the late 1970s. In the past, Libya's small population could be accommodated in public sector jobs. With rapid population growth (half the population is under twenty), increasing unemployment is frightening Gaddafi, who recognises that it has the potential to threaten the foundations of his regime. Drastic action is required to bring more and better jobs to Libya, so that the gains of the revolution are protected. Mending fences with the West was a step taken with money in mind: these days the Libyan regime is pursuing reform, chasing foreign investment and talking positively about some of the sweeping political reforms that will undoubtedly be needed to protect a truly competitive economy.

★

There is one economic truth about Libya that often gets left out of the story. This is that, by and large, the nation's oil industry has been run smoothly, efficiently and relatively conservatively. The oil sector is the foundation upon which Gaddafi's entire revolutionary society rests, and it has been protected at all costs. Ironically, of course, the main force from which it has needed protecting has been Gaddafi's own revolution. The sudden policy reversals, the vindictive manoeuvrings and the xenophobia that have characterised Gaddafi's wider rule have largely been absent from the world of oil. This is because, of course, while the oil money flowed in, Gaddafi had no need to tax anyone and hence no compelling need to account to the citizenry for his actions. So long as he kept money flowing into people's bank accounts, he retained the intoxicating freedom to shape and reshape his eclectic *jamahiriyya*. The National Oil Company (NOC) has been the one branch of the Libyan state left to the control of knowledgeable, skilled experts and largely protected from the violent interventions of the revolutionary committees.

Upon taking power in 1969, the Colonel renegotiated contracts with the foreign oil companies in Libya, using either nationalisation or modified participation agreements to obtain a majority stake in all of them. He then pursued an aggressive oil-pricing policy, and encouraged his fellow members of OPEC to do the same. At Gaddafi's instigation, by 1973 OPEC had destroyed the traditional system of pricing, led by the major oil companies, instituting a new regime much more favourable to the producer countries. This was the radical Colonel's first experience of the international spotlight, as the Western world reeled at his bold challenge to the status quo. His successes in the resource economy won him a highly valuable new legitimacy: these early victories meant he would now be taken seriously. Gaddafi's pricing revolution and the nationalisation of many of the oil companies working in Libya worked to Libya's advantage, and the oil industry became even more profitable.

Sadly, everywhere else in the economy a storm of chaos descended relatively soon after Gaddafi took power. The first warning of things to come was in 1973, when Gaddafi delivered a speech calling for a cultural revolution, and lamenting the population's lack of revolutionary fervour. As part of this cultural revolution, Gaddafi called on the workers of Libya to take over the running of businesses and government. Ahmed, the Libyan businessman I interviewed in June 2009, told me that he turned up one morning at the large company he worked for to find that the junior clerks had put themselves in charge. In his company, this only lasted a short time, because the clerks proved unable to run things and welcomed the reinstatement of authority. The shock of this bizarre policy, however, reverberated through both the economy and society, a terrifying indication of the intentions of the new leadership.

With the publication of his *Green Book*, Gaddafi moved to ban shops, wages and rent, all of which in his view perpetuated the exploitation of the masses. Unsurprisingly, the people had not felt themselves particularly exploited by the availability of consumer goods, and were distressed to find themselves forced to shop in depressing, under-stocked government supermarkets, even if the first one had been personally opened by Yasser Arafat. Ahmed told me:

> In 1978, when *The Green Book* came out, that's when the real disaster happened. There weren't any shops from 1979 to 1986. In the early days

the shops had been full of goods . . . In the later years, many essential goods disappeared and you had no choice – only one type of tea, only one type of pasta.

A flourishing black market developed, and Libyans also travelled often to Tunisia to buy up as much as they could. It was an odd plight – living in a rich country, with plentiful income, there was so little available to buy that in the worst times people even struggled to feed their families properly.

According to *The Green Book*, 'a person living in another person's house in return for rent, or even without rent, is not a free person', and so, in 1978, Gaddafi decreed that tenants should seize ownership of their rented homes. Overnight, thousands of Libyans who had invested in property found their security whipped away from under them. The financial turmoil continued in May 1980, when Gaddafi declared all currency denominations invalid other than the one-dinar note, causing a mass stampede to deposit imminently obsolete currency in the nation's banks. People were then told they could withdraw only 1,000 dinars of currency annually. The next year, private bank accounts were banned, and thousands of people watched their life's savings melt away. The trauma of this was immense, and many decided the regime had become totally untrustworthy and fled, taking exile in the West. With them went expensive educations, vital skills and invaluable experience. By 1981, it is thought that there were between 50,000 and 100,000 Libyans living abroad.

Each year on 1 September, Gaddafi celebrates the anniversary of the revolution in 1969. The 1980 celebration saw the delivery of a crucial speech, in which he announced that all of Libya's entrepreneurs and traders were parasites, who contributed nothing to national productivity. As a result, small businesses were banned, and all of the shops that had held on throughout the turbulent events of the late 1970s now closed. Corner shops, souks, jewellers, restaurants – all shut down for much of the 1980s, making Libya's towns and cities feel grey and moribund. Most Libyans relied almost entirely on the black market to supply themselves with everyday necessities and luxuries. Meanwhile, slogans emblazoned on the billboards and plastic water bottles of Libya proclaimed the lucky citizens to be freed from the exploitation of private sector employment, being 'Partners not Wage Workers'.

It was rumoured that by 1986, there was more money under Libyan citizens' beds than in the nation's banks. This cash was needed for the black market transactions on which many relied for day-to-day needs. Moreover, the excesses of the revolution – the banning of retail trade, seizures of bank accounts, random transfer of property ownership – meant that most felt their cash was safer at home. Guma el-Gamaty gave me a powerful overview of the people's experience of Gaddafi's management of the economy:

> Libyans enjoyed for at least three decades, the fifties, sixties and seventies, a relatively stable life, free to pursue commercial activities, buy cars, travel abroad, because Libya has a small population with a huge oil wealth. However, in 1980 Gaddafi decided to impose his own brand of socialism, his own economic order, his *Green Book*, which meant that he came out with very harsh steps. He changed the currency just like that, said the old currency was worth nothing, and a lot of Libyans kept a lot of cash, so suddenly those people with tens of thousands of Libyan dinars in their house, it became worthless. It was a ploy to strip people of wealth. Then he started this rule that you were only allowed to own one house, and people were stripped of property. His own people, they started grabbing villas and houses and just living in them. He nationalised all the shops and businesses and companies. Even corner shops were closed down and he replaced them with people's marts, absolutely crazy, just like China and Cuba. This plunged the country into deep economic misery and suffering. Even toothpaste was not available. Imports just stopped, the private sector was just completely cancelled. The 1980s were very tough in Libya; anyone who lived there will tell you how miserable and tough things were. People reverted to the old days of cleaning teeth with charcoal, little sticks of it . . . About 1988 or 1990, Gaddafi realised his own brand of socialism had failed miserably and had made people very unhappy, very angry, so he slowly went back on this brand of socialism. He slowly began to allow small shops, small properties to come back. Today, nineteen years on, I would

say Libya is much better in terms of economic and social activity. *The Green Book*, which was applied very vigorously and harshly, failed miserably. And Gaddafi now, without saying it, has completely backtracked. Publicly he wouldn't say that . . . but practically it's not there. Today people are allowed to own companies, to set up shops, to run businesses.

Despite his preoccupation with socialist economic experimentation, Gaddafi could not avoid confronting the obvious problems of an economy and society entirely structured around oil. Oil was the main industry, and it was mainly staffed by foreigners. Small businesses had been banned. There were thus very few options left for employing people. Moreover, oil would certainly one day run out. As things stood in 1969, and as they stand today, if the oil and gas dried up, Libya would have virtually nothing. Accordingly, Gaddafi paid hundreds of thousands of pounds to consultant after consultant, seeking advice on how best Libya's economy could diversify.

Before the discovery of oil, development aid from the West had poured into efforts to make Libyan agriculture viable. Some progress was made, and Libya's farms gradually became more productive. Agriculture has since been one of the areas consistently targeted for development by Gaddafi, mainly through wild, destructive schemes for irrigation. Since Gaddafi took power, truly astonishing amounts of money have been spent trying to make Libya's farms successful. Mansour el-Kikhia, a professor at the University of Texas and an expert on Libya, has written that an average of $33 million per month was spent on agricultural projects between 1970 and 1997, with the money going on wells, fruit trees, irrigation pipes, forestation and infrastructure. By 2000, relatively optimistic estimates suggested that agriculture supplied just 7.6 per cent of Libya's GDP. Libya still imported 75 per cent of its food needs.

The agricultural sector illustrates the limits of Gaddafi's regime well. As with his nuclear weapons programme, money was poured into high-end farming technology, but little attention was given to the careful study of local conditions. Much of Libya is not suitable to be farmed at all, and costly projects to irrigate tracts of desert ended up wreaking environmental devastation, leading to the near-collapse of the country's water table. The government developed showy, expensively irrigated sheep and grain farms, but every single component of production needed to be imported, and Libyans did not want to work on the farms – Tunisians, Egyptians and even south Asians did the manual labour. When Gaddafi suddenly expelled thousands of foreign workers in 1985, agriculture in Libya pretty much collapsed. In general, agricultural schemes were badly managed, almost hilariously so. I say almost, because the cost of all this was immense, and the damage to the water supply was a serious crime in a desert nation.

Gaddafi's tendency towards ill-advised technological excess is powerfully illustrated in the ongoing project of the Great Man-made River, an enormous water pipeline project under development since 1983. The project aims to provide fresh water to Libya's cities, as well as to irrigate nearly 2,000 square miles of agricultural land. It is projected that by completion, it will have cost at least $30 billion, but probably significantly more. The first phase was finished in 1994 and is said to supply two million tons of water daily to Benghazi. In 1996, the second phase was completed and now delivers 2½ million tons of water to Tripoli each day.

The Great Man-made River was from the beginning the subject of rumour and cynicism. Many suggested that the cavernous labyrinth of underground tunnels it justified were in fact more likely to serve questionable military purposes. More prosaically, others dined off stories about the stunning inefficiencies and blunders that had accompanied its construction. A rumour is currently doing the rounds that the pipes were made of an unsuitable material and are now reacting with the soil around them, meaning that every single pipe will need to be dug up and replaced.

★

The story of economic reform in Libya begins with a population deeply angry at the excesses of the 1980s. Over this decade, Libyans grew increasingly unhappy with the squandering of national income on war in Chad. Oil prices also fell precipitously during this period, fostering even more discontent. Oil revenues had totalled $21 billion in 1981; by 1986 this had fallen to just $5.4 billion. Gaddafi, aware of the political dangers of economic want, in 1987 began an early experiment with economic liberalisation, which he called 'the Revolution within the Revolution'. He demanded modernisation in the management of state enterprises and an overhaul of agriculture and industry. He also called for the development of a strong private sector. Small businesses began to open again, to the gratitude of citizens who had spent years frustrated by the paucity of food and goods on offer. Reform at this time was not, however, hugely popular. Many Libyans feared that the regime's call to scale back the public sector would mean they would lose their jobs and the guaranteed standard of living they had become accustomed to. The population was without initiative, clinging to security within a state characterised by constant turmoil: this was to be an impediment that would also dog the reform programmes of the 2000s. The Revolution within the Revolution was anyway to be swiftly derailed by the economic and political storm of Lockerbie.

The 1990s proved a grey decade for Libyans. While the wild political excesses of Gaddafi's regime during the 1980s were curbed, UN and US sanctions brought isolation and economic stagnation. Economic growth slowed to just 0.8 per cent per annum between 1992 and 1999, while per capita GDP fell from $7,311 to $5,896. By the end of the 1990s, government-set wages had been frozen at the same amount (about 250–300 dinars per month) for nearly twenty years. Libya also faced a high rate of population growth and an almost non-existent rate of job creation. For the young Libyan, relatively few exciting options presented themselves. Gaddafi's determination to open Libya to the world, politically and economically, was substantially fuelled by his awareness of the need to find gainful employment for the growing ranks of Libyan youth.

Libya also faced the problem of a generally weak infrastructure that got even worse during the period of sanctions. Sanctions banned the import of new oil machinery, meaning that the industry had to get by on outdated, run-down equipment. Libya's electricity supply, its port facilities, its air transport capacity and its telecommunications infrastructure were all of poor and worsening quality. In Libya, things often still just don't work. Walking the streets, you see piles of rubble and garbage stacked up literally outside the doors of flashy five-star hotels. Potholes don't get filled, hospitals that run out of bandages or needles wait months for new supplies. I have sometimes waited hours to get a telephone connection to Tripoli as the network is so prone to failure. Opening up to the wider world, it was hoped, would help to address the moribund state of the infrastructure, and inject some much-needed dynamism into the country.

From the early 2000s, therefore, Gaddafi allowed his advisors to launch a programme of economic reform that would allow Libya to profit from its international reintegration. Libyans were promised that this reform would create a lively, exciting private sector and a much better business environment. Commitments were made, particularly under reformist Prime Minister Shukri Ghanem, a highly experienced economist educated in the US, to increase transparency in state finances, to undertake extensive privatisation and to encourage foreign investors. Libya's new economic strategy also looked forward hopefully to developing prosperous industries in agriculture, construction, energy, tourism and transit trade.

Positive steps were taken to encourage foreign investment, including cutting the minimum amount required of foreign companies from $50 million to $1.5 million, so that many more could pursue a greater range of business opportunities. Banking reform has been judged relatively successful, with BNP Paribas allowed in 2007 to take a 17 per cent stake (with an option to increase this to 51 per cent) in the Sahara Bank, Libya's biggest state-owned commercial bank. The mobile phone sector has also been privatised. A Free Trade Act was passed to ensure attractive conditions for foreign investors in key sectors of the economy. In July 2005, 3,500 goods became free of import duty. In March 2007, a Libyan stock market was established.

Reform in the oil and gas sector was hailed as successful, to the extent that many observers now feel that Libyan reform is a two-track process, with one set of effective, consistent policies for oil and gas and another set of unreliable, erratic polices for all other parts of the economy. The first track, energy sector reform, has been greeted with enthusiasm by the international industry. To great excitement, in 2004 the Libyans put up for sale a new set of Exploration and Production Sharing Agreements (EPSAs). The process of auctioning these EPSAs to foreign companies was noted for its transparency, openness and efficiency. In 2010, Libya is exporting 1½ million barrels of oil per day and has ambitions to lift this to two million barrels per day. Profits from natural gas have also taken off. The Western Libya Gas Project was launched in 2004, with the completion of a pipeline between Libya and Sicily. Libya has 53 billion cubic feet of proven natural gas reserves, and its unproven reserves may amount to over 100 billion cubic feet.

Recently, however, there has been new concern about Libyan plans for further nationalisation in the oil industry. Attempts have been made by the NOC to acquire the Libyan arms of international companies, and burdensome new regulations have been introduced forbidding offshore engineering, through which foreign companies are able to conduct a sizeable part of their operations from outside Libya. All of this is probably designed to ensure that the Libyan workforce finds jobs in the oil industry, but it is also likely to induce nervousness in many of the oil majors.

Outside the oil industry, things initially looked exciting. A Harvard management guru, Michael Porter, was appointed by Saif Gaddafi as an advisor and prepared a 200-page report arguing that tourism, agriculture and construction should be the focus in moving away from the dominance of oil and gas. Porter's work envisaged that by 2019, Libya could be fully integrated into the international economy, the home of numerous globally competitive local firms, a centre of entrepreneurship, a leader in environmentalism and the site of an excellent IT infrastructure. Following on from the report, Saif Gaddafi was permitted to set up an Economic Development Board to push reform forward so as to achieve this rosy vision.

There is certainly a wealth of possibilities to create a really productive economy in Libya. Tourism stands out as one of the most under-realised sectors. Libya's landscapes are breathtaking, its beaches spectacular, and its historical heritage fascinating. The Roman ruins of Leptis Magna, near Tripoli, are frequently visited and have been well restored and maintained. In contrast, other sites are dramatically decaying. The ruins of Cyrene, said to be one of the most impressive Ancient Greek sites in the world, are falling into disrepair. Cyrene was founded in 632 BC, and its visitors can wander through the arches and corridors of a city once vibrant with the trade and culture of not only the Greeks, but also their Roman successors. But Cyrenaica is the ancestral home of King Idris and the Senussi, and it has traditionally harboured the most opposition to Gaddafi. Its cultural heritage has suffered accordingly and, in recent years, looters have wandered in and out of the World Heritage Site at Cyrene, stealing or even just smashing ancient treasures.

The process of economic reform offers the hope that Cyrene and other neglected sites from Libya's rich past will be preserved for the cultural and the economic benefit of its citizens. In 2006, just 130,000 tourists came to Libya. In comparison, Tunisia, Egypt and Morocco now each host well above six million tourists annually. Saif Gaddafi, in particular, has promoted Libya's potential to match its more tourism-savvy neighbours. In 2007 he exhibited his plans for the 'Green Mountain Sustainable Development Area', a tourist development focused on the spectacular Greek and Roman ruins at Cyrene and the surrounding Green Mountain region. The development is to include protected wilderness, boutique eco-lodges, organic farms and archaeological sites restored according to international best practice guidelines. The celebrated British architects Foster & Partners have been employed to plan the project. The goal of the development is to attract moneyed high-end tourists to sites along the coastline, in the process, hopefully, employing up to 70,000 Libyans.

It will be fascinating to wait and see whether the Gaddafi family's ambitions are realised. This will be a real test of commitment to openness and to a more relaxed, peaceful rule, for tourists will certainly be deterred by any reports of ugly excesses in what is effectively a police state. Can Gaddafi allow foreigners to troop in and out, interacting with the locals, forming their own opinions of his achievements? Will the world trust Libya enough to visit in large numbers? Already, the signs are mixed. In May 2005, the regime stopped demanding that visitors have their passports translated into Arabic, a major structural impediment to tourism. But in November 2007, the cumbersome rule was suddenly reintroduced. Forty Swiss and 170 French visitors to Libya were turned back from Tripoli airport the day the new rule was announced, presumably returning home to relate stories of a somewhat disappointing holiday. One is left wondering how strong the commitment to the tourist trade really is at the top.

In general, Libya's commitment to economic reform and its ambition to create a freer, more dynamic business environment outside the oil industry seem questionable. The dream of a diversified economy with a prosperous, dynamic private sector fuelled by foreign investment has remained distant. Oil and gas continue to make up 97 per cent of exports and more than 75 per cent of government revenue. Aspects of reform appear halting and uncertain. A free trade zone, for example, officially opened in Misurata, Libya's third largest city, in 2004 was still not operating by the end of 2008. The plans look good, but the policy environment is, as ever, hazardous and stormy.

A major obstacle to reform and economic diversification is undoubtedly Gaddafi himself. He continues to enjoy encouraging a state of uncertainty, dramatically reversing policies and strategies and ensuring that no reformist plan can be pursued with confidence. A recent example was his stunning announcement in September 2008 that he would abolish most of the institutions of government: no more education and health departments, just money paid directly to people to allow them to take care of their own needs. This was in response to what he saw as the complete failure of Libya's lethargic, moribund bureaucracy to spend new oil revenues effectively so as to improve state services. Under the Wealth Distribution Programme, small local bodies would be set up to replace central government ministries. Gaddafi told the nation: 'Each one of you, prepare to take your portion of the wealth and spend it as you wish. As long as money is administered by a government body, there will be theft and corruption.'

Libyans are thus now facing up to the prospect of the meagre state infrastructure that does exist being dismantled, leaving them with cash in hand but a chaotic and ungoverned set of hospitals and schools to spend it on. This is free-market capitalism Gaddafi-style: the gradual reform proposed by others wrested out of shape into a festival of productive revolutionary disorder. As yet, little progress has been made on the dismantling of government, and it is to be hoped that this remains the case. Nonetheless, the incident illustrates some of the difficulties and uncertainties that private companies will encounter in dealing with the mercurial policy environment created under Gaddafi's regime.

Libya's regulatory environment is also something of an impediment to the encouragement of investment. The judicial system is exceptionally weak and the rule of law absent. If things go wrong, recourse to the Libyan legal system is an unattractive option. There is much work yet to be done on creating the transparent, strong, independent institutions needed to win the confidence of business. A big question mark remains over the extent to which Gaddafi's autocratic regime will allow this. The Colonel may want privatisation and a booming economy, but not as much as he wants his own totalitarian rule to be protected from such threats as an active judiciary or critical regulatory agencies. Markets need freedom. Capitalism inevitably brings some level of social inequality. The ability of Gaddafi's state to accommodate such realities is deeply questionable.

Support for economic reform is said to be quite low inside the Libyan state. Most bureaucrats have witnessed the dramatic failures of earlier schemes and, understandably, few are willing to go out on a limb to enact the institutional reforms needed to create a safe, predictable environment for entrepreneurs. Reform has stumbled against the serious inefficiencies of a state weakened by decades of despotic, unpredictable rule, which naturally encouraged a 'lie low, line your pockets and save your own skin' mentality throughout government. The armies of foreign consultants working in Libya note that it is difficult to find assertive decision makers among the timid ranks of Libyan politicians and civil servants, which makes it hard to drive projects to completion. As well as timidity when it comes to decision-making, government corruption is also reported to be a problem throughout the economy, and those setting up businesses in Libya regularly face demands for bribes.

To understand the difficulty of reforming Libya's economy, you need to understand the problem of its workforce. The government and its agencies have historically employed almost everyone in Libya, offering reasonably paid and completely secure jobs. In 2005, it was estimated that the public service employed nearly 75 per cent of the workforce. Manual labour is viewed as undignified in Libya, and Libyans have become used to seeing foreigners doing all menial work. Their beleaguered education system was unable to provide them with the skills needed to work in the oil industry, and even today just 3 per cent of Libyans have jobs with the oil companies. Although Gaddafi's regime legislated requirements for foreign companies to employ locals, there were simply not enough suitable local candidates. So, while the oil and gas industries bring cutting-edge technology and enormous, exciting projects to the country, its nationals are mainly working in dull, meaningless bureaucratic jobs.

Providing jobs in the public sector bought Gaddafi a certain degree of stability and has probably been key to the political survival of his dictatorship. The cost has been an enormous payroll, an army of under-employed public servants and a thoroughly inefficient bureaucracy. Any plan to slim down this bureaucracy carries an immense, probably unsustainable political cost. Meanwhile, the population has grown, and even Libya's massive public sector cannot keep providing jobs for everyone. Unemployment is estimated to be at least 30 per cent, a considerable political and economic worry for Gaddafi. In 2006, the then new Prime Minister, al-Baghdadi al-Mahmudi, said he would make some 400,000 public sector workers redundant. This was accompanied by a commitment to find opportunities for them in the private sector. Quickly, though, Libya's leaders backtracked. It was announced that those made redundant would be paid their salaries for an astonishing three years after their jobs ended.

Other tentative steps have been made towards addressing the problem. In 2005, Shukri Ghanem launched a 'crash programme' to create a skilled workforce. The forthright Ghanem (now head of the NOC) told the BBC that 'Libya's schools and universities unfortunately stopped teaching English for a long time, which affected the abilities of Libyans to work for foreign companies and also their ability to comprehend what's running around them in this world'.[1] To make up for past mistakes, extensive language coaching was made available, and Tripoli is now one of the most prosperous places to be for the world's English teachers.

The government has also made generous loans available to people wishing to start up businesses. It was reported that $2.3 billion had been allocated for potential entrepreneurs. It remains to be seen, however, how willing Libya's historically scarred population, witness to frequent crusades against indigenous small business, will be to come forward and take part in such a policy. In general, though, the cumbersome state bureaucracy is a problem that remains to be solved, and it is somewhat doubtful whether Gaddafi's or any other regime will muster the political courage to do so.

★

What is certain, however, is that there is money to be made. Lord Foster's involvement with the Green Mountain project exemplifies the myriad possibilities for British involvement in Libya's economic revival. Such opportunities are not confined to the oil industry or to tourism. Cranes loom wherever you go in Libya, and the sounds of drilling and hammering are to be heard everywhere. A construction boom is already underway, and more is forecast: there are plans to spend $50 billion on public works by 2012, particularly on housing and infrastructure. No doubt the worldwide economic slowdown will mean the scaling back of some of these plans, but there will nevertheless be an unprecedented number of new construction projects in Libya in the near future.

Britain is particularly well placed to benefit from Libya's revival. While our respective governments have often been at loggerheads, thousands of Libyans have travelled to the UK for education and are familiar with Britain and its people. We have the right kind of skills: in construction, we are particularly experienced in specialist consultancy services. Libya currently plans to spend $5 billion on twenty-eight new universities, all of which will require staff and know-how in construction and planning from beyond its borders. In healthcare, we can provide extensive expertise. At the moment, Britain is somewhat under-represented in the new flowering of Libyan industry, with some British companies put off by an unusual business environment and the extensive bureaucracy and red tape that remains. I encourage them to take the plunge anyway. Patience in Libya is rewarded, even if the work needed to get through the door is considerable. Meanwhile, one key measure to reverse the appalling economic mess in which Britain finds itself is to export – but on a scale hitherto unseen. Libya is just three hours away by air, and with its extraordinary wealth could be a hugely important trading partner for us. The next government must do everything possible to promote Anglo-Libyan trade.

Of course, to do business in this kind of world is to cross an ethical minefield. No less than anyone else, I feel the strength of the argument that by working with the Gaddafi regime, we may seem to give our tacit approval to political repression. But what is the alternative? Removing ourselves from Libya means that we lose our chance to be part of the process of rebuilding the economy of a really important oil-producing state, which has the potential to be a stable partner to Britain. Michael Porter, the Harvard professor of business who has worked closely with Saif Gaddafi on reform, has commented in the press that he sees working with Libya as a unique opportunity, a sort of test case to gauge the possibilities of engaging with problematic regimes seeking reform. I agree with his view that by sending talented British businessmen to work closely with their Libyan counterparts, we have a really valuable opportunity to make Libya's economy and society work better. Moreover, the hard reality remains that Libya's oil is key to world stability. It is in our interests to keep her close. Inevitably, the current regime will eventually give way to another, and if Britain is to play a role in a post-Gaddafi Libya, we need to be there now, building up our networks and our knowledge.

This is not to say that I advocate a self-interested silence on the human rights abuses that undoubtedly take place in Libya and on the troubling issues of our mutual past. Rather, I believe that an engaged friend has more chance of causing change than a distant, critical Western stranger. Tripoli now boasts outlets of British chains including Marks & Spencer, Bhs and Monsoon. The British Council provides English language teaching to thousands of pupils. As we become more interdependent, culturally and economically, the chances for honest, productive conversations on all the issues that both unite and divide us grow ever greater.

# 13

# AFTER GADDAFI

The leader you cannot change. You can change everything except the leader because he is a leader.

Saif el-Islam Gaddafi, 2004 [1]

At sixty-seven, Gaddafi is approaching old age. His revolutionary fervour is now thoroughly out of fashion. By all accounts, few Libyans now feel any fondness for his leadership, and many onlookers describe Libya as a society in which a façade of calm disguises seething (if almost completely unorganised) political tension. All those with an interest in Libya wonder what the future will bring.

Gaddafi's police state is so strong and so effective that challenges to his rule are unlikely while he lives. But how does a society under the iron control of a charismatic, despotic leader make a successful transition when that leader inevitably passes? Libya has no institutions that can help to make that transition. Popular committees feed their ideas up to the General People's Congress in an odd system of supposedly democratic involvement, but there is no capacity for the Libyan people to make a choice between different leaders with different ideas about their country's future. There is no free press where debates can be held, conflicts worked out. Indeed, the question of Gaddafi's leadership has been explicitly ruled by his son Saif el-Islam to be a 'red line', one of the subjects Libyans are forbidden to discuss.

In the absence of public debate, Libyans and international observers are left to speculate. Could the country exchange the stability of its dictatorship, nearing half a century old now, for the uncertain waters of a multi-party democracy in which the participating parties would have to be built almost from scratch? Will Libya be taken over by the Islamic groups who have been at work there almost as long as Gaddafi himself? Will one of the Gaddafi children step forward, leading a seamless Syria-style transition from dictator to son? Will coup be followed by countercoup until someone builds up enough influence to hold onto power? Or will one of Libya's highly educated, knowledgeable technocrats step forward to guide the country slowly to a more open, stable and prosperous future? Whatever happens, a great fear remains that a wave of violence may follow Gaddafi's departure, with these competing tensions in society being worked out on the streets.

Gaddafi himself appears to take little interest in the issue. Guma el-Gamaty, the Libyan dissident I interviewed in London in June 2009, commented of the Colonel's attitude to his succession:

> No-one can tell, simply because of the erratic nature of Gaddafi's personality. I think he feels he is a great ruler who will rule Africa and will rule forever, make this United States of Africa that will take on the world, take on the United States of America. The man is delusional. I don't think he wants to talk about who will succeed him, he doesn't want to admit that day is coming.

Gaddafi's ventures into fiction suggest he is deeply perturbed by the prospect of his own demise. In one of his short stories, he spends a page wondering whether death is male or female, and concludes:

> Death is a male who is on the offensive all the time. He has never been on the defensive even when he is beaten. He is brave, fierce, cunning and sometimes cowardly. Death attacks but gets beaten off badly at times. He does not emerge victorious in every attack as some people seem to think.[2]

It is not surprising that, unlike Fidel Castro or even Kim Jong-il, Gaddafi is doing nothing to indicate how he would like to see Libya ruled when he has gone. Of course, he is a healthy man who is likely to be with us for many years yet. At the same time, the deafening silence over the question of succession leaves many wondering whether the Colonel is even capable of contemplating a world in which he does not lead Libya. As things stand, he continues to set his ministers, his sons, and his followers against one another, so that none is likely to be left with a clear mandate to take over.

★

Despite his lifelong crusade against the principle of inherited rule, Gaddafi has done little to assuage fears that he will pass the reins of dictatorship on to one of his children. One or other of the eight young Gaddafis plays a role in almost every aspect of life in Libya. For many of the thousands of Libyans living abroad, watching and desperately hoping for change, this is a source of the greatest sorrow. Ahmed, my Libyan businessman friend from London, felt despondent about the role of Gaddafi's children, and what it may mean for his country:

> The country is in a mess. So much corruption, so much negligence. People
> have lost hope; he [Gaddafi] will never change. He is much stronger, even
> more powerful. Even if he dies, he has eight children. His children, they are
> holding everything. In every field, they are controlling everything. People
> are desperate. They don't believe in the opposition because they believe
> it to be useless. They have no faith in any group outside the country. For
> years we hear of this group or that group. They are all useless.

Gaddafi's children are indeed, as Ahmed told me, omnipresent in Libyan society. It is likely that they will play some role in a post-Colonel Libya, but at the same time, none is clear favourite. Gaddafi's Libya is a place characterised by division and fear, and his children have not been immune from their father's tendency to play one sector of society against another. None of the children has consistent cross-institutional support.

Nevertheless, several of them are in a strong position and, in the absence of a clear alternative, it may be one of them who takes the reins.

Saif el-Islam Gaddafi, Gaddafi's second son and the eldest by his second wife, Safia Farkash, has been far and away the most credible and the most consistently ambitious of the siblings. Saif's position is not unique and perhaps reflects a new regional tendency. Syria's current President, Bashar al-Assad, a relatively moderate leader with a keen focus on economic reform, stepped smoothly into the breach after his father, Hafiz, died in June 2000 following a thirty-year rule. Over in Egypt, meanwhile, 81-year-old Hosni Mubarak is grooming his reformist, anti-poverty son Gamal to assume the leadership. Gaddafi will thus not be alone among the republics of the Arab world if he does push ahead with plans to install a favoured son. Regional politics, it seems, may increasingly be conducted by dapper, expensively suited, Western-educated heirs, all fluent in the language the US most likes to hear. If they are men of strength and principle, this may be to everyone's benefit. If, however, they are unable to reach out to their people, if they cannot contain the many tensions of each society, then interesting times may lie ahead.

Saif undoubtedly has many strings to his bow. He graduated in 1993 from al-Fateh University in Tripoli, where he was a student of engineering and design. He has undertaken postgraduate degrees at the IMADEC University in Vienna and at the London School of Economics and Political Science (LSE). Saif is also an artist. In 2002, his exhibition 'The Desert Is Not Silent' toured the world, to mixed reviews. His paintings recorded such subjects as galloping Arab horses, sunsets, roses, and Colonel Gaddafi floating in the sky over a beach circled by an eagle. A reviewer from *The Guardian* rather cruelly commented that the exhibition served to reinforce the 'depressing connection between bad art and megalomaniac regimes'.[3]

Saif has carved out a public role for himself as a reformer, with the desire to work for progressive change in both politics and economics. His vehicle for promoting this change has been his non-governmental organisation (a loose term in this context, given that most such organisations are banned in Libya, and the ones that do exist are almost all under the stewardship of one of the Gaddafi children), the Gaddafi International Charity

Foundation. The Gaddafi Foundation advocates progress on human rights and humanitarian work, and promotes societal development. It also says that it wants to foster civil society and stronger political institutions, something of a challenging remit in a country where some would say neither exists at all. Nevertheless, it might be argued that the foundation's very existence and its willingness to use the language of human rights bode well for Libya's future.

Saif has championed some groundbreaking plans for reform. In a televised speech from Benghazi in August 2008, he asked for an independent Libyan central bank, a high court and an independent media. He has also pushed plans for a Libyan constitution, telling a *Newsweek* journalist it was required because 'nothing is well defined. And because nothing is well defined, you open the door for rumours, speculation, expectations, you know, because nothing is clear and transparent.' When asked whether his father backed him in his constitutional quest, Saif replied, 'I think so. Maybe not 100 per cent.'[4]

Additionally, Saif has emphasised his ability to connect with young Libyans, who are more and more a really worrying demographic for the leadership. As mentioned above, Libya has an extremely youthful population, and a large proportion of its youth are unemployed. These are the young men and women most likely to heed the calls of the Islamic fundamentalists dreaded by Colonel Gaddafi, and if Saif can find ways to address their concerns, this will be a point in his favour. Saif portrays himself as a media-savvy moderniser, with a slick website and a number of television stations under his belt. In a regime where lengthy readings from *The Green Book* are still screened on state television nightly, Saif may be welcomed by the younger generation as the face of a more exciting modernity.

Saif also has considerable experience of international politics under his belt, especially through his central role in shepherding Libya's return to international respectability. He was at his father's side during negotiations over the Lockerbie and UTA bombings, and has helped to build Libya's profile as a broker of world conflicts. In 2001, for example, he played a part in the negotiations to free aid workers held hostage by the Taliban. Through the Gaddafi Foundation, he negotiated the release of Western and Malaysian hostages seized by Abu Sayaf, a radical Islamist and separatist group based in the Philippines. He is thought to have been central to Libya's decision to free the medics detained on charges of infecting Benghazi children with HIV, and to the negotiations over the surrender of Libya's nuclear arsenal.

Looking at video footage of Saif in 2008 and 2009, one can see that this role alongside his father on the world stage has not necessarily been easy. Repeatedly interrogated by journalists about Lockerbie and his father's record of sponsoring terror, Saif has had to confront his country's poor reputation head on. He has certainly made mistakes – labelling the Lockerbie relatives 'greedy' and after 'blood money' in an August 2008 BBC interview was a gift to journalists all over the world – but all in all, he has mainly demonstrated composure and dignity in the face of questions from journalists who are almost always under-informed about Libyan affairs and who tend to patronise him as a sort of tinpot dictator's mouthpiece.

There are, however, clear limits to Saif's chances. Is a PhD graduate of the LSE trained to talk in the often banal and gentle jargon of international development, a habitué of foreign capitals, really able to take on the leadership of Libya? Compared to regime insiders with decades of experience of running Libya's economy and government in the most stressful and uncertain of conditions, Saif is radically inexperienced. Pitted against the tough, revolutionary old guard after his father's rule is ended, Saif is likely to struggle. He is often judged as under-estimating the strength of this brutal set of survivors as opponents to his liberal vision of the future. For the revolutionary committee men and the military leaders, Saif's vision of a freer, fairer Libya spells a political obsolescence they will not accept easily.

It will be all too easy for his detractors to paint Saif as a decadent, liberal favourite of the West. His hobbies include falconry and playing with his four pet tigers (which travelled with him to Vienna when he went to study there, obligingly accommodated by the local authorities in Schönnbrun Zoo). All of this is unlikely to win him popularity with the Libyan people, who although not by and large fundamentalists, are often devout Muslims who take pride in their country's religious heritage. Nor, indeed, would they need to be religious to feel that this kind of showy excess smacks of corruption.

Saif has been riding the wave of Libya's economic reforms, so far mostly with success. Yet recently it has seemed that this might be less of a route to popularity than might have been supposed. The oil sector is working better, but the rest of the economy in many ways languishes. Regulation, transparency, reform and change are needed to make the economy work properly and to create better opportunities for Libyans. Within the context of a dictatorship, all this is unlikely and economic reform may disappoint. If so, Saif will be the public face of this disappointment.

Saif himself regularly denies that he will succeed his father. He was quoted in the *New York Times*, for example, saying of Libya that 'this is not a farm to inherit'.[5] In August 2008 he even declared that he was withdrawing from politics entirely. Few Libyans or observers really believed this, but for Saif, the decision was perhaps a recognition that his political future may be brighter if he stays aloof from the fray of everyday politics. Many continue to feel that despite his denials Saif will play an important role in a post-Gaddafi era.

Having watched Saif's career with interest, it is my feeling that he is unlikely to lead Libya for long, if at all. He comes across as sensitive, conflicted and too thoughtful, a completely different creature from his impulsive, macho father. It strikes me that despite widespread cynicism towards his advocacy of human rights and political reform, Saif himself believes what he says, and even believes that it can happen under his father's rule. There is a strong sense that this student of international politics has been living a life of the most relentless doublethink. He has been completely unable to confront the truth of his own position as the favoured son of a ruthless, often irrational dictator, while touring the globe promoting civil society, democracy and human rights. Sad as it is, the West has also proved again and again that what matters to it most is Libya's oil, not human rights or the freedom of its people. Saif may not be seen as the strong man required to hold Libya together in a post-Gaddafi landscape, protecting vital energy interests.

What, then, should we make of Saif's siblings? His main rival seems to be Moatessem Billah, Gaddafi's fourth son, rumoured to be a strong man, but without the intellectual talents of his older brother. Moatessem spent his early career in the military and is said to have led a failed coup against his father. He returned to Libya from Egypt after a reconciliation with the Colonel, and is now working as an advisor to the National Security Council. While Saif has been a very public crusader for reform, Moatessem has carved out a more traditional career path, generally keeping a low profile, carefully building up alliances among Libya's 'old guard'. It is said that Moatessem has important supporters, including his uncle Abdullah Senussi, Libya's very powerful head of military security, and Musa Kusa, Libya's foreign minister and one of the most influential and long-serving members of Libya's elite. Of late, Moatessem has been more visible: in October 2008 he attended high-level meetings in Russia with his father, and he met Condoleezza Rice to discuss shared security concerns in 2007. Saif has been entertained in the drawing rooms and offices of Washington on a number of occasions, but never officially received, suggesting that Moatessem's star may be in the ascendant.

Gaddafi's eldest son, 39-year-old Mohammed, has occasionally been mentioned as a possible successor. In general, however, he is felt to suffer from lower status because he is the son of Gaddafi's rarely mentioned first wife. Nonetheless, he remains an important figure in the landscape of Libyan politics. He has headed the Libyan Olympic Committee and the General Post and Telecommunications Company. Like his siblings, Mohammed is no stranger to controversy. In 2006, a Saudi newspaper reported that he had called on Pope Benedict XVI to become a Muslim, after the Pope apologised for making a speech critical of Islam. He also found notoriety when he banned Israel from taking part in the 2004 World Chess Championship in Tripoli (Libya had won the right to host the event only after having made a promise that the Israelis would be allowed to attend).

The Colonel's third son, Saadi, is a flamboyant character on the international football scene. Aged thirty-four, he seems less serious without much interest in politics. Saadi invited Diego Maradona to his wedding, is a good friend of the Brazilian superstar Ronaldo and dreams of hosting the

World Cup in Libya. He has had a professional football career, and was a long-serving member of the Libyan national team. His abilities, however, have often been disparaged. The dismissed national Libyan coach Franco Scoglio (given the sack after putting Saadi on the bench once too often) said of him, 'As a footballer he's useless. With him in the squad we were losing. When he left, we won.'[6] Saadi then spent some time in Italy pursuing his football career, and was signed to Perugia between 2003 and 2005 (he was thrown off the team after failing a drug test), moving on to Udinese for the 2005/6 season and to Sampdoria for 2006/7. He took to the field only twice during his Italian career, and unkind rumours circulated that the Italian clubs were keener to profit from Libyan sponsorship than from Saadi's footballing talents. Football in Italy has certainly benefited from the Gaddafi connection: at Saadi's urging, in 2002 the Colonel spent £14 million to acquire a 5.3 per cent stake in Juventus.

Saadi has been an uncertain influence on football at home in Libya. He has certainly raised the profile of the sport, and it is said that it was he who talked his father into lifting the national ban on the game back in the 1980s (football and the watching of all organised sport were considered against the egalitarian, anti-competitive spirit of the 'third way'). In 2000, he invited Middlesbrough, with Paul Gascoigne as captain, to Libya to play a friendly match against the Libyan national team (Libya won). Libya was said to have paid £1 million to host the English team. On the other hand, Saadi has not been widely seen as an ambassador for good sportsmanship. It has been reported that during his career with the Tripoli team al-Ittihad, the opposition would turn and run away rather than tackle him. Not surprisingly, he achieved a stellar record in the Libyan league.

The eastern city of Benghazi is traditionally the centre of opposition to Gaddafi, and al-Ahli Benghazi, one of its football teams, was reported to have suffered some seriously skewed refereeing during matches with al-Ahli Tripoli, for whom Saadi played before al-Ittihad. In 2002, the Benghazi players walked off the field after the Tripoli team were awarded two highly suspect penalties, but Saadi's armed guards ordered them to return. A similarly biased decision the same year led to a pitch invasion by enraged Benghazi fans. These fans later burnt down the local offices of the Libyan

Football Federation, which is headed by Saadi. The regime responded by dissolving al-Ahli Benghazi, arresting fifty fans and razing its clubhouse to the ground.

Off the sports field, Saadi has also worked as a film maker and in the oil industry. It is not entirely clear whether he is interested in politics, but at a press conference in Sydney in 2005 he spoke of his father's desire for him to step outside the world of football to play a more important role. Dressed in a powder blue suit, posing in front of a large photograph of his father garlanded with lilies, Saadi told the Sydney journalists he was there to establish the Libyan–Australian Friendship Society. A small start, perhaps, but one which indicates the possibility that Saadi may emerge as a political player. This suspicion was reinforced in 2006, when Saadi announced that he would be involved in the development of a 'Libyan Hong Kong', a free trade and investment zone to be located on the coast near the Tunisian border. The zone would aim to overcome Libya's labyrinthine bureaucracy and poor social infrastructure by effectively starting from scratch, providing exemption from many of the nation's more obstructive regulations. Saadi, it seems, may be closer to his brother Saif's worldview than to that of Moatessem.

Hannibal, the fifth son, is, to put it bluntly, a frightening character, with a record of brawls and punch-ups in foreign countries. He is most notorious for having single-handedly derailed Libya's relationship with Switzerland. In July 2008, he and his heavily pregnant wife, Aline, were arrested and held in jail for two days for abusing domestic staff in a luxury hotel in Geneva. Libya has since been embroiled in hostilities with the Swiss: immediately after the incident, Tripoli stopped issuing visas to Swiss nationals, threatened to stop supplying the Swiss with oil (half of Switzerland's oil comes from Libya) and talked of expelling all Swiss companies from Libya. Hannibal seems a relatively unlikely successor in a context where a steady hand at the tiller is likely to be what Libyans most value.

The two youngest sons, Khamis and Saif al-Arab, as yet have low profiles. Saif al-Arab still seems to be vigorously sowing his wild oats. In 2007, *Der Spiegel* reported that he had been accused of threatening to throw acid in the face of a bouncer who had ejected his girlfriend from the 404 nightclub in Munich, and that he had controversially claimed diplomatic immunity when the police launched an investigation.

Khamis, on the other hand, is a very serious player, and is increasingly emerging as the son with the strongest combination of strength, ruthlessness and intelligence. These days, Khamis is said to be in virtual charge of the military, heading up the 32 Brigade, a powerful regiment with a massive arsenal at its disposal. In 2006, a huge demonstration against the Gaddafi regime erupted in Benghazi, and the security men panicked, shooting demonstrators outside the Italian consulate. For two days, it was rumoured that Benghazi was under the control of the mob. Khamis was the one to lead his forces in to surround the city, a dramatic demonstration of his growing power and of the extent to which his father relies on him. Khamis is said to resemble his father exactly and to be possessed of the same ruthless cunning. The army and the revolutionary committees support him, and he is free of what the old guard sees as the taint of liberalism.

Gaddafi's daughter, Aisha, has a master's degree in international law and is reputed to have had some success as a business ambassador for Libya. She has worked as the head of Libya's Tourism Investment and Promotion Board. She is best known, however, as one of the hundreds of lawyers throughout the world who stepped forward to volunteer to defend Saddam Hussein during his trial in Iraq. Like Saif al-Islam, Aisha has focused strongly on charity work, heading the human rights charity Wa Attassimou, which has promoted causes such as women's rights. Wa Attassimou achieved considerable publicity when it gave a special award for courage to Muntazar al-Zaidi, the Iraqi journalist who hurled his shoes at outgoing US President George W. Bush in 2008. Aisha is popular in Libya, and the odd report has touted her as a possible successor. She clearly has a strong interest in politics: it was even reported that while in London in 2000 she took to the podium at Speaker's Corner to deliver a fiery speech in which she described the IRA as 'freedom fighters'. Libya remains a socially conservative country, however, and it is unlikely that Gaddafi would try to anoint a daughter as his successor.

★

Gaddafi is careful to spread power and influence thinly. His children are powerful figures in the land, but others, too, have power, counterbalancing each other in a delicate, shadowy dance. Some of the most powerful in the land are the men known as the *Rijal al-Khaimah* (Men of the Tent). The Men of the Tent are effectively the ones who have run things on the Leader's behalf, even though many have had no officially recognised role. The criterion for membership is trust, and Gaddafi ensures that the Men of the Tent oversee every aspect of national life: the media, the economy, tribal politics and culture. After countless unsuccessful coups against him and a particularly dicey decade back in the 1990s, these days the Men of the Tent are largely from the Leader's own Qadhafiyya tribe. Scrabbling for men he can trust, Gaddafi now places more faith in those to whom he is tied by blood or tribal allegiances. After he passes, the Men of the Tent will certainly play a role in whatever new regime follows. One of the most prominent among them has been Abdullah al-Senussi, Gaddafi's brother-in-law, who was for many years regarded as his second in command. Senussi, who worked closely with Libya's security agencies, is a somewhat sinister character, having been convicted *in absentia* by a French court of the 1989 UTA Flight 772 bombing (see Chapter 3).

Gaddafi's cousins, the Gaddaf al-Dham brothers, have also come to wield considerable influence. Ahmed, the younger brother, is known as the Libyan Prince, and is renowned for his charm. He is Gaddafi's personal envoy, and delivers in person the regime's most sensitive correspondence. His particular remit is Egypt, and he is known as the 'special co-ordinator' of the Libya–Egypt relationship. He has funnelled billions of dollars into the Egyptian economy, the conduit of Gaddafi's determination to maintain a powerful Libyan influence over the border. Ahmed's brother, Sayed, heads the Popular Socialist Leadership Organisation, which gives tribal leaders representation in government.

Other Men of the Tent include Khalifa Haneish, another Gaddafi cousin, who has no formal position but who is heavily influential in the security apparatus. Masoud Abdul Hafid, from the Qadhafiyya, is also an informal player in the security apparatus, who looks after the volatile south of the country. Omar Ishkal has been entrusted with leading the revolutionary committees for the last three years, a position of considerable power. Ahmed Ibrahim runs a Centre for Green Book Studies and is seen as the top ideologue of the regime. He is a veteran of the draconian crackdowns on university students in the 1970s, and has publicly described Libya's reformists as weak failures.

These are the men who can bring into play the institutions of real power – the revolutionary committees, the military and the security agencies. Libya has many men of talent working within the ranks of its government and bureaucracy, in particular inside the oil industry, but when it comes to the ruthless violence that is likely to be required to secure a hold on power in the wake of Gaddafi, they will be able to do little. For the weakest of the institutional players is the government. Gaddafi has worked assiduously to ensure that his departmental secretaries and bureaucrats have little chance to build up any reputation or following. Elites are moved from post to post in quick succession, with regular stints overseas to remove them even further from the public consciousness. Government departments and state agencies themselves are frequently attacked, and few high-up officials have any confidence in the longevity of the organisation in which they work, let alone of their own careers. With the exception of Gaddafi, his family and some of the Revolutionary Command Council originals, journalists in Libya seldom bother to mention politicians by name, as it is unlikely that the public will make the effort to remember who is doing what when things change so regularly.

Recent years, however, have seen Libya's technocrats, economists and reformers gain somewhat in influence, because their know-how was needed to modernise the economy and to reap the benefits of the increased foreign presence in Libya. One of the lead reformists is the former Prime Minister Shukri Ghanem, who previously held the powerful position of head of research at OPEC. Ghanem was made Prime Minister in 2003 and assembled a cabinet of fellow reformers to work with him. His attempts to invigorate the sluggish, enormous state bureaucracy, to reform government and to launch a campaign of privatisation were viewed positively by the business community and by Western governments. Ghanem was a man of action, not just words: in 2004 alone, he privatised 160 publicly owned companies. His plans for political reform were ambitious. According to the Libya expert Dirk Vandewalle, he called for a strengthened legislature and judiciary, an increase in the Prime Minister's independence, and safeguards to ensure that decision makers were protected from what he referred to in shockingly direct terms as 'invisible' forces.[7]

Gaddafi, however, began to feel that the benefits of reform were not reaching the people quickly enough, while politicians and an inflated, corrupt bureaucracy prospered. In his usual way, therefore, he intervened to adjust the balance of power, putting the reformers once again on the back foot. In 2006, Ghanem was sacked as Prime Minister. His reforms had apparently been blocked by 'revolutionary' opponents of privatisation, and he was reported to have declared that he should either be allowed to implement change properly or be let go. Let go he was, as was another reformer in 2009, when Mohammed Abderrahman Shalgham, a close ally of Ghanem, was replaced as foreign minister by Musa Kusa. Kusa, of course, was the former diplomat notorious for having been kicked out of Britain in 1980 for calling on Libyans to murder dissidents abroad. Shalgham, by comparison, was internationally respected for his openness and effectiveness in carrying out the substance of the Lockerbie negotiations.

Reformists were reshuffled, not purged, and their talents continue to benefit the regime. Nonetheless, it is clear that the old guard, with their power vested in the army and the revolutionary committees, are significantly more powerful in the land, despite the fact that their fortunes wax and wane in comparison to the reformers. In the end, dictatorships run on armies and spies, and are by their very definition challenged by reformists and supporters of liberalisation. Technocrats and economists play their role as Gaddafi sees fit, but they are on a tight rein indeed. Unfortunately, it is unlikely to be these moderate men that we should look to understand the immediate post-Gaddafi fate of Libya.

*

What, then, of the army? After all, for many years, observers hopefully watched Libya's generals for signs of a challenge to Gaddafi. The Americans, when they attacked Tripoli in 1986, secretly hoped that the chaos created by their bombardment would furnish the perfect opportunity for a countercoup from the ranks of the military. The problem was that Gaddafi, too, expected this. He has been the survivor of more coup and assassination attempts than have been counted, with a resurgence of resistance in the army occurring regularly every five years. The early 1980s were a particularly restive period, followed by a clampdown in the middle of that decade. The 1990s then saw another reinvigoration of the military opposition; in October 1993 senior leaders in the army were involved in yet another failed coup (followed by the arrest of close to 2,000 suspected dissidents and 12 known executions). Yet another coup attempt followed in 1995.

To reduce this sizeable and frequently demonstrated risk, Gaddafi has weakened the army command considerably. During the late 1970s and 1980s, he vested increasing power in the revolutionary committees, part of whose job has been to monitor and infiltrate the military. He makes sure constantly to rotate commanders from post to post, and often orders early retirements (occasionally en masse), to stop individuals building a power base. Gaddafi also ordered regular restructuring of the army so that segments of it were divided and set against one another. In the late 1970s, he created paramilitary organisations, including people's militias, in an apparent attempt to counterbalance the power of the army. Despite all of this, the army remains an obvious centre of power in that it commands the arsenal of the state, and it is certainly likely to play a role in deciding the post-Gaddafi balance of power. What is unlikely at this point is a challenge to the regime while Gaddafi lives.

As with his military commanders, Gaddafi has been very suspicious of the traditional tribal leadership, whose authority is vested in the aeons-old Bedouin system of tribal social organisation. In the early years, he sought to keep the tribal leaders, many of whom had prospered under King Idris, well away from the corridors of power. Since the 1990s, however, the tribal leadership has been welcomed back into the political arena, in another of the Colonel's striking policy reversals. In 1993 Gaddafi created a new political body called the Popular Social Leadership System (PSLS), purpose built to give tribal leaders a strengthened role in national politics. In giving the leaders a formal political role, it seemed Gaddafi had moved to bring tribal politics in from the shadows, to some extent making it part of the system. He has not, however, encouraged the traditionally excluded, restive eastern tribes, hailing from King Idris's Cyrenaican heartland, to play much of a role. One expert on Libya has written that only two out of the thirteen general co-ordinators of the PSLS since the inception of the system have been from the east.[8]

Since the tribes have been restored to political favour, observers have noted that what political choices Libyans do have — in electing representatives to popular committees — have been increasingly decided by tribal allegiances. Professor Mansour el-Kikhia has noted that 'bloody battles between tribes have taken place over land or political posts'.[9]

Tribal loyalties thus continue to influence people's political fortunes. They have powerful meaning for ordinary men and women, and are part of their self-definition. They have strengthened rather than weakened in modern times, as people seek the safety and reliability of a part of their lives that Gaddafi has not really been able to touch. They represent, therefore, one of the more powerful lines along which a new Libyan politics might be organised in a post-Gaddafi era. Whether Libya opts for continuing dictatorship or for democratic revival, tribalism is one of the few strong principles of social organisation, and it will certainly play a part in the deal-making that will follow Gaddafi's departure from power.

Libya's army, its tribes and its dictator's children: all will play some part in working out a post-Gaddafi future. What is currently certain, however, is that none are being encouraged to voice ideas or to debate any such future. Although Libya has been relatively freer since the early 2000s, criticising the government is still a no-go area, a truth some have discovered to their cost.

Fathi al-Jahmi provides the best-known example of this. Jahmi, a 66-year-old former provincial governor, was imprisoned in 2002 after he publicly criticised Gaddafi. His case was publicised by human rights organisations, and considerable pressure has been exerted on Libya to free him. He was briefly released in 2004 after US Senator Joseph Biden visited Libya and personally requested he be freed. When Biden departed, the unfortunate Jahmi was swiftly returned to incarceration. The official Libyan government line is that he is 'mentally disturbed' and is being held for his own protection.

★

We must also, of course, look outside the nation's formal institutions. There is also the possibility that in a power vacuum, underground opposition forces could emerge to stake their claim on power in Libya. Gaddafi has long feared this and has built a police state of such strength and security that it seems unlikely he will be challenged while alive. After he dies, things will be different.

Abroad, a variety of opposition groups have flourished during Gaddafi's rule. This international opposition has encompassed supporters of Idris's monarchy; disillusioned Arab nationalists who had no truck with *The Green Book* or socialism; purged elites from the army and the state; disillusioned technocrats stunned by the mismanagement of the economy; religious elites resentful of Gaddafi's attacks on conventional Islam; and members of the Muslim Brotherhood (of which more below). These groups have at times banded together, with lines of organisation criss-crossing in a complicated and ultimately disappointing history of attempts at resistance. For none of them has managed to mount a consistent, coherent challenge to Gaddafi. Their heyday was back in the 1980s: between 1980 and 1983 eight coup attempts were reported, many backed by such organisations as these. Nowadays, however, the story of the opposition abroad is mainly one of crashed websites, infrequently published newsletters and sporadic meetings in conference halls. Few any longer expect overseas organisations of Libyans in exile to play a role in any successor regime.

The most high-profile opposition group was the National Front for the Salvation of Libya, founded in Sudan in 1981 by Mohammed Yusuf al-Magariaf (see Chapter 6). The National Front managed to some degree to overcome the chronic division in the ranks of Libya's opposition, bringing together Islamists and secular opposition groups. It launched a major attempt to overthrow Gaddafi in May 1984, but ultimately failed. Although it is a weaker organisation these days, it continues to publish its newsletter, *Inqadh*, and to broadcast its radio programme, Voice of Libya, out of Cairo.

Dissident organisations abroad have, as we know, faced considerable violence from the Gaddafi regime. Gaddafi launched his high-visibility 'stray dogs' campaign back in the early 1980s, in which he called on Libyan dissidents overseas to be murdered. In line with his general move away from violence and terror, the threat against dissidents decreased from the late 1980s. Nonetheless, the lives of those opposing Gaddafi from a distance have not been easy, and periodically the 'stray dogs' approach has come back into favour. In November 1993, for example, Gaddafi made a speech declaring that overseas opponents were 'worthy of slaughter'. In the wake of this speech Mansour Kikhia (not to be confused with Professor Mansour el-Kikhia), a prominent dissident and former diplomat who had defected to the US and whose family had American citizenship, was kidnapped in Cairo. He was then handed over to Libya, where it is thought he was executed.

At the end of 1995, the British Foreign Office expelled Khalifa Bazelya, a diplomat working on Libyan affairs in the Saudi Arabian embassy in London and one of Gaddafi's most powerful spooks. Bazelya was accused of intimidating dissidents and recruiting spies. MI6 had itself tried to turn Bazelya, and it was reported in *The Observer* that he had 'led them a merry dance'.[10] It was widely suspected that his expulsion was linked to the murder a month before in London of Ali Abuzeid, a well-known Libyan dissident.

Gaddafi thus continues to fear dissidents abroad, but he fears even more the forces of radical Islam, which he has described as 'more dangerous than AIDS'. Fundamentalist Muslims confront his tattered, exhausted ruling ideology with forceful claims of religious purity that undoubtedly find resonance with some Libyans. Deprived of a civil society, disillusioned by the failures of their government, much of the population may well be persuaded to trust the militantly religious, the visibly non-corrupt.

Gaddafi has been dogged by Islamists throughout his rule, an eternal irritation that has provoked regular, violent clampdowns. An early challenge came from the Muslim Brotherhood, an international intellectual Sunni movement that was exported to Libya from Egypt under King Idris, who gave it free rein. Although Gaddafi vigorously repressed its members, the Brotherhood continued to be a presence in Libya into the 1980s and 1990s. It was a non-violent movement that in Libya was mainly restricted to a small number of men from an upper-middle-class intellectual elite. Given that Gaddafi's security apparatus watched over every aspect of Libyan life, and that ordinary society was virtually non-existent, there was almost nothing the Brotherhood could do to build up a popular following, and it was plagued by division, poor organisation and constant anxiety. Nevertheless, Gaddafi raged against it, hurling insults and often exaggerating its significance immensely. He has at various times labelled the members of the Brotherhood delinquents, cowards, hooligans, marijuana addicts, alcoholics, liars, bastards and rotten agents of Western imperialism. Although weak in Libya, the Brotherhood clearly pushed important buttons.

In 1998 the Colonel was able to unleash a final revenge on his historic enemy. His security men, armed with new intelligence on names and addresses, mounted a sweeping campaign of arrests that saw 152 alleged Brotherhood members jailed. Most members who escaped arrest left Libya for good. In February 2002, two Brotherhood leaders, Dr Abu Hanek and Dr Abdullah Izideen, were sentenced to death, thirty-seven members were dealt life sentences, and the remainder got long prison terms. The Brotherhood's presence in Libya is now much reduced.

The Brotherhood, with its intellectual roots and its genteel, privileged membership, was a different proposition entirely from the next generation of Islamists. These men had more radical means and more radical ambitions, and were spurred on by the worldwide resurgence of fundamentalist Islam. The 1980s saw jihadist cells springing up all over Libya, often inspired by the many Libyans who had travelled to Afghanistan to support the insurgency against the Soviet invaders (Gaddafi was on the side of the Soviets, labelling the Afghan mujahideen 'lackeys of the Americans'). Libyan jihadists at home in Libya were few in number and weak in organisation, but were nonetheless ambitious, convinced that the religious, oppressed Libyan population was more likely than most to rise up against its corrupt government. In a prominent demonstration of the growing threat they presented, six jihadists were publicly hanged in Benghazi in 1986, accused of having tried to kill a leader of the revolutionary committees, Ahmed Musbah al-Warfali.

The 1990s saw the jihadist threat grow better organised and more lethal. The Libyan Islamic Fighting Group (LIFG), mainly veterans of the war against the Soviet Union in Afghanistan, was probably the main group responsible for the periodic Islamist-sponsored unrest seen in Libya throughout the 1990s. In October 1995, they called for Gaddafi to be overthrown, and bravely declared this to be their *raison d'être*.

In general, 1995 was a turbulent year, marked by blustering threats and aggressive action against the many expatriate workers and refugees resident in Libya. Behind all of this, many saw the work of the LIFG. Hazy reports emerged of ongoing clashes between police and demonstrators in Benghazi between June and September. Some sources identified the demonstrators as fundamentalists, some as political opponents, and others as football rioters. It was rumoured that a July riot had left sixty protestors dead.

A Libyan tourist advertisement informs us that Brak is an administrative town in western central Libya, boasting a campground, a men's hostel and some historically interesting abandoned mud huts. This sleepy oasis town was in November 1996 the site of a jihadist attempt on Gaddafi's life. An LIFG member called Mohammed Abdullah al-Ghrew hurled a grenade at the Colonel as he progressed through the town with his official cavalcade. It was not a strong or a particularly convincing attack, but the regime responded with force. In the ensuing clampdown, it is thought that all LIFG members deserted the country. Gaddafi took to the airwaves to denounce the LIFG as servants of the Americans, who had prospered by stashing away CIA money while in Afghanistan.

The LIFG, as with other radical Islamist groups in Libya, had little success. They were poorly organised and chaotic, and enjoyed relatively little popular support. By the end of the 1990s, neither they nor the more moderate Brotherhood were any longer a significant presence in Libya. Gaddafi's fear of fundamentalism persisted, however, and he seized the chance to benefit in this respect from closer relations with the West. As a partner in the war on terror, Gaddafi found some genuinely powerful assistance in his quest to eradicate fundamentalists from Libya. The

Americans agreed to return to Gaddafi two LIFG leaders, Emir Abdullah Sadeq and Abu Munder al-Saidi, who they had arrested in Asia in March 2004. Britain installed the LIFG on its official list of terrorist organisations, and arrested five members living in Britain.

Libya's jihadists and the Muslim Brotherhood have, as I write, been all but completely neutralised. Yet Islamic fundamentalism, or so Gaddafi must fear, is a force bigger than the organisations that exist to promote it. From time to time, violence continues to erupt in Libya, and it is often attributed, rightly or wrongly, to jihadists. Gaddafi's regime still reacts brutally to any hint of fundamentalist involvement: it was reported in 2006 that 23 people were killed and 100 wounded in Benghazi when the police shot at demonstrators protesting against the notorious cartoons mocking the Prophet Mohammed published in Denmark that year. An activist alleged that most of the demonstrators that day were teenage boys.

Saif, meanwhile, has persuaded his father to follow a different road, attempting to engage the Islamists, both jihadists and members of the Muslim Brotherhood, in a dialogue with the regime. Talks, ongoing since 2006, have periodically stumbled and resumed. It may even be that dialogue with the regime proves the final blow to the organisations involved, as they are forced into dramatic compromises to secure the release of their leaders from Libya's prisons. On the other hand, the talks might give these organisations a legitimacy and a public profile otherwise unattainable. Saif's olive branch to the Islamists presents a positive show to the watching world, but at the same time the government is known to be holding 100 political prisoners associated with banned Islamist groups, mainly in the prisons of Tripoli. Some human rights organisations and diplomats feel that this number may be only the tip of the iceberg. Figures of up to 2,000 political detainees have been cited, many of whom are likely to have been held for years without trial, and among whom there are sure to be numerous alleged Islamic fundamentalists.

The forces of fundamentalist Islam are very likely to play a role in Libya's future. Many observers of Libyan affairs feel their claims will continue to resonate with the people, for whom religion has been an undoubted consolation through decades of cultural and social impoverishment. At the same time, though, Libyans have shown relatively little appetite for violence, and it is likely that the more extreme of the Islamist groups have been held back in Libya by popular lack of interest as well as political repression. It remains to be seen how capable religious establishments will be of constructing credible and effective organisations capable of winning support in a post-Gaddafi future.

★

The story of organised opposition to Gaddafi, therefore, is somewhat underwhelming. The twentieth century furnished so many stories of heroic resistance to dictatorship, colonisation and exploitation. In Poland, Lech Wałęsa and his Solidarity movement led a heroic resistance to communism, of which I heard much from my grandfather when I was a child. In Romania, a massive popular uprising toppled Nicolae Ceauşescu. Why, I ask myself, has no such movement emerged from Libyan society? One reason, at the simplest level, is that the population is very small. The task of ruthlessly and intrusively policing six million Libyans is eminently feasible. Also, the country is rich, so Gaddafi has been able to fund a behemoth of a security apparatus that has done its job well. More importantly, the country's wealth means that people have not, since Gaddafi came to power, gone to bed hungry, without a roof over their heads, or without knowing that they will get free medical care. The desperation that might fuel resistance has in the main been lacking. In comparison, the Romanians who rose up against Ceauşescu had suffered hunger and deprivation, and had little to lose.

Another problem is that so many potential leaders of an opposition have left the country. Compared to other dictatorships, people have had more money and better access to the West. Some of those who might, if forced to stay, have devoted themselves to resistance have understandably seized on the chance to build fruitful lives elsewhere. My interviewee Ahmed is a case in point – he has built a rewarding, interesting career in the UK, he has educated children who are now leaders in their fields and who are good, strong people who contribute to society. If Ahmed had been a black South African, oppressed by apartheid rather than by Gaddafi, he would have found it impossible to leave – frustrated by the immoral regime, he might have turned his considerable talent to resistance. In the case of Libya, escape was relatively easy. Ahmed can even continue to return to the country on visits to his family. The only price he has paid for this (and I do not underestimate the personal cost) is to keep a studied political silence.

While it is now fashionable and indeed right to talk about nations taking responsibility for their own fate – with even Barack Obama making speeches in Africa about moving on from talk of blaming colonisers – colonisation also has a part to play in understanding why Libya has not produced a convincing opposition. Italian colonisation effectively tore Libyan society to pieces, and left little to replace what was broken. There was no heritage of organised politics, no legal system and only a very weak education system, and local resistance was crushed brutally. As Libya achieved independence, there was almost no aspect of society around which a new politics could be organised. It was not a promising base from which to oppose a dictator.

I asked Guma el-Gamaty for his opinion on why Libya had produced such weak resistance to Gaddafi. He answered with passion:

> The key difference, in Poland and Czechoslovakia and Romania, there they had an essential infrastructure of civil society. In the Czech Republic, Václav Havel was organising to meet secretly with colleagues. This critical infrastructure was not there in Libya, even the seeds were stopped. From 1977 Gaddafi completely clamped down, he eradicated every sort of organised opposition. I think that disabled Libyans, it denied them this ability to organise. And Libyans hate him, they all say this behind closed doors, but they cannot organise, the potential leaders would be taken away immediately and killed. There is huge fear. In 1984 he hanged people simultaneously in about ten cities, and it was like a public ceremony, people were forced to come and watch, and they sort of froze. People were telling their children, 'Don't get involved, because we'll lose you,' and things just accumulated. So that now, Libyan society is very fragmented, very weak, it really feels the weight of oppression. And add to that, Libya is a huge country with a very small population, there are no concentrations of

people. I mean a lot of people tried, students, military officers, but they all failed and then they were all arrested and killed.

One thing about Gaddafi I will give to him is he does not compromise his position at all, he is absolutely ruthless, he probably realised to stay in power you would have to be like that. Plus he is not a mutt; he is very smart, he has a natural Bedouin intelligence. He is not intellectually very elaborate, but he is cunning and ruthless.

Gamaty hits on another key aspect: Gaddafi's amazing instinct for self-preservation. He is a master of dividing and conquering, an impresario at balancing power. Competing sections of society – his children, the army, Libya's Islamic establishment, tribes, the security forces, the popular committee pyramidal structure, revolutionary committees, bureaucrats – all have been divided internally and set against one another. No-one has had the opportunity to build up any sort of support or following. As the lurid billboards picturing the great Leader dotted all over Libya suggest, the only permissible focus of loyalty is Gaddafi himself. At the moment, the only possibility if the Colonel departed this world would be a complete power vacuum, a landscape of utter uncertainty. Gamaty says that as things are at the moment, with no clear line of succession and no leader with an uncontested power base, Gaddafi's departure would mean Libya 'would be like a pressure cooker, on the boil for forty years, and suddenly the lid goes off'. Perhaps the result would be a productive chaos, a working out of tension, a chance for the people of Libya to refuse further subjugation. For if Gaddafi does decide to spell out a succession, setting up one of his sons to take over, the future appears no more promising than a depressing, barren series of coups and countercoups, with all the country's potential continuing to be squandered, and the energies of the leadership devoted to their own power and influence and not to the welfare of a citizenry that has profited so little from its nation's wealth.

It remains to be seen how Gaddafi will approach the question of what will follow him. At the moment, he seems to be in a state of profound denial of his own mortality. But Gaddafi's major achievement is to have kept Libya stable, at least in comparison to many of his neighbours, and to have kept the oil flowing out and the money flowing in. His obituaries will doubtless have to acknowledge this, as well as documenting his violent excesses. Will he be willing to remain in denial, allowing the prospect of anarchy, the trashing of his legacy of stability by an explosion of tumult and conflict? Unfortunately, like Gamaty, I feel that he will. Gaddafi is not the man to step back into quiet retirement in order to ensure a smooth transition.

It is my hope that Britain will continue to build person-to-person links, to do more and more business with the Libyan state, to make friendships with those who have been forced to work under Gaddafi for so long. In this way, as the inevitable transition takes place, we can be at hand as a genuine friend, capable of giving advice if asked and proud of having demonstrated an engaged but principled interest in the future of this unique north African state.

# ACKNOWLEDGEMENTS

First of all, I would like to thank Madelaine Healey for the immense support she has given me in researching and writing this book.

I had the honour of meeting the family of PC Yvonne Fletcher and was humbled by their courage and dignity. I will do everything I can in Parliament to ensure that her killer is finally brought to justice. Her tragic death reminds us how grateful we should all be for the professionalism and dedication of our police and how they put their lives at risk for us every day.

My heartfelt thanks go to my wife Kate and daughter Alexis for being so supportive during the course of writing this book.

# NOTES

**Chapter 1: The making of Gaddafi**

1. E. D. Morel, *The Black Man's Burden: The White Man in Africa from the Fifteenth Century to World War I*. Manchester: National Labour Press, 1920, p. 100.

2. Geoff Simons, *Libya and the West: From Independence to Lockerbie*. Oxford: Centre for Libyan Studies, 2003, p. 9.

3. David Blundy and Andrew Lycett, *Qaddafi and the Libyan Revolution*. London: Weidenfeld & Nicolson, 1987, p. 39.

4. Mirella Bianco, *Gadafi: Voice from the Desert*, tr. Margaret Lyle. London: Longman, 1975.

5. Blundy and Lycett, *Qaddafi and the Libyan Revolution*, p. 40.

**Chapter 2: Gaddafi's revolutionary experiment**

1. Quoted in Alyssa Fetini, '2-Min. Bio: Muammar Gaddafi', *Time*, 3 February 2009.

2. Quoted in Mirella Bianco, *Gadafi: Voice from the Desert*, tr. Margaret Lyle. London: Longman, 1975, p. 67.

3. Quoted ibid., p. 24.

4. Lisa Anderson, 'Libya's Qaddafi: Still in Command?', *Current History* 86, February 1987, p. 67.

### Chapter 3: Guns and money

1. 'Master of Mischief', *Time*, 7 April 1986.

2. Donald Trelford, 'My meeting with Gadaffi', *Observer*, 28 March 2004.

3. See Daniel Pipes, *In the Path of God: Islam and Political Power*, rev. ed. New Brunswick, NJ: Transaction, 2002.

4. 'I am a mixture of Washington and Lincoln', *US News & World Report*, 10 November 1986.

5. See Patrick Seale, *Abu Nidal: A Gun for Hire*. London: Hutchinson, 1992, p. 148.

6. See Martin Sicker, *The Making of a Pariah State: The Adventurist Politics of Muammar Qaddafi*. New York: Praeger, 1987, p. 114.

7. See Brian L. Davis, *Qaddafi, Terrorism, and the Origins of the US Attack on Libya*. New York: Praeger, 1990, p. 11.

8. Seale, *Abu Nidal*, p. 136.

9. See Pierre Péan, *Manipulations africaines: l'attentat contre le DC10 d'UTA, 170 morts*. Paris: Plon, 2001.

10. See Ion Mihai Pacepa, *Red Horizons: Chronicles of a Communist Spy Chief*. Washington: Regnery Gateway, 1987, p. 98.

11. See Lauren St John, 'The years of loving dangerously', *Sunday Times*, 29 March 2009.

12. Jon Swain, 'Scargill in secret talks with Gadaffi's regime', *Sunday Times*, 28 October 1984.

13. Quoted in Sicker, *The Making of a Pariah State*, p. 119.

14. See 'Master of Mischief', *Time*, 7 April 1986.

15. 'Tracking the Children of God', *Time*, 22 August 1977.

16. Nelly Sindayen, '10 Questions: Imelda Marcos', *Time*, 26 June 2006.

17. See 'Gaddafi to visit Indonesia', *The Australian*, 24 January 2004.

18. See 'Thai militants "trained in Libya"', BBC Online, 13 October 2005.

19. K. Wong, letter to the editor, *Far Eastern Economic Review*, 24 February 1978.

20. See Shanti Nair, *Islam in Malaysian Foreign Policy*. London: Routledge, 1997.

21. Quoted in Trelford, 'My meeting with Gadaffi'.

### Chapter 4: The IRA's Tripoli connection

1. Brendan Anderson, *Joe Cahill: A Life in the IRA*. Dublin: O'Brien Press, 2002, pp. 273–4.

2. Quoted in Geoff Simons, *Libya: Struggle for Survival*. Basingstoke: Macmillan Press, 1993, p. 316.

3. Quoted in 'Death of Press Gallery Member – Libyan Support for IRA: Motion (Resumed)', Historical Debates of the Oireachtas, Seanad Éireann, vol. 117, 25 November 1987.

4. See Ed Moloney, *A Secret History of the IRA*, 2nd ed. London: Penguin, 2007.

5. Liam Collins, 'Gun-running IRA chief hid behind guise of "simple farmer"', *Irish Independent*, 9 October 2005.

6. See Toby Harnden, *Bandit Country: The IRA and South Armagh*. London: Hodder & Stoughton, 1999, p. 240.

7. Ibid., pp. 242–3.

8. See Donald Trelford, 'My meeting with Gadaffi', *The Observer*, 28 March 2004.

9. 'Death of Press Gallery Member – Libyan Support for IRA: Motion (Resumed)'.

10. Quoted in Simons, *Libya*, pp. 289–90.

11. Liam Clarke, 'Gadaffi's lesson to the IRA: cling onto power', *Sunday Times*, 28 March 2004.

### Chapter 5: Arab and African dreams

1. Gamal Abdel Nasser, *Egypt's Liberation: The Philosophy of the Revolution*. Washington: Public Affairs Press, 1955, p. 87.

2. Robert Fisk, 'A very weird leader: Profile – Moammar Gaddafi', *The Independent*, 26 August 2000.

3. Brian Cathcart, 'Obituary: Jean-Bedel Bokassa', *The Independent*, 5 November 1996.

4. Nelson Mandela, speech at a banquet hosted by Colonel Gaddafi, Tripoli, 22 October 1997. See www.anc.org.za/ancdocs/history/mandela.

5. See Geoff Simons, *Libya: Struggle for Survival*. Basingstoke: Macmillan Press, 1993, p. 276.

## Chapter 6: Death in St James's Square

1. See David Blundy and Andrew Lycett, *Qaddafi and the Libyan Revolution*. London: Weidenfeld & Nicolson, 1987, pp. 186–7.

2. Sir Geoffrey Howe, 'Libya (Diplomatic Relations)', Hansard, HC Deb, vol. 59, col. 209, 1 May 1984.

3. Ibid., col. 210.

4. Denis Healey, 'Libya (Diplomatic Relations)', col. 213.

5. 'On This Day 1950–2005: 17 April', BBC Online.

6. See Paul Keel and Gareth Parry, 'Softly, softly at the siege of St James', *The Guardian*, 19 April 1984.

7. Howe, 'Libya (Diplomatic Relations)', col. 211.

8. Geoffrey Robertson, 'Diplomatic immunity should end', *The Guardian*, 9 July 1999.

9. Margaret Thatcher, 'Libya', Hansard, HC Deb, vol. 95, col. 877, 16 April 1986.

10. Quoted in Ian Black, 'Machine gun burst echoed for 15 years', *The Guardian*, 8 July 1999.

11. See Robertson, 'Diplomatic immunity should end'.

12. Quoted in 'Dismay over Libyan PM's claims', BBC Online, 24 February 2004.

13. See Black, 'Machine gun burst echoed for 15 years'.

14. Tam Dalyell, 'Lockerbie', Hansard, HC Deb, vol. 298, col. 1005, 23 July 1997.

## Chapter 7: Reagan versus Gaddafi

1. See 'Reagan decides it had to be done', *The Economist*, 19 April 1986, pp. 17–21.

2. See 'I am a mixture of Washington and Lincoln', *US News & World Report*, 10 November 1986, p. 32.

3. See Bob Woodward, *Veil: The Secret Wars of the CIA 1981–1987*. London: Simon and Schuster, 1987, p. 190.

4. 'The most dangerous man in the world', *Newsweek*, 20 July 1981.

5. 'I am a mixture of Washington and Lincoln', p. 31.

6. Larry Speakes with Robert Pack, *Speaking Out: The Reagan Presidency from inside the White House*. New York: Charles Scribner's Sons, 1988, p. 180.

7. Quoted in 'President's news conference on foreign and domestic issues', *New York Times*, 8 January 1986.

8. 'La France garde ses distances', *Le Figaro*, 16 April 1986.

9. See Craig R. Whitney, 'London Journal: A veteran of the great Tory wars exits No. 10', *New York Times*, 26 March 1991.

10. Saif al-Islam Gaddafi's statement to the High Court, in the case between Saif al-Islam Gaddafi and Telegraph Group Ltd, 2002. Available at the Libya Our Home website, http://www.libya-watanona.com/news/n21aug2a.htm.

### Chapter 8: Libya and Lockerbie

1. Quoted in Claire Gardner, 'The final moments of Pan Am Flight 103', *The Scotsman*, 8 December 2008.

2. Jim Swire and Peter Biddulph, 'There's a plane down, an airliner', *Sunday Times*, Scotland, 8 December 2002.

3. Michael P. Scharf, 'The Broader Meaning of the Lockerbie Trial and the Future of International Counter-terrorism', *Syracuse Journal of International Law and Commerce* 29, Fall 2001, p. 57.

4. Tam Dalyell, 'Lockerbie', Hansard, HC Deb, vol. 298, cols 999–1000, 23 July 1997.

5. UN Security Council Resolution 731, 21 January 1992.

6. UN Security Council Resolution 748, 31 March 1992.

7. US Department of Commerce, Bureau of Export Administration, *Annual Report*, 1997, p. 224.

8. Adel Darwish, 'What costs more than six years of sanction?', *Mideast News*, 1 May 1999.

9. Quoted in 'Mandela dismisses US opposition to his Libyan visit', *Business Day* (South Africa), 23 October 1997.

10. Quoted in 'Anglo-US agreement on Lockerbie trial', BBC News Online, 24 August 1998.

11. Scharf, 'The Broader Meaning of the Lockerbie Trial and the Future of International Counter-terrorism', p. 57.

12. Hans Koechler and Jason Subler, *The Lockerbie Trial: Documents Related to the IPO Observer Mission*. Vienna: International Progress Organization, 2002, p. 18.

13. Ibid., p. 22.

14. Michael Scharf, 'How the Lockerbie trial paid off for US security interests', *Boston Globe*, 10 February 2001.

15. Robert Black, 'A prison visit', The Lockerbie Case website, 1 November 2007, http://lockerbiecase.blogspot.com.

16. Anthony Sampson, 'Mandela says UK must drop Libya sanctions', *The Independent*, 9 February 2001.

17. Quoted in Mark Macaskill, 'Fraser: my Lockerbie trial doubts', *Sunday Times*, 23 October 2005.

18. See 'Lockerbie case: British Foreign Office corrects information on its Libya web site and affirms the Scottish Court's right to order disclosure of "sensitive" material', International Progress Organization website, 1 September 2008.

19. Gareth Peirce, 'The framing of al-Megrahi', *London Review of Books* 31, no. 18, 24 September 2009.

## Chapter 9: A Gaddafi for our times

1. Oliver Miles, 'Tony Blair, peacemaker?', Guardian website, 28 June 2007.

2. Robert Fisk, 'Gaddafi vows to expel a million', *The Independent*, 19 October 1995.

3. Quoted in Aidan Lewis, 'Profile: Muammar Gaddafi', BBC Online, 28 August 2009.

4. Muammar Qaddafi, 'The one-state solution', *New York Times*, 21 January 2009.

5. Quoted in 'Gaddafi visit seals French deals', BBC Online, 10 December 2007.

6. Quoted in Christopher Dickey, 'The politics of blackmail', *Newsweek*, 1 August 2007.

7. Quoted in Peter Popham, 'Two leaders united in prejudice', *The Independent*, 12 June 2009.

8. Ian Sample, 'Nightmare in Benghazi', *The Guardian*, 31 October 2006.

9. Quoted in Dickey, 'The politics of blackmail'.

10. Quoted in Ian Black, 'Gadafy repairs relations with the West', *The Guardian*, 24 July 2007.

11. See George Joffé, 'Libya and Europe', *Journal of North African Studies* 6, no. 4, Winter 2001, p. 86.

12. Quoted in David Pallister, 'Condoleezza Rice meets Gadafy in Libya', *The Guardian*, 5 September 2008.

13. See Bill Gertz, 'Libyan sincerity on arms in doubt', *Washington Times*, 9 September 2004.

14. Robert Fisk, 'Libya's weapons of mass destruction: reinventing Gaddafi', *The Independent*, 22 December 2003.

15. See Ellen Knickmeyer, 'US, Libya neither friends nor enemies, Gaddafi says before Rice's visit', *Washington Post*, 2 September 2008.

16. Mahan Abedin, 'Libya, Radical Islam and the War on Terror: A Libyan Oppositionist's View', *Spotlight on Terror* 3, no. 3, May 2005.

17. See Patrick E. Tyler, 'Two are said to tell of Libyan plot to kill Saudi ruler', *New York Times*, 10 June 2004.

18. 'The Arab League summit: unity of a kind', *The Economist*, 2 April 2009.

## Chapter 10: African King of Kings

1. Quoted in Adrian Hamilton, 'Muammar Gaddafi: exporting revolution from an Arabian desert', *The Independent*, 10 August 2002.

2. Quoted in Basildon Peta, 'Gaddafi aims to "hijack" African Union organisation', *The Independent*, 15 June 2002.

3. Lydia Polgreen, 'Qaddafi, as new African Union head, will seek single state', *New York Times*, 2 February 2009.

4. See 'Gaddafi has "own way" of doing things, jokes Zuma after AU meeting', *Cape Argus*, 5 July 2009.

5. Robert Fisk, 'A very weird leader: Profile – Moammar Gaddafi', *The Independent*, 26 August 2000.

6. Quoted in Angela Eager, 'Gaddafi sends thugs to help Mugabe fight election battle', *Daily Telegraph*, 14 October 2001.

## Chapter 11: Living in Libya

1. 'Gaddafi invents "rocket car"', BBC News Online, 6 September 1999.

2. See Mary-Jane Deeb, 'Great Socialist People's Libyan Arab Jamahiriya', in David E. Long, Bernard Reich and Mark Gasiorowski (eds), *The*

*Government and Politics of the Middle East and North Africa*, 5th ed. Boulder, CO: Westview Press, 2007, p. 434.

3. Quoted in Eliza Apperly, 'On another planet: how Italy's women saw Colonel Gaddafi', *The Guardian*, 13 June 2009.

4. See Maria Graeff-Wassink, 'The Militarization of Women and "Feminism" in Libya', in Elisabetta Addis, Valeria E. Russo and Lorenza Sebesta (eds), *Women Soldiers: Images and Realities*. Basingstoke: Macmillan, 1994, pp. 137–49.

5. '2008 Human Rights Report: Libya', US Department of State website, 25 February 2009.

6. See *Libya: Human Rights in Socialist People's Libyan Arab Jamahiriya 2008*. London: Amnesty International, 2009.

7. '2008 Human Rights Report: Libya'.

8. *Country Report: Libya*. London: Economist Intelligence Unit, April 2009.

9. *Libya: 'We Can Criticise Allah but not Gaddafi'*. Paris: Reporters without Borders, 2006.

10. Kate Adie, *The Kindness of Strangers*. London: Headline, 2002, p. 333.

11. *Country Report: Libya*. London: Economist Intelligence Unit, January 2009, p. 19.

12. Quoted in 'Libyan government nationalises reform media', Magharebia website, 3 June 2009.

## Chapter 12: Paying for the Revolution

1. Quoted in Rana Jawad, 'Libya grapples with unemployment', BBC Online, 5 May 2005.

## Chapter 13: After Gaddafi

1. 'Saif Gaddafi's vision for Libya', BBC Online, 16 November 2004.

2. Muammar al-Qadhafi, *The Village. . . The Village. . . The Earth. . . The Earth. . . and the Suicide of the Astronaut, with Other Stories*. Sirte: Dar al-Jamahiriya, 1996, p. 53.

3. Jonathan Jones, 'Dad, you're in my painting!', *The Guardian*, 23 July 2002.

4. Quoted in Christopher Dickey, 'The Politics of Blackmail', *Newsweek*, 1 August 2007.

5. Quoted in 'Qaddafi's son declares he's leaving politics', *New York Times*, 22 August 2008.

6. Quoted in Richard Owen and Rory Campbell, 'Why Gaddafi's son can dictate the midfield', *The Times*, 17 June 2003.

7. Dirk Vandewalle, 'Libya in the New Millennium', in Dirk Vandewalle (ed.), *Libya since 1969: Qadhafi's Revolution Revisited*. New York: Palgrave Macmillan, 2008, p. 229.

8. See Amal S. M. Obeidi, 'Political Elites in Libya since 1969', in Dirk Vandewalle (ed.), *Libya since 1969: Qadhafi's Revolution Revisited*. New York: Palgrave Macmillan, 2008, p. 110.

9. Mansour O. el-Kikhia, *Libya's Qaddafi: the Politics of Contradiction*. Gainesville: University Press of Florida, 1997, p. 103.

10. Martin Bright and Anthony Barnett, 'Libya hunt for embassy killer suspects', *The Observer*, 18 June 2000.

# INDEX